From Reviews* of Dutch and French Editions of ~~Dutch~~ ~~~~

'The authors, Barkman and De Vries-van der Hoeven, both knew [Van Gulik] personally... their book contains a wealth of previously unknown material...' **I. Sitniakowsky**, De Telegraaf, January 29, 1994.

'...that Van Gulik was a bewilderingly versatile and creative personality becomes clear when one reads this biography...(which) is perhaps even more compelling than the detective novels that he wrote.' **Kees van Kempen**, Dagblad Tubantia, April 1, 1994.

'Sinologists and former diplomats Barkman and De Vries-van der Hoeven have provided an excellent portrait of an extraordinary man.' **Margreet Hirs**, De Volkskrant, Jan. 12, 1994.

'A restless genius... Robert van Gulik was, as the expression in English goes, "larger than life"...' **Dick van der Pol**, NRC Handelsblad, December 11, 1993.

'This biography is as exciting and abundant as the life of its subject.' **Christine Nguyen Thi**, Revue Bibliographique de Sinologie, Vol. 15, 1997.

'...this polyglot, this great lover of women, this collector of drawings and erotic prints... curious about everything... leaves behind a rich and complex work, respected by scholars and specialists of Eastern cultures and languages, adored by lovers of police literature...' **Daniel Walther**, Dernières Nouvelles d'Alsace, March 7, 1997.

'...a beautiful biography...the man was no doubt a genius; he wanted to see everything, to learn everything, to meet everybody...' **Marc Henry**, Le Soir, February 19, 1997.

'...if mental precocity and a multiplicity of gifts are the signs of genius, then Robert Hans van Gulik (1910-1967) was one of them...' **Isabelle Martin**, Journal de Genève et Gazette de Lausanne, February 9, 1997.

* translated from the original languages of the reviews

DUTCH MANDARIN

Dutch Mandarin
The Life and Work
of Robert Hans van Gulik

C. D. Barkman (1919-2006)
&
H. de Vries-van der Hoeven

English Translation by Rosemary Robson

ORCHID PRESS

DUTCH MANDARIN: The Life and Work of Robert Hans van Gulik
C. D. Barkman & H. de Vries-van der Hoeven
English Translation by Rosemary Robson

First English edition, Orchid Press, Bangkok 2018.
Originally published in Dutch as *Een Man Van Drie Levens*; Forum,
Amsterdam 1995.

Copyright © 2018 C. D. Barkman & H. de Vries-van der Hoeven
Copyright © citations from the works of RH van Gulik: The Robert van
Gulik Estate

ORCHID PRESS
P.O. Box 19,
Yuttitham Post Office,
Bangkok 10907, Thailand
www.orchidbooks.com

All rights reserved. No part of this publication may be reproduced,
copied or stored in a retrieval system, or transmitted, in any form or
by any means, electronic, mechanical, photocopying, recording or otherwise, without the prior written permission of the copyright owner.

Front cover image: Robert van Gulik with the gibbon Ginger, in the
garden of the embassy in Tokyo. (see p. 278)

Back cover image: Ante-chamber to the library, Tokyo 1967. Note
the calligraphy in large characters on the left, which bore the seal of
Emperor Ch'ien-lung. (see p. 266)

ISBN: 978-974-524-200-5

CONTENTS

FOREWORD AND ACKNOWLEDGMENTS

No, nothing shall remain. Not our names [which] become empty sounds, at the very most recalling a personality who never existed for those who come afterwards. Not what we said or what we did; because, as soon as words are uttered, actions performed, they become alien to us, chill and detached; they go their own way, without ever looking back.

Robert van Gulik,
from *At the Hot Springs of Odawara.*

People of genius cannot be summed up in a single formula. They are gifted with an extra dimension that sets them apart from others who are merely talented. Their genius imbues them with something unexpected and intangible. Robert van Gulik, diplomat, multi-facetted scholar, Sinologist, calligrapher and author of Chinese detective novels, fits into this category.

The absence of a biography of Van Gulik was the incentive for some of his friends and his eldest son to gather material about the life and work of this exceptional Dutchman; the present work is the result of this effort. There is a short description of his life in Chinese by Dr Chen Chih-mai, entitled *Ho-lan Kao Lo-p'ei* ('The Dutchman Robert van Gulik') and there is another, also short, by Janwillem van de Wetering (*Robert van Gulik: His Life, His Work*), neither of which can really be called a biography. Unlike Dr Chen, the second author did not know Van Gulik personally; in spite of this, even with the scanty material at his disposal, he succeeded in producing an extremely personal sketch of some distinction about Van Gulik and his work. In 1981, the academic journal *Orientations*, published in Hong Kong, devoted the whole of its November issue to Van Gulik.

It is not uncommon to find authors, or poets and scholars for that matter, among diplomats, but among his twentieth-century colleagues Van Gulik occupies a unique place. Not only was he a truly extraordinary ambassador, he was also one of the greatest scholars, indeed perhaps the most versatile, of Chinese culture. He learned about and experienced China and Japan from the inside, and felt completely at home in the cultures of both countries.

Moreover, every time his Chinese calligraphy, seal-carving, lute playing and learned papers on extremely diverse subjects arouse the admiration of the intellectual elite in China, this raises such questions as: What sort of person was he? How did he live? How did he achieve all this? These questions become even more insistent when we note that the interests of this *uomo universale* were not restricted to the already immense field of Chinese studies.

As a schoolboy of only eleven he produced a study of the Javanese *wayang* or shadow theatre. Later he learned Sanskrit and Tibetan, Japanese, Korean and Mongolian and thereafter he studied Islam and Arabic. He thus mastered an astonishing breadth of knowledge. This knowledge was not in itself his highest goal, as is the case with many academics. His overriding interest was always in *people*, Eastern people in particular. He wanted to learn about how they thought and how they functioned, so that he could think and work this way himself.

Robert van Gulik did not restrict his studies to languages; he was even more interested in ethnography and the fine arts. Whatever the circumstances, his cultural activities took priority over those arising from his job. Imperturbably and with great perseverance, he followed his own path; when he lost his library, manuscripts and artefacts during the Second World War, he simply began again.

Among the general public he acquired worldwide fame above all for his Judge Dee detective novels and stories, of which more than a million copies have been published in a large number of languages. They are a fascinating synthesis of Van Gulik's comprehensive knowledge of Chinese culture, art, jurisprudence and society. The fictional protagonist, Judge Dee, based on a historical Chinese magistrate of the same name, is the principal character in the numerous exciting plots, many of whose elements Van Gulik had come across in Chinese literature. The author also produced the illustrations, which were drawn in the Chinese style. These novels have won great popularity both in the West and in Asia because of their originality and authenticity, their thrilling plots and incisive style.

So he was diplomat, author and scholar, but what struck those who knew him best was that he actually led three lives: his own Dutch life, and also his Chinese and Japanese lives.

It is virtually impossible to describe and understand a man as versatile as Robert van Gulik completely. Anyone who has the audacity to attempt the task and is undeterred by the thought that a biographer of Van Gulik may only be able to conjure up a personality which was not him, often stumbles across unexpected and surprising twists and turns and uncovers questions which are sometimes difficult to answer.

Partially, and usually even then only cautiously, Van Gulik answered a number of these questions in his own autobiographical notes—written in English—which he committed to paper in 1964 at the request of the British publisher of his Judge Dee novels. In these notes, with a few rare exceptions, he far more often reveals the external side of his life rather than his internal world. Thus he remains an elusive figure who invariably seems to have shrouded himself in a veil of secrecy. Nevertheless, when these notes, together with the contents of a large number of his pocket diaries, as well as his academic and other publications, are combined with what many of his contemporaries can say about him, and are all taken into consideration, one finds enough material for a biography which conjures up an incredibly intriguing personality. While he might never be known fully, this image of a personality is indisputably Van Gulik's.

In this volume, two authors who knew him well have recorded the life of this great Dutchman who died in 1967, in his fifty-eighth year.

Leentje de Vries-Van der Hoeven wrote the two last chapters; Carl Barkman the rest. Mrs De Vries also collected a huge amount of data and was always an inexhaustible source of information which was essential to the completion of this book. As the basis for their work, they have drawn on the autobiographical notes Dr Van Gulik left and these have been included in this volume, almost without alteration, in his own words in English. To these have been added his diary entries (written in Dutch and translated here). Almost throughout his entire career he kept a pocket diary in which he would note down where he was, whom he had met, etc., on a daily basis. The selection of photos in this book is also largely based on Van Gulik's own choice; namely, they are the photos which he had incorporated into his own autobiographical notes. Although there is no autobiographical report covering his third period in the Netherlands or his final sojourn in Japan, he did continue to keep a pocket diary and his contemporaries were also prepared to make their own contributions. Mrs De Vries was present during Van Gulik's final stay in Tokyo and thus her recollections of this period are first hand.

Both authors are profoundly grateful to the following individuals for their diverse, important contributions and co-operation (including making available the autobiographical notes and pocket diaries): the late Mrs Frances van Gulik (Shih-fang); as well as Willem (Professor Dr W.R.) van Gulik, who supervised the entire work, and also Pieter, Pauline and Thomas van Gulik, and those whose initiative set the whole project in motion—Dr H.N. Boon, who unfortunately did not live to see this book in print, and Iwan Verkade.

They would also like to thank the following people for their valuable contributions and suggestions: Mea Wheatley-Bakker, R. Borgerjoff Mulder, Professor C.R. Boxer, J.G. Bruggman, A.F. Calkoen LL.M., Dr Chen Chih-mai, L.W Claassen, A.H. Croin LL.M., Prof. Dr Wisse Dekker, G.J. Disselvelt, A.H. Duijf, J.H. van Gemert, W. Gout, W.J. van Gulik M.A., Mrs A. Henny, Mrs C.W. Heijbroek-De Valk, Prof. Dr W. Idema, Prof. Dr A.E. Kersten, F. van Kispal, J.G. Kist LL.M., Mrs N.K. Kist-Tanser, F. Koopstra M.A., R.H. Count van Limburg-Stirum LL.M., A.H.J. Lovink, H.J. du Marchie Sarvaas, M. Ondei M.A., Mrs A. Reuchlin-Blom, Mrs A. van Roijen-Snouck Hurgronje, E.L.C Schiff LL.M., Mrs J. Schwarz LL.M., Ch. van der Sloot, J. van der Steen, Jonkvrouw I.F.A. Taets van Amerongen, Mrs Etsuko Teruyama, S.J. Baron van Tuyll van Serooskerken LL.M., Mrs G.A. Vixseboxse-Besier, Prof. Dr F. Vos, G.W. Baron de Vos van Steenwijk, J.W.M.H. Waalkens and C. van Wermeskerken M.A.

An exceptional contribution was made by Mrs A.M. Evers, who some time ago compiled a bibliography of the complete oeuvre of Dr Van Gulik and had it published. It is now in the Mugar Memorial Library of the University of Boston.

We are also grateful to Henk Figee, Marijke Bartels and Gerrie Lindenburg for their encouragement and editorial assistance and to all the many others who have, in some way another, facilitated our task as authors.

Of course, it goes without saying that the authors are completely responsible for the text of this biography.

Finally a word of special thanks to the Board of the *Stichting ter Bevordering van de Culturele Betrekkingen tussen het Koninkrijk der Nederlanden en China* (Foundation for the Encouragement of Cultural Relations between the Kingdom of the Netherlands and China) for its financial support and also to the M.A.O.C. Countess van Bylandt Foundation.

In this work, in remaining true to Dr Van Gulik's notes and other writings, as well as those of his contemporaries, the Wade-Giles system of Chinese transcription has been used. The few exceptions are in the cases of established geographical and other names, the transcriptions of which are now widely known in *Hanyu Pinyin*— indicated where appropriate by the abbreviation '*p.y.*'.

Chapter 1

THE BEGINNING

Robert Hans van Gulik was born on 9 August 1910 in Zutphen, in the Dutch province of Guelders, while his father was in charge of reorganizing the Royal Dutch East Indies Army (KNIL—*Koninlijk Nederlands-Indisch Leger*) military hospitals in The Netherlands.

Robert's autobiographical notes reveal that his grandfather, Willem Jacobus van Gulik (1834-1910), was the first in the family to show an interest in the Orient, which Robert personally attributed to his grandfather's deeply held belief in reincarnation.

This grandfather, through self-tuition, had developed a reasonable knowledge of electrical engineering, at that time a newly emerging area of study. The competence he thus acquired enabled him to obtain a position as a technical advisor at the Central Post Office in Utrecht. Religion played a dominant role his life, and he was also attracted to spiritualism—it was said that his constant preoccupation with telegraphy had aroused his interest in 'invisible communications'. He was the founder of the spiritualist society *Veritas*, gave lectures and wrote extensively on this subject, and devoted a great deal of his spare time to what would now be called parapsychological experiments. He has been described as a tall man of imposing, dignified appearance, who had the gift of clairvoyance. He often stayed with his brother-in-law, the well-known theologian the Reverend J.C.W. Quack (1826-1904), in his beautiful old manse in Ravestein, a small town on the Meuse in the province of North Brabant, where they would sit until deep into the night discussing supernatural phenomena.

Robert's grandfather loved Oriental art and had a special partiality for Japanese and Chinese lacquerwork. He passed his interest in the East on to his own two sons as well as to his grandsons, Robert's three elder brothers and Robert himself. Robert's father, who was named Willem Jacobus like his father, studied medicine in Utrecht. Despite his affinity with animals and biology, he had a strong military streak. Hence it is not surprising that, after passing his medical finals, he chose to join the KNIL Medical Service. This was the time he also met

Bertha de Ruiter, who was to become his wife. She was the daughter of a merchant in Arnhem (the provincial capital of Guelders) whose German mother came from a family which had produced a number of talented artists and musicians.

In 1897, Willem was posted to the Dutch East Indies (present-day Indonesia) with the rank of captain in the KNIL Medical Corps. He and his wife remained in the colony until 1909 and four of their children were born there. When they returned to the Netherlands, they settled down in Coehoornsingel 58 in Zutphen, an old Hansiatic town in Guelders, where Robert was born. When he was three years old, the family moved to Nijmegen, where the largest colonial army military hospital in the Netherlands was located.

As a toddler, Robert's older brothers were already regaling him with colourful, enthralling stories, telling him about everything they could and could not in the Indies—a word imbued with a magical allure for him. His parents were also hoping to return to that distant country with which they had fallen in love, even though their initial years there had been a difficult time for his mother.

When she first arrived, she had had the greatest difficulty in adapting to her new, unaccustomed way of life (humid, oppressive heat, the busy social calendar, servants, the foreign language, the hundred and one things which might make one feel awkward, including the wrap-around skirt or *sarong* which kept slipping down the first time she tried to wear it and the chignon which refused to stay in place). Precisely at this unsettling time the family had to move several times and three sons were born in very quick succession: Willem Jacobus, born 10 January 1897 in Batavia, then the capital of the Dutch Indies, now Jakarta, Pieter Johannes, born on 15 July in Batoedjadjar (now Batujajar, then a KNIL barracks, north-west of Bandung in West Java) and Ben Adolf, born on 31 July 1899 in Batavia. A daughter, Bertha Lina, was born on 18 May 1905 in Makassar, the colonial and present-day capital of the south-western part of the island of Celebes (now Sulawesi).

Robert's mother found herself frequently left to her own devices. Her husband was away participating in various colonial military expeditions, among them, the Boni Campaign against the Buginese in South Celebes and in the Aceh War in the northern tip of Sumatra, in which he distinguished himself. His courage and martial appearance, accentuated by a moustache, earned him the nickname of Willem the Cossack, which he would keep throughout his military career.

In spite of all their vicissitudes, Robert's parents had enjoyed a pleasant life in the large, comfortable colonial-style houses, surrounded by high white walls and graced by spacious front verandas decorated with exotic plants in Chinese porcelain pots. Father enjoyed a glass of beer or a tot of Dutch gin after he returned home from his duties and had made himself comfortable, stripping off his uniform, taking a bath to freshen up (splashing dippers of water over himself: *mandiën*) and donning short batik trousers and a light-weight *badjoe tjina* (long Chinese shirt).

Sometimes, once night had fallen they might drive around for hours in their comfortable carriage in the moonlight under the darkened palms. There were plenty of house parties from which mother sometimes had to excuse herself because of her pregnancies. The men enjoyed sociable gatherings at the club exchanging tall stories, the latest news and snippets of gossip as they relaxed over a drink. Colonial society was fairly rigidly divided, primarily by rank and position, but there were also horizontal divisions, into groups which exchanged greetings but did not socialize with each other. The women tended to be the strictest guardians of the sharply defined boundaries. The Van Guliks were members of one group, the military officers, but because father was a doctor as well as being an officer,

Pl. 1.   Robert van Gulik's parents with their three sons and Uncle Piet in a carriage, Batavia 1900

Pl. 2. Father, well-known by the nickname 'Willem the Cossack', Celebes
        1904.

their social circle was less restricted, a happy coincidence which
allowed them to indulge in a far wider range of interests than would
have been usual in an average officer's family.

By present-day standards, life in the Indies was still fairly
primitive, but around the turn of the century Batavia had already
begun to assume a more modern air. The hissing, swaying steam
tram (the *tjèbol*—dwarf) was replaced by an electric model. Shops
selling ladies' fashions and department stores with brightly lit
windows had made their appearance. *Deleman* and *sado* (horse-
drawn taxis) drove around and could be hailed when required.

The Van Guliks were not unduly bothered by the climate, and
the eternally green, unchanging landscape dominated by the blue
mountains never palled. Robert's father was a member of the 'colonial
school'. He was absolutely convinced that the Dutch administration
was the best for both the 'natives' and the Dutch. He was completely
impervious to Indonesian nationalist aspirations for independence
within the foreseeable future. Nevertheless, despite his conservatism,

he was profoundly interested in the languages and cultures of Indonesia, and he had acquired a wealth of in-depth knowledge about them.

As mentioned above, Robert's father was transferred back to the Netherlands in 1909, first to Zutphen and then to Nijmegen. Robert could remember the back garden of the large house on the Bergendalscheweg in the latter town better than the house itself. He played in the shrubbery with his dog Tippie and closely observed the behaviour of the hedgehogs, lizards and tortoises which his older brother Piet kept in various terraria.

In 1914, his father was posted back to Java. He travelled out ahead alone. Robert's mother remained behind a little while to ensure that the three oldest boys, who were now at secondary school, were safely boarded with one of their teachers. In 1915, Mother, Bertha (Bep) and Robert also boarded a Dutch steamship to sail to the Indies. The First World War had broken out and Robert remembered the large piles of sandbags on each deck and that everybody had to remain in their cabins as they sailed through the Suez Canal.

Later when he wrote about his parents Robert said that

> …my parents were a well-matched couple and their marriage went better than average. By nature and by his profession Father was inclined to be rather authoritarian, and he was always the undisputed head of the household. Mother was by nature pliable, but she got her way in her own quiet manner, especially with regard to our education and household matters. Her children and her house were the centre of her interest, her hobbies reading and music. Later I learned that from time to time there had been conflicts, but these were of a minor character and my parents always took good care that we, the children, never noticed that there were difficulties. Although it seems terribly trite and outmoded nowadays to say so, I wish to state that I loved and respected my parents, and cherish their memory. Reading other persons' autobiographies it strikes me how often the writers state that they violently hated either their father or their mother, and I consider myself lucky that I for one had a perfectly normal, happy childhood.

Chapter 2

ELEMENTARY SCHOOL IN JAVA
1915-1923

The happiest years of Robert's youth were those he spent in the Indies. His father's first posting was for a year in Surabaya, the provincial capital of East Java, but after his promotion to colonel and appointment as Director of the Military Medical Service whose headquarters were in Batavia they moved to the capital of the East Indies.

Pl. 3. Robert, Batavia 1922.

At first Robert was troubled by the heat and often ill, but once he had become acclimatized, he rapidly grew into a sturdy boy, mad about football and other sports.

> Father was assigned an official residence that even in those days of the grand colonial style was considered very large; after Father's retirement the Topographical Service was housed there. I retain a vivid picture of our home: spacious, marble-tiled rooms, a huge pillared central hall where Father put his ever-growing collection of Indonesian arms and Chinese porcelain on display, an extensive garden full of high fruit trees and where stood two guest-pavilions (furnished by me and my playmates as robber nests), and all kinds of animals including my Father's favourite white horse, parrots, singing birds (Mother's hobby), and my favourite brown monkey. A host of quiet and friendly native servants, and their numerous offspring, definitely not quiet, but excellent playmates! And the ever-present image of Mother, dressed in the native sarong (batik long loincloth/wrap-around skirt) and kabaya (white-lace, long-sleeved jacket), the sensible and becoming garb then worn by all Dutch ladies when at home. When in the course of the twenties they took to humdrum European dresses, life on Java lost much of its former charm.
>
> Father's main orderly and groom was a Javanese sergeant who was a lover of the *wayang*, the ancient Javanese shadow-play. The puppets he had hung on the wall of his room caught my fancy at once (these stylized puppets constitute as a matter of fact one of the finest expressions of Javanese artistic genius) and prompted by me he began to relate to me the stories enacted on the shadow stage. The *wayang* thus became the dominating passion of my childhood. My parents knew that I expected no other birthday present than a new *wayang* puppet, and I built up a small collection of the main characters, with which I gave performances against a bedsheet hung across the room, and under the guidance of the Javanese groom.

The name of Robert's friend and instructor in the art of the shadow theatre (*wayang*) was Wongso, but Robert also often addressed him as *Oppas* (Caretaker), his function in the household. When not on duty, he exchanged his uniform for a simple batik coat and a head-cloth. This quiet, gentle man, who seemed so frail and vulnerable, was actually gifted with great physical strength and intrinsic poetical power. When he manipulated the puppets, which could be made to express tender or fierce emotions, his slender hands were eloquent. Yet, those same hands and arms were so sinewy he could keep a grip on the strongest man. His movements were unhurried and predictable, hence reassuring. Wongso was delighted that Robert showed such an intense interest in his favourite form of theatre. Never before had he had come across the son of a *Belanda* (Dutchman)—a colonel no less—who was so absorbed in Indonesian culture, and he assisted young Robert when the latter gave performances in his bedroom, where he hung up a bed sheet to make a screen on which to project his *wayang* characters.

The delicate Wongso had a resonant voice. Alternating narration and song, he would recount sections of an ancient story enshrined in a Javanese epic poem, sometimes in the rounded cadences of the beautiful, sonorous High Javanese or at other times in the shriller, staccato tones of Low Javanese, punctuated by the angry beating of gongs. Robert thrilled to it and would join in the drama, making his puppets laugh or cry. There is a photo of him in Javanese costume taken during a *wayang* performance in Nijmegen in 1925.

Pl. 4. Robert gives a wayang performance, Nijmegen 1925.

The family often spent its holidays in a government bungalow amid the breathtaking mountain scenery of the Priangan Highlands, south of Batavia. He and his five-year-older sister Bertha, a cheerful child who loved plants and animals and was very knowledgeable about them, would go for pony rides. The small, fast, tough local mountain ponies would carry them from one tea or rubber plantation to next; wherever they went they were welcomed with open arms. The snacks which could be bought from the *warung* (roadside stalls) tasted much better than the food at home: *saté* (meat grilled on a stick), rice steamed in a banana leaf which could be kneaded by hand into edible balls, the most delicious fruit, *cendol* (thick syrup containing pieces of coconut flesh mixed with finely shredded ice), plus a host of other delicacies.

Sometimes in the evening Robert was allowed to accompany his father to a village feast, where *wayang golek* was performed to the accompaniment of a small *gamelan* (orchestra composed mainly of bronze percussion instruments). Darkness falls early in the tropics and the whole village would be lit by the light of kerosene lamps. The villagers would be dressed in their best clothes, newly washed and starched. The mood would be animated and festive. The music of the *gamelan*, which sounded so enchanting in the open air, would accompany the drama, this time not told by shadows as at home but by large wooden puppets carved in the round, conjured into life by the *dalang* (puppet master) and his assistants. Robert and his father, so well-acquainted with these figures and knowing the stories inside out, could never have enough of it. Father was a man of few words, but father and son had no need of verbal communication, they understood each other.

These holiday weeks were made even more special for the children because on such occasions their father had more time for them. Usually they only saw him at the evening meal, so there was seldom an opportunity for any long conversations.

> Father spoke little of religion and we did not go to church, but he had us follow a Bible class, and he taught us his simple code of right and wrong, and the importance of doing our duty; he always told us that we would have to make our own choice in due time as to our religion, our profession and our marriage-partner. Later I understood that Father's views on all these matters had been strongly influenced by Grandfather. Despite Father's military strain and curt manner he was at heart a mystic; it was probably therefore that the Indonesians liked and respected him, although they violently disagreed with his colonial views.

Robert thoroughly enjoyed his elementary school. His classmates were a mixture of Dutch, Indonesian-Dutch and Chinese-Indonesian children. Even then he had a thirst for knowledge and paid great attention to the lessons, even though this did not stop him enjoying all the mischief he and his friends got up to before and after school. Above all else, Robert and his friends valued feats of physical daring and courage. Their heroes were the silent film actor Eddy Polo, Buffalo Bill, Nick Carter, the master detective, and Raffles, Lord Lister, the gentleman thief ('my mother dismissed the books about the last two', he was to write later, 'as pennydreadfuls, but as I remember it, the 'plots' were often very good'.) Girls were a waste of time.

Their chief interest was fighting. This was taken very seriously. They studied and practised the holds and throws used in *pencak silat* (one of the Indonesian martial arts) and organized proper contests, umpired by a referee. The more informal bouts were held behind the bicycle stand in the school playground, the more serious contests were decided in the old abandoned fort close by. They had three sorts of competitions: boxing (punches only), a combination of boxing and wrestling and (the highest grade) boxing, wrestling and kicking. No wonder Robert often came home with a black eye! Only later did it dawn on him how miraculous it was that no serious accidents had ever happened. The art of fighting could also be turned into a sort of duel. For instance, sometimes as Robert and his mates cycled past a small group of Indonesian boys they would stare at them provocatively. Eventually, in order to challenge him, one of them would call out: 'Why are you staring at us, Fatty?' Naturally an insult like that could not be ignored, so he would get off his bike and make an appointment for a fight: 'Tomorrow afternoon 4 o 'clock at the old fort...'

Football came second only to fighting and took precedence over kite-flying (preferably from the neighbour's roof) and hunting birds and the larger species of bats with air-guns. In the mind of a Dutch *totok* (someone born and bred in the Netherlands), the word kite-flying conjures up a picture of these boys simply launching their kites into the air and then placidly following the course of their flight. For Robert and his friends it was a very different matter. First they boiled a small pot of glue and crushed a piece of glass into fine shards, using the mortar and pestle used to prepare *sambal* (chilli relish). After they had mixed the glue and the glass, they pulled the tails of their kites through the mixture. If ordinary kite-flying was a question of skill, the real fun began when they could manoeuvre their kites so that they could cut the tail of someone else's kite. When that happened, they shouted *Láyangan pedót!* (Kite cut!) and everybody chased after it armed with long bamboo poles. Even if a boy still happened to be at home when the cry went up, he would race outside, of course with bare feet and perhaps even still in his pyjamas, through gardens, over hedges and walls, in pursuit of the kite. The boy who found it, kept it. This point was never disputed.

Life was full of adventure, *branie* (daring) or what was called dash in the west. People observed a communal code of honour, which was particularly important in a multiracial society. There was never any question of racial conflict among these boys. What was of overriding importance was that a boy was a chap who was not afraid to do things and abided by the rules.

Robert hated hunting, he loved animals far too much to indulge in it, but he did find the hunting trips which he and his friends made into the jungle on the outskirts of the town exciting. He was also thrilled by the covert bike rides he and his friends made to the Chinese quarter to buy their air-guns and ammunition, an expedition strictly forbidden by their parents.

In the Chinese quarter, Robert was intrigued by the Chinese characters on the signboards and scroll paintings, the same strange signs he admired so greatly on the porcelain in his father's collection. He was fascinated by the mysterious, shadowy interiors of the Chinese temples which housed exotic statues of a whole pantheon of gods, as well as incense-burners standing on richly decorated altars. He interrogated his Chinese classmates about all such matters, but they tended to be very shy and reticent about their own culture, and pretended ignorance.

The Javanese shadow theatre, the *wayang kulit*, continued to be his main hobby. As long as he was doing well at school, his parents raised no objections. In fact, they constantly stimulated his intellectual and artistic development:

> On my tenth birthday Father and Mother presented me with a bulky blank ledger, nicely bound, and told me to write down there all I knew about the *wayang*; they hoped that thus my hobby would serve the useful purpose of improving my handwriting and my Dutch style. I set to work with relish, and in the course of the ensuing year covered all its 200 folio pages with notes and coloured drawings. I completed it on my eleventh birthday, and then added a solemn 'Preface'. Later I thought that the book had become lost,

but Mother had preserved it and I was much amused when I got it back in my University days and I found I had stated blithely in the Preface: "Everything recorded in this book is completely true.".

The contents of the manuscript are organized so systematically and in such an academic manner that only the letter N on the title page, which occasionally faces the wrong way, betrays that the author was only eleven years old. He deals with the current variations of the *wayang*, meticulously describes the puppets, the musical instruments and decor, sketches the substance of the plays and gives insights into the roles of the principal characters.

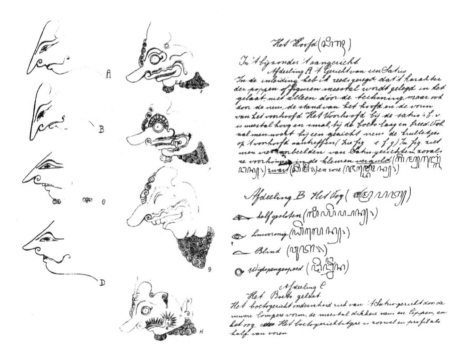

Fig. 1: A description of the face and eyes of *satrias* (knights) and *butas* (demons or monkeys) in the *wayang*. From *De Wajangs*, a manuscript completed by Van Gulik at the age of eleven.

When I entered the 7th and last grade, I happened to read Jules Verne's novel [*Tribulations of a Chinaman in China*] and was fascinated by its description of the life and ideals of the Chinese. I realised that besides the Javanese culture I so much admired there were other, superior cultures. These doubts were strengthened when I read the Dutch version of Sister Nevadita's fine book *Myths and Legends* [*of Hindus and Buddhists*], and found that nearly all of the stories of the *wayang* are based on the ancient Indian epics Mahābhārata and Rāmayāna. Moreover, the Indonesian way of life and the language were familiar, whereas Chinese life and language were an unknown mystery. I was beginning to think of ways and means for learning more about this mysterious culture when my years on Java came to an end.

In the summer of 1923, shortly after Robert had completed elementary school and had sat his grammar school entrance examinations, his father reached the end of his army career and retired with the rank of major-general. They made the voyage home to the Netherlands on a large Dutch passenger ship. Robert and his mother wept as they stood at the ship's rail and watched the coast of Java disappear.

Chapter 3

GRAMMAR SCHOOL IN NIJMEGEN
1923-1930

Back in Holland we settled down in an old country-house called
Severen in the village of Beek, near Nijmegen. I got the turret-room
from where on clear days I could see Germany across the border.
Father and Mother had always wanted to devote their remaining
years to country life, and Severen with its extensive grounds on
the edge of the forest was ideal for that. Father kept a riding horse,
dogs, poultry, and a host of other animals, Mother looked after the
flower garden. Father's oriental collection was housed in the large
reception hall.

I went to the Municipal Gymnasium in Nijmegen, half an
hour's bicycle ride from *Severen*. It was an attractive 19th century
building near the quay of the river Waal, and with a competent
staff. Having a nice home and going to a good school I should have
been happy, but I kept comparing life in Holland with that in Java,
and was sulky and morose most of the time; puberty will have been
a contributing factor. I looked down on the other boys because they
would not fight (fighting was considered in Holland fit only for
guttersnipes) and sniggered about sex which we, grown up in the
east, considered as something quite natural. I still feel ashamed
when I think of the beastly way I used to treat the other boys.

When they went to the boat to meet his brother Wim and his
family, he held his four-year-old nephew over the rail for a moment
in his outstretched arms. Robert also liked to tell the tall story of how
his jaws had grown so powerful as a result of his boxing practice,
that while a tooth was being extracted not he, but the dentist, fainted,
from exhaustion. Robert had all sorts of gymnastic equipment with
which to work out in his turret room in *Severen*.

My acting as "school-bully" had only one good result; I took under
my protection a boy called F.M. Schnitger (Martijn), a thin fellow
with a harelip who also came from Java and was the target of the
other boys' teasing. We exchanged nostalgic memories of Java,

and bought books on the Javanese language and history which we studied together before and after classes. Martijn also assisted me in staging *wayang* performances at home when I dressed in native garb.

I liked the classes, especially those in the Classics and modern languages, and could not help noticing that Javanese literature, though not lacking in a certain artless charm, yet could never be compared to the great western literatures. So I turned again to Chinese, and bought the Chinese volume in the Marlborough Self-taught Series. Later I realised that this is about the worst handbook ever written, and the print was so small that it made me nearsighted. At that time, however, it was a gate to paradise: the study of Chinese characters, combining profound meaning with perfect beauty of form, brought me in a trance of happiness. Having read somewhere that Sanskrit is the basis of all languages, I bought a Sanskrit grammar too. Martin, who did not do too well in class, kept to Javanese and in later years continued his studies in Vienna. He acquired fame because of his pioneering archaeological explorations on Sumatra (v. his book *Forgotten Kingdoms of Sumatra*, Leiden 1938, reprinted 1964) and we remained close friends till his untimely death during the war which cut short a brilliant scholarly career.

Robert's father raised no objections to his son's extra-curricular studies because they did not interfere with his schoolwork, but he: 'wisely insisted that I devoted the remainder of my spare time to physical exercise, all the more necessary since I was growing fast and was getting on for six feet when I was fifteen. Reading voraciously, I took to reading till after midnight, a habit that has stayed with me ever since.' He read western literature and began to write his own poems, which were occasionally published in the school magazine, but his studies were his chief absorption. Everything Asian seemed to fascinate him. Although his love of Java did not dim, his main focus of interest now shifted to China. It seems he had lessons from a Chinese student who later became a professor in Wageningen (the Agricultural University). He had already learned a great many Chinese characters before he went to university.

The Chinese name he used and was to keep for the rest of his life, by which he is known in Chinese circles, Kao Lo-p'ei, (*p.y.* Gao Luopei, 高羅佩) dates from this period. Chinese is a monosyllabic language; *Kao* stands for *Gu*(lik) and *Lo-p'ei* is the pronunciation which approximates *Robert* best. Later he was also given a Chinese literary name.

Fig. 2: Seals of Van Gulik's Chinese name, from the last page of *Ch'un Meng So Yen*, 1950 (left) and the title page of *Chinese Pictorial Art*, 1958 (right).

Because he devoted so much time to Chinese, he had to repeat one year, either the fourth or the fifth, which meant it took him seven years to complete grammar school, a study normally done in six. During the holidays his father sent him to work for a farmer, paid employment, 'to earn his own living'.

He also devoted much of his time to studying Sanskrit, partly as a linguistic exercise but also, as he said himself, to obtain better access to the world of Buddhism. However, chance played a role in this as well:

> Then I had the great good fortune to meet the famous linguist and Sanskrit scholar Professor Dr C.C. Uhlenbeck, who had just retired from Leyden University to settle down with his wife in Nijmegen. Our meeting was brought about by a lucky accident: I had bought in a curio shop a bamboo-leaf inscribed with a script [neither] Martin nor I could identify, so I paid a visit to the professor to ask him what it was. He corresponded in every respect to my idea of a learned professor: a thin man with a slight stoop and a straggling beard, and the high dome of a bald head. He was very kind, told me the script was Burmese, and questioned me about my studies. Thereupon he offered to teach me general linguistics and Sanskrit, once a week on Wednesday afternoon when there were no classes. At first Father objected, saying that this was imposing on the professor's kindness, but he replied that upon retiring he had not realized how much he would miss lecturing to students and that moreover he thought he could make me into his special pupil who would in years to come continue his own school of linguistic thought.

Soon I went there Saturday afternoons too, and the Uhlenbecks being childless themselves, came to consider me more or less as their adopted son. The professor did not know Far Eastern languages, but he pointed out to me the best Chinese handbooks to use and the right approach to Chinese studies. He gave me a sound grounding in general linguistics, even going over with me my Latin and Greek homework, and taught me Sanskrit and later also Russian. When in 1928 the First International Linguistic Congress was held at The Hague and when he was elected President, he took me along as his secretary.

He was a scholar of remarkably wide interests, being an expert also in anthropology and sociology and comparative religion and what is more a fine pedagogue who could explain the most complicated problems in a simple and crystal-clear manner. He encouraged me to write essays and articles on Chinese subjects, so as to get experience in formulating my thoughts.

When Robert was in his sixth year there, the school moved to a larger building and, on the evening on which it was inaugurated, the students performed two plays: *Orpheus*, a comedy accompanied by modern melodies, was the contribution of the lower classes, and *Ajax* by Sophocles, also to a modern musical accompaniment, was the offering of the seniors. Robert played the protagonist and a girl whose surname was Van Enk, a born actress, played his wife and co-star. The daughter of the Headmaster, Dr Schwarz, who was then twelve years old and in her first year, recalled it all very well. She also played the role of Ajax's son. She did not have to say anything, but when Robert took farewell of his wife and child, he solemnly laid his hand on her head while he addressed his last words to them. Robert was an impressive Ajax, a mighty warrior. With his serious character accentuated by his height and sturdy build, he made an older, more mature impression than his fellow students. His maturity was also betrayed by the way he behaved. He had no girlfriends. It seems as if he found schoolgirls too childish. The Headmaster, who shared his interest in Sanskrit, had a soft spot for this outstanding student, and Robert was often invited to visit him at home. He made friends with Jaap R.W., a boy who lodged in the headmaster's house. He was a rather weak character and was very persuadable. Dr Schwarz sometimes tended to worry a little— needlessly as it would turn out later—when Robert took this boy to the pub to play billiards and perhaps have a couple of beers.

In those days, these sorts of entertainment were thought to be rather precocious for a boy at secondary school.

As I was about to commence the sixth and last grade of the Gymnasium, I had an opportunity for showing Prof. Uhlenbeck my gratitude. He and his wife had formerly lived for one year with the Peigan tribe of North American Algonquin Indians and for the first time recorded their language; their notes were written on thousands of cards which filled two large suitcases. When he told me his failing eyesight prevented him from working this material out into a dictionary, I offered to do it for him. He accepted because he thought it would broaden my linguistic insight if I came to know also a language of a so-called "primitive people". He gave me a brief course on the structure of the language and on the phonetic system he had used, Father bought a typewriter for me and I set to work. I had finished the typescript of the first, English-Blackfoot part in six weeks, and it was accepted for publication by the Netherlands Royal Academy of Sciences. I had hoped that the Professor would mention my name in preface as the one who had typed out the book, but on receiving the first proofs I saw to my astonished delight that he had put my name next to his on the title-page, as co-author! (Later, in my student days, I also prepared the second Blackfoot-English volume, also published by the Royal Academy; it is on this—very slight!—foundation that my name appears also on lists of scholars of Americanologists).

Professor Uhlenbeck's generosity made it all the more difficult for me to tell him about a decision I had made shortly before passing my final exam of the Gymnasium. He as well as my parents had taken it for granted that after that exam I would be enrolled at Leyden University as a student of philology, as the beginning of a purely academic career, and I myself had also come to accept that. Then, however, I saw an advertisement in the paper of the Netherlands East Indies Government; they were needing junior officials in the Bureau of Far Eastern Affairs at Batavia (the capital of the Indies), and offered to pay for three years Chinese and Japanese studies at Leiden University, and one year studying in China, the candidate thereafter to be appointed at the said Bureau (which resembled that of the British Office of the Protector of Chinese in the F.M.S [Federated Malay States, now part of Malaysia]). I came to the conclusion that this was the career I really wanted, and for which I was best suited. For although I had a certain facility for learning languages, my aim in doing so was primarily to come to know more about the people who used these languages, and not to become an accomplished philologue. Also, I wanted to live in the Orient, not temporarily as visiting lecturer or in some other academic position, but for many years, and in an official capacity which would enable me to take an active part in their life. Finally, I wanted to be independent, and to earn my own money.

My decision astonished my parents, and it was a great blow to Professor Uhlenbeck. But great man as he was, he said that he appreciated my honesty, and that after I had gone to Leiden he would always welcome my passing part of my holidays with them, when he would continue his teaching of Sanskrit and Russian—subjects that would later always come in useful, even if I would keep to an official career. I did indeed stay every University holiday one week or so with the Uhlenbecks, till I left Holland in 1935, and we corresponded regularly till he died in Switzerland many years later. I never regretted my decision, for I am by temperament unsuited for a sedentary life and although I like to deliver occasional lectures on subjects that interest me, I lack the patience to guide students through a long-term course; to put it frankly, I am keener on learning than on teaching, and thus am lacking one of the chief qualifications for becoming a really good professor. Up to date (1964) I have twice acted as Honorary Professor, but each time for one year only, and charged with a course for advanced students on subjects that particularly interested me, and this I enjoyed very much.

Although Robert's decision about his future career had been made, he still had to sit his final school examinations. He passed them without any difficulty on 14 June 1934, after which he spent a gloriously peaceful summer at *Severen* with his parents.

In September Robert left for Leiden, where he enrolled in the Faculties of Arts (Chinese and Japanese) and Law, as prescribed by the terms of the contract which he had signed with the Dutch East Indies Government. His scholarship was not large (around 80 guilders a month), but enough for his board and lodgings and a few small expenses, yet out of this he still managed to save around 30 guilders. He used the books in the University Library. His father offered to supplement his scholarship, but he refused. He wanted to be completely independent.

Chapter 4

STUDENT IN LEIDEN
1930-1935

Although Robert van Gulik had been something of an odd man out at elementary and secondary school, while he was a student at the University of Leiden his lifestyle certainly was the absolute opposite to that of the general run of his contemporaries. Like other students he lived in digs, but in his case for less than a month. He never became a member of the Corps, the elite student society, nor any other student association.

In the notes he made we read:

> Looking back after thirty years, I think I understand what exactly made me so keen on complete independence. I was vaguely thinking of a bohemian style of living, where "wine, women and song" would play an important role. To put it plainly, I longed for sensual pleasures, but intended to pay for those myself. Thus my desire for independence was partly a typically adolescent dream, partly a natural reaction to six years of over-strenuous, purely intellectual pursuits with sport as the only outlet. A kind Fate decided that I would get all I wanted—though in a quite different manner from which I imagined.

Nowadays the fate which fortune had in store for Robert would not be considered unusual by students (with the exception perhaps of the age difference), but for those who studied before the revolution of the sixties, it is astonishing to learn that, instead of indulging in a free and easy student life unencumbered by any ties, Robert chose to live with a widow who was eighteen years his senior and had a young son of seven, and that he rapidly showed signs of developing a sense of responsibility for being a fellow breadwinner.

> After I stayed about one month in a small rented room, I met Nelly R[emouchamps], the widow of a well-known archaeologist who had died very young, and this meeting was to prove the first turning point in my life. She was 38 at the time, had a son of seven,

and supplemented her modest pension by working as an assistant in the University Library. Nelly was a remarkable woman, well-read in Dutch, French and German literature, a more than average amateur pianist and singer with a wide knowledge of modern art; far from being a bluestocking, she had a great zest for life. She had travelled with her husband all over Europe, visited the great art collections and many archaeological sites, and digested what she had seen. Since she looked at least ten years younger than her actual age, and I ten years older, we did not make an incongruous couple. We decided to pool our meagre resources, and I moved into the small house she had inherited, and where her late husband's fine collection of books on archaeology and art took up nearly all the available space. There I stayed until my departure from Holland five years later.

Nellie was a vivacious woman, with a French air about her. She had a cheerful, open face, wreathed in smiles, beautiful eyes, a strong, prominent nose (just like Robert's mother's); her dark hair was cut in a bob and she was just a tiny bit on the plump side. In contemporary photographs, she seems rather younger than thirty-eight, and Robert certainly appears at least ten years older than he actually was.

Pl. 5. With Nellie Remouchamps, 1932.

Now that he had taken the plunge directly from being a secondary school pupil to being the head of a household, as he described it himself, he needed more income than that provided by a student scholarship. Nellie helped him to earn a little extra in a way which also benefited his studies (it is amazing how strongly considerations of what might be useful played a role both with Robert personally and with the people who cared for him). Nellie, who had a wide circle of acquaintances in artistic and literary circles in The Hague and Amsterdam, introduced him to newspaper and magazine publishers. It was not long before his articles and book reviews about oriental art and literature were earning them a satisfactory extra income. This money gave them the opportunity to make trips to Brussels and Paris, two cities which Nellie knew very well.

He later told his son Willem that it was possible to live quite well in Paris with the extra 75 guilders a month which the publishing house Elsevier paid for his contributions to its magazine. The time he spent in the French capital was among the most carefree in his whole life. He thoroughly enjoyed going riding in the Bois de Boulogne with the famous song-writer Lucienne Boyer, both wearing a sort of Russian Cossack uniform, which was then all the rage. When he wrote the Judge Dee novel, *Poets and Murder*, thirty years later shortly before his death, he drew his inspiration from the lyrical, bohemian background of this Paris interlude and from the song *L'âme des poètes*. Evening after evening while he was writing this book, he played gramophone records of Juliette Greco, who included this Lucienne Boyer composition in her repertoire.

In Paris he and Nellie often stayed in small hotels in Montmartre. They talked until deep into the night with artists and writers, visited collections of Eastern art and went to operas and concerts. Nellie was deeply interested in his Chinese studies and encouraged him to practise calligraphy. It was she who pointed out to him the link between this form of writing and modern abstract art.

In the summer, during long walks and cycle rides they would explore the countryside in the east and south of the Netherlands. They were often joined by Martijn Schnitger. Robert, who was a life-long gastronome, was lucky in this respect too: '[Nelly] was also an excellent cook and instilled in me the subtleties of French food and wines.'

Although his private life was 'completely satisfactory' (as Robert said himself), he was far less pleased with his Chinese lectures. They were given by a 'fairly young professor who taught Chinese as just another job and was interested in history rather than in Chinese art and literature'. Apparently, even though he was a Chinese scholar of world renown, Professor Duyvendak inevitably suffered in any comparison with Uhlenbeck. He was certainly far more interested in Chinese history and philosophy and was more a competent classical philologist than a connoisseur. Duyvendak also tended to be a know-all, but in that respect, young Van Gulik, with his own private study and lessons from the great Uhlenbeck behind him, probably far outstripped him.

Nevertheless, Professor Duyvendak did take Robert's private study into account and his acknowledgement of this enabled the latter to pass his bachelor's exams in Chinese, with Japanese as a minor, which would normally have taken three years, on 19 February 1932, after barely two years' study. He passed his bachelor's exam in Indies Law at the same time, after submitting a thesis entitled *De ontwikkeling van de juridishce positie van de Chinezen in Nederlands Oost-Indië* (The Development of the Juridical Position of the Chinese in the Dutch East Indies). His professor in this subject was the eminent scholar Cornelis van Vollenhoven, founder of the Adat (Traditional) Law School, with whom he got on very well.

He also liked his professor of Japanese, Professor Dr J. Rahder. An 'absent-minded Buddhologist who lived in a world of his own of Tantric mysteries', who also taught him Tibetan. What Robert fails to record in his notes is that Rahder also gave outstanding, absorbing lectures on the modern and most recent history of the Far East, and in his background material in all of them he dealt with the whole political game played by the Great Powers. In his attitude to women, Rahder was certainly far from absent-minded. At one conference of Japanese scholars he gave a learned address in the language the use of which is restricted to Japanese women, much to the delight of the Japanese who were present. Any student who happened to visit him at home would come across an attractive lady, who would introduce herself in a Russian accent as: '*Je suis la maîtresse de Monsieur*', which hinted that she gave him Russian conversation lessons, among her other duties.

Shortly after Robert had passed both his bachelor's examinations, the Dutch East Indies Government decided to retrench (the peculiar quasi-euphemism 'reorganization' had not yet come into use) and the cadets' contracts were cancelled. After this blow, he found a job as an assistant at the *Rijksmuseum voor Volkenkunde* (National Museum of Ethnology) in Leiden, where he was put in charge of the Southeast Asian section. He spent many enthralling hours sorting out the fine collection of *wayang* puppets—his old love— and he wrote a series of articles about the shadow theatre in Asia. He gave up his law studies and concentrated on Chinese, Japanese and Tibetan. Whenever he went to stay with the Uhlenbecks, he continued his studies of Sanskrit and Russian.

During one of these holidays with his old preceptor, Van Gulik completed his Dutch translation of a Sanskrit play by the great Sanskrit dramatist Kālidāsa and a publisher who was prepared to print it was found. Robert chose the type face, designed the dust jacket and drew the illustrations, and in doing so discovered that 'taking care of the make-up of a book is nearly as great a joy as writing it'. This book, entitled *Urvaçi,* was his first published work (he did not count his co-authorship of the Blackfoot dictionaries).

In his notes, Robert explained his reasons for choosing to attend the University of Utrecht to do his master's degree and his doctorate:

> I mentioned already that I didn't get on well with my Chinese professor, Dr J.J.L. Duyvendak—partly my own fault, for I was a cocksure and opinionated youngster. Although Duyvendak does not rank among the great Chinese scholars, he did a tremendous lot for the organization of Chinese studies, and conducted himself splendidly during the German occupation. His main interest, however, was ancient Chinese history and philosophy, while I was attracted by the later great periods of the flourishing of Chinese art and letters (Tang, Sung and Ming dynasties), and contemporary China. The University of Utrecht appointed Thos. Ferguson as Professor of Chinese, a man who had spent more than forty years in China (lastly as Commissioner of Customs), and was an authority on modern Chinese history and modern Chinese. Therefore I enrolled at that University to follow his lectures. I remained in Leiden, however, and went every Friday to Utrecht for Ferguson's lectures, and those in Sanskrit by Prof. J. Gonda. It was there that on April 21, 1934 I obtained my MA in Oriental languages with honours, having previously submitted a thesis on the famous 12th century Chinese painter and art-critic Mi Fu and his treatise on ink-slabs (*Yen-shih*).
>
> In consultation with Prof. Uhlenbeck I chose for my doctoral thesis horse-cult in China and Japan, and its origins in India and Tibet—a subject that covered the entire field of my studies, while my love of horses and horse-riding inherited from Father would act as an extra incentive. I estimated that it would take me about a year to write this book, so now the time had come to think about what to do thereafter. The Netherl. Indies Government again needed officers for its Bureau of Far Eastern Affairs. I still cherished my childhood memories of Java, and the idea of going there as an official, treading in the footsteps of Father, Uncle Piet and my brothers Willem and

Ben, was very attractive; however, I now knew that China itself, and also Japan, were the great centres of Far Eastern culture, and I preferred to go there, and as soon as possible. Nelly suggested the Foreign Service, because she thought that a diplomatic post would give ample scope to both my scholarly and practical interests. I presented myself at the Foreign Ministry in The Hague, and was told that since our missions in China and Japan were in great need of oriental experts, I could enter the foreign service directly after I would have obtained my doctor's degree, without having to pass the regular Foreign Service examinations.

In those days, the Foreign Service was still divided into three sections: the diplomatic, the consular and the interpreting services. The highest rank which officials posted to the legations or consulates in China and Japan in the last-mentioned service could attain was secretary-interpreter. Robert commenced as an assistant-interpreter but it would otherwise have been impossible for him to enter the diplomatic service without having first passed the compulsory entrance examinations.

Pl. 6. Dinner in a Chinese restaurant in Utrecht after conferral of doctorate, March 1935 (on the right both parents).

Chapter 5

FIRST PERIOD IN JAPAN
1935-1942

TO JAPAN VIA HARBIN, CHINA

On 7 March 1935, Robert van Gulik was awarded his doctorate in philosophy and literature with first class honours for his thesis entitled *Hayagrīva: The Mantrayānic Aspect of Horse-cult in China and Japan* (Leiden, 1935). It was a sound, excellently documented study about an original topic. Hayagrīva is a horse-headed tantric deity whose ritual spread from India throughout Tibet, Central Asia, China and Korea as far as Japan—countries whose languages he had studied. The Sanskrit scholar and philosopher Frits Staal later wrote: 'It was typical of him that he did not choose to follow the familiar path which another person might have made his life's work, but immediately embarked on other topics.' (*De Gids*, No. 10, 1989). This is true, even though in later publications Van Gulik also revealed evidence of his interest in Tantrism.

The period between the award of his doctorate and his departure for his first foreign posting on 3 May 1935 was completely taken up by preparations for his journey and saying good-bye to his family and friends. On 27 March he was sworn in as assistant-interpreter by the Minister of Foreign Affairs. He also paid a courtesy call on the Chinese envoy.

It is noteworthy that one of the friends he took his leave of was the poet J. Slauerhoff, to whom he had given Chinese lessons. He had dinner with Slauerhoff and his wife at the restaurant *Zomerzorg* in Leiden, another time he dined with him alone and they played chess. He even spent the evening before his departure with Slauerhoff. They had a great deal in common and this was what attracted them to each other. Van Gulik had a feeling for poetry and Slauerhoff, the great nomad, had, like Van Gulik, fallen under the spell of Asia and of Chinese culture. Consequently, it was no coincidence that the journal *China*, for which Van Gulik had written on such topics as Chinese literature and in which he published poems he had translated from

Chinese, had also printed a story by Slauerhoff, 'Het Lente-Eiland' (Island of Spring) about an island in the vicinity of Amoy (now Xiamen), and a number of poems from his anthology *Oost-Azië* (Eastern Asia).

In Het Lente-Eiland, Slauerhoff published these verses about the Chinese lute:

> *In my mouldered frame*
>
> *And my time-worn strings*
> *Slumber the songs, once*
>
> *Admired, now long disdained.*
> *Dimmed the jade keys,*
> *The golden studs stolen.*
> *Dust clogs my once resonant insides.*
> *The notes still linger on.*
> *But, Oh, who still plays me?*
>
> *The song is ignored*
> *And as time passed I've grown lonely.*
> *Poets are wanderers, their number few.*
> *The people now clamour for*
> *Shang's flute, Chin's flageolet*
> *Shrill and barbaric.*

In the same journal (*China*, vol. 5, 1930), in a translation by the first-year student Robert van Gulik, the great Song dynasty poet Su Tung-p'o:

> I mourn the impermanence of our lives... I wish that human life was as inexhaustible as the great river, then I would keep company with the soaring Immortals, arrest the moon in her course, and be eternal... I know now that this cannot be granted me, hence I have cast my song to the melancholy wind.
>
> [From 'Het gedicht van den rooden muur' (Poem of the Red Wall)]

Young Van Gulik was an accomplished writer, even though his style could sometimes verge on mawkishness, but the quotation below from his article 'De Wijze der Vijf Wilgen' [The Sage of the Five Willows] (*China*, vol. 8, no. 1, 1933) does show that at that time, like his friend Slauerhoff, he did occasionally come across a Chinese lute, the instrument to which he would later devote himself with great commitment.

Lingering in the memory, it faded to no more than the enchanting, musical lilt of melodious Chinese verse. It was a song of a lute, a garden full of roses and chrysanthemums. there was a little wine and a hint of melancholy. Nothing more.

Although Slauerhoff liked the lute, so much cloying sentiment irked him. Once, as they sat playing chess, they had had talked and shown each other some of their verses. 'Not bad', said 'Slau', 'but enough of the roses and silk, and that melodious, scented business. Reality, even a dream, is more brutal.'

Hence the lute remained but eventually, except on a few rare occasions, Van Gulik abandoned poetry because, as he said himself, he knew how beautiful and how perfect Chinese poetry could be, and realized that such heights were beyond him.

After a trip to Paris with his companion Nellie to revisit old haunts and to say good-bye to their many friends there, Van Gulik left the Netherlands on 3 May 1935. He took the shortest route to Japan at that time, by rail through Siberia, Manchuria (as the three north-easternmost provinces of China were then called) and Korea, from where he took a ship. With mixed emotions, a pleasurable sense of excitement, probably mixed with the dull ache caused by the final farewell from Nellie, he finally boarded the train on his way to China, the country of which he had dreamed ever since he was a child, to whose language and culture he had devoted years of study. The journey took nine days. Neither at the time nor later did he give any description of the trip. Obviously he was not in the mood to do so. The abrupt, final parting from the woman with whom he had spent five happy years was still too grievous.

The idea was that Nellie and her son would follow me later, after the ministry had specified my final destination. However, she had only encouraged this idea to spare me pain. When she accompanied me to the station to say good-bye, at the very last moment she said that, for both our sakes, this must be the end; gradually the difference in age would assume disastrous proportions and that we should therefore grow apart from each other. She made me promise that I would destroy all her photographs and letters, would never write to her and never ever attempt to see her again. I did never see her again because she died, ten years later, of a heart attack during the war while I was serving in China. The only photographs of the two of us which I have are those which I recently received from her son. Only as the years passed did I fully begin to realize what a wonderful woman she had been and how much I owed her.

The photograph of my PhD dinner shows mother sitting on my left, behind her stand father and Uncle Piet. Mrs Ferguson is sitting on my right and Nellie is next to her. She was there as my landlady; as if by tacit agreement, our real relationship was never broached between me and my parents. Father had always said that we were completely free in the choice of our women, and he abided strictly by his word. Professor Uhlenbeck was unable to be present; his health, his eyesight in particular, was deteriorating and he no longer ventured out very much. I was not aware that the photographer had pressed the shutter, and this photo shows me precisely as I was: a self-satisfied stripling. With my PhD diploma in my pocket at the age of twenty-four (a normal university study took eight years and a PhD was rarely attained before a person was thirty) and the glamour of the prospect of a diplomatic career, I considered myself as a rather remarkable young man. However, a few weeks in the Far East were enough to bring me sharply back down to earth with both feet on the ground.

But first there was the long train journey from Europe to Asia.

The Trans-Siberian offered neither the glamour nor the luxury of the Orient Express. The wide railway gauge in the Soviet Union meant that the carriages were certainly more spacious and comfortable (Robert actually had a whole compartment to himself and only had to share the washroom between the two compartments with another passenger), but everything was simpler, the people, their clothing and the food (not by candlelight!), which to make matters worse was terribly monotonous. With the exception of the area around Lake Baikal, the landscape was also monotonous and soporific—endless plains and birch forests—and an air of poverty hung over the towns and villages through which the train passed. Nevertheless, the length of the journey and the immersion in, or at least the passing by, of a completely different world, elicited a fascination all its own.

At the Chinese border station of Manchouli (now Manzhouli), Van Gulik was immediately confronted with the complicated situation into which that part of China had been plunged. Rail traffic was organized by Soviet personnel (the Trans-Siberian and the Chinese Eastern Railways were still in Soviet hands) but the day-to-day work was done by Chinese. Japanese soldiers kept guard and Japanese customs officials checked the passports and searched the luggage. Japan had occupied the whole of Manchuria in 1932, and had proclaimed the state of Manchukuo in the region, with Emperor Pu Yi as nominal head of state. (The film *The Last Emperor* tells his story).

Naturally, Robert van Gulik did not want to let slip the chance to make his first acquaintance with China (apart from a train). As the official reason for his week-long visit to Harbin, he alleged that the local Dutch consul had been struggling with a staff shortage and was in need of assistance. The daughter of the consul, Mrs H. De Vries-Van der Hoeven, says that this was absolutely not true. This 'need of assistance' was obviously a pretext Van Gulik used to justify his week-long stay in Harbin. However, his visit there was rather a disappointment.

> Harbin shocked and baffled me. It was the most dismal city in the dismal puppet-state of Manchukuo. I felt completely at a loss, also because my Chinese, Russian and Japanese colloquial knowledge proved sadly inadequate. In the cavernous Hotel Modern where I was staying, suave Soviet officers (then still attached to the Chinese Eastern Railway) rubbed shoulders with grim-looking Japanese agents, in the squalid streets Chinese hooligans brawled with pauperized poor White Russians, under the indifferent eyes of slovenly clad, insolent Chinese soldiers, and smartly turned out, contemptuous Japanese military police; the bars were crowded by blowzy Russian prostitutes, and the noisy Chinese women in the shops and in the streets were drab and ugly. Everywhere one was met with hostility and suspicion. Where were the refined Chinese scholars, writing poetry in their elegant miniature gardens, where their dainty damsels? It was a terrible disillusion.

It is hardly surprising that his high expectations of his first acquaintance with China should end in disappointment. After all, Harbin was not a Chinese city but a Russian enclave on Chinese soil, constructed by Russians when the Trans-Siberian railway was being built across Northeast China to Vladivostock (and Port Arthur). At the end of the 1920s and the beginning of the 1930s, the Russian population of Harbin was approximately half a million and it was full of typically Russian buildings, including many churches, and Russian (or rather a sort of pidgin Russian) was the main means of communication between Russians and Chinese. There was even a separate Chinese quarter on the Sungari River near the railway bridge.

Van Gulik's outpourings should be taken with a pinch of salt according to Mrs De Vries. The hotel in which he stayed, the Hotel Modern in the main street (the Kitaiskaya) of the Pristan quarter, was certainly not as bad as he depicted it. It was one of the three best hotels in Harbin. Nor, in contrast to some in the outer suburbs, could the streets in the centre be qualified as squalid. During the Russian Revolution, a large number of intellectuals, artists, businessmen and the clergy had fled to Harbin, where they contributed to the cultural life, education, religion, the press and commerce, all of which were flourishing in the Russian community just at that period.

Later Van Gulik also realized that,

> Harbin had always been a Russian, never a Chinese, city in the true sense of the word, that virtually all the decent Chinese had fled south with the arrival of the Japanese army, that the rapes and kidnappings had become such daily events that the small number of decent Chinese women who did remain did not leave their houses.

As the decorative, fragile Chinese ladies had withdrawn from public view, the presence of attractive, elegantly dressed Russian girls, in the street, hotels, shops, restaurants, nightclubs and bars, was made all the more apparent. They must have made an impression on Robert, so recently bereft of any ties. If so, why does he not make a single mention of them in his notes? In hindsight, there is an explanation. Actually, something miraculous had happened, something about which in later years he was only prepared to talk about with a very select number of people. He met a Russian girl who swept him off his feet so completely he wanted to marry her, right away, there and then in Harbin! It was completely out of character for him to want to tie himself down so suddenly. Was it the parting with Nellie which prompted him to seek a new, permanent relationship, perhaps to show Nellie that he could make his own way without her? Whatever the reason may have been, he confided his intention to Consul Van der Hoeven, who, after a long conversation in which he had to use enormous powers of persuasion, was able to convince him to abandon the plan.

Later, Van Gulik divulged a more detailed, and, perhaps with hindsight, rosier version of what happened to a colleague. Van der Hoeven's attempts at persuasion were not the only reason he had dropped his matrimonial plans. Another incentive had been his visit to a place of entertainment where he met another, even more attractive Russian girl, who was importantly even more skilled in the art of love-making. The many facets of this art always fascinated him and it was years before he actually married.

IN JAPAN

After a hectic week in Harbin, Robert left to take up his official appointment, Tokyo, where a second shock awaited him. The huge, half-Japanese, half-Western city confused him, and his new chief, the Dutch Minister, General J.C. Pabst, although competent, was also, in Robert's eyes at least, a dour old martinet.

> He told me at once that he had expected an experienced diplomatic officer. I might hold a doctorate of oriental languages, he barked at me, but I didn't know the first thing about Japanese politics or economics, so that the only way I could make myself useful was to keep the Legation's accounts in order; deficits would be subtracted from my salary.
>
> Thoroughly chastened, I set to work. Every morning, as soon as I had finished the accounts, I studied the back-files and found them fascinating; politically, Japan was poised to return to a military dictatorial rule resembling that of Tokugawa Shogunate, economically it was exercising increasing pressure on the Netherl. East Indies; and there were clear signs suggesting aggressive plans.

Indeed, although in practice Japanese imperialism at that time was principally directed against China, Tokyo was showing signs of taking greater political and economic interest in the Dutch East Indies. During the 1930s the indigenous population there was fairly sympathetic towards Japan. These sentiments were assiduously cultivated by Japan through propaganda radio broadcasts and by awarding Indonesian students scholarships. It was becoming increasingly more obvious that Japan had also assigned Indonesia a place in its Asian 'New Order'. Tokyo made economic demands on the Dutch East Indies government, for instance, to do with the export of petroleum to Japan, which could be only partially satisfied. These demands were invariably accompanied by a covert threat of violence.

In the Legation archive Van Gulik found plenty of instances of this. A year earlier, the Minister had received a visit from the patriotic association, *Meirinkai*, whose representatives included both a retired general and a retired admiral. This party had handed over a memorandum about the forthcoming economic conference between the two countries in Batavia (capital of the Dutch East Indies, present-day Jakarta). The Dutch government was urged somewhat aggressively to ensure that the outcome of the impending negotiations would be successful. Should they not be so, 'dark clouds' would hang over their relations. Pabst had categorically rejected this threat as well as another unacceptable passage.

In this period, the gradual breakdown of the parliamentary democracy of the 1920s in Japan was slowly gaining momentum, ceding to an increasingly arrogant military administration. Military leaders had difficulty tolerating the limitations imposed on them by civilian governments. Junior officers, the majority of whom were from poor rural families, distrusted their own leaders, especially prominent politicians, whose luxurious, corrupt life-style (as they saw it) they despised. Puritanism, chauvinistic nationalism and self-denial drove some to commit violent acts and sow confusion in order to instigate the fall of the 'un-Japanese' democracy.

In fact, the military was divided and the goals for which the various factions were striving were not always the same, often leading to compromises in politico-military matters. One of the powers to be reckoned with was the Kwantung Army stationed in Manchuria. As far as Japan was concerned, the principal purpose of Manchuria was to act as a buffer against the Soviet Union, but it also did not underestimate its economic importance. Japanese money constituted 75 per cent of all foreign investments there and 40 per cent of all Japanese trade with China was connected to Manchuria. There was universal agreement among all the parties in Japan about the need to protect these Japanese interests, but the time had come when the military leaders preferred action to diplomacy. With at least the tacit consent of the general staff, the Kwantung Army was able to instigate a growing number of incidents, pretexts for more aggressive actions and the occupation of ever larger areas of China. Because of its actions, successive Japanese governments were being held to what could only be called ransom by the military. One after another moderate politician vanished from the stage.

A fiercely nationalist current in Japan insisted that the country be accorded a position equivalent to that of the other great powers as well as a leading role in Asia. At the First London Naval Conference in 1930, Japan had still agreed to accepting a fleet division of 5-5-3 (United States, United Kingdom, Japan), even though this acquiescence had unleashed a torrent of bitterness and outrage on the home front. Although the terms of this treaty remained in force until 1936, by 1935 Japan was no longer willing to accept any restrictions greater than those imposed on the other countries and withdrew from the Second London Naval Conference. The end of co-operation with the other naval powers, preceded by the occupation of Northeast China (Manchuria) and secession from the League of Nations were just so many more steps on the road to further aggression.

The Japanese believed that the western powers had been their forerunners both in their occupation and exploitation of parts of China and in establishing colonies in Asia. Japan had not escaped the world-wide depression of 1929, which had raised arguments in support of the hypothesis that expansion by military conquest would deliver the country from its economic problems. Many were convinced that, by securing more outlets and the supply of essential raw materials not found at home and creating more *Lebensraum* for Japanese colonists (by 1930 the population had more than doubled since the beginning of the century), Japan would attain greater prosperity.

In Japan in principle there were two imperialist schools of thought: the first advocated territorial expansion on the continent (China and Russia); the latter was (also) in favour of looking farther southwards overseas. When the time was ripe, the second school would succeed in making its voice heard. The Dutch Legation was utterly convinced of this and scrupulously dispatched repeated warnings to The Hague. However, in the world of Dutch politics there was little interest in spending money on defence. Even when the Fleet Law was being debated in the 1920s, far greater interest was raised by the burning matter of the freshly baked bread rolls on Sundays, which meant allowing bakeries to open on the Sabbath, than in building up the strength of the Royal Dutch Navy.

At grammar school and again at the university, Robert van Gulik had shown that he was not afraid of hard work. In Tokyo, he threw himself enthusiastically into his study of Japanese and later even more of Chinese. This turned out to be a critical decision because at that time practical knowledge of modern languages tended to be neglected in Leiden and Utrecht, at least in the case of Chinese and Japanese.

Now that he was a free man, a fancy-free bachelor, he also seized every opportunity to enjoy himself with both hands. His studies still left him plenty of time for life's pleasures, playing billiards, dining out with friends and exploring the night life.

All his small, personal affairs are noted in Robert's tiny pocket diaries, which he kept meticulously at this time. For instance, 3 August 1935:

> 1 o'clock lunch with Abo [the Japanese tutor] in Manyasurō, 3.30 to Yokohama. Looked at furniture with Md. [Mulder from the *Nationale Handelsbank/* National Commercial Bank], then played billiards at the Y.U. Club. Drinks and dinner at the Roof Gardens, the New Grand [Hotel]. Afterwards to K.2, Star and K.1 [nightclubs/hotels]. x [followed by the characters for Shizuko, a girl's name, which frequently re-occurs after this in the diaries; it is not difficult to guess the meaning of these x's. They are used only in the pocket diary for 1935, the activities they indicate certainly did not diminish later, but are seldom still noted].

Or another day, 12 March 1936:
> 2-4 Abo [tutor], 4-6 Narita [tutor], half-past five De Visser [Arie de V., a businessman who drank copiously] arrives, went together to dine at Lohmeyer's [restaurant in the Ginza]. Afterwards played billiards at the Ginza Club and won the 1,000 point game. At 9 o'clock fetched [Theo] Rocqué from the train. Had a drink at the Imperial [Hotel] and then ate at the Grill.

Or 20 May 1936:
> Worked at home. Mulder arrives at half-past six to have a drink, De Visser comes later. Together to Mulder's house, where found the Mullers. Had a drink together. Afterwards to Lohmeyer's where we ate with De Visser. Then to Yamada where played billiards until half-past nine. To Tokyo Eki [Station], dropped Adolfs off, met Fabius there. Together to Asakusa [a pleasure quarter], then to the Cotton Club and to Fledermaus [a western restaurant].

In the mornings he worked at the Legation, but the office was closed in the afternoons. He used this time to take lessons in colloquial Japanese and journalistic style from the former chancellery clerk, later supplemented by lessons in Japanese literature, later again in Chinese and everything to do with Chinese culture (literature, calligraphy, history and so forth). Every so often he would learn another language

(Mongolian, Hindi, Korean). By dint of countless visits to bookshops and antiquarian book-sellers and conversations with connoisseurs of Eastern art, he added to his personal, not inconsiderable knowledge in this field. He was developing a pattern of living and working which he was to maintain throughout his seven years in Japan, which he later resumed in China, in Japan on his later return there and in other countries.

Robert made a number of Dutch friends, whom he saw on a regular basis, and only showed an interest in foreigners if they could converse about his—extremely broad—field of interests. He played billiards on an almost daily basis, skated in the winter, was an avid cinema-goer and was very fond of good food—Japanese, Chinese or western, but Chinese was his favourite. Making love (an expression which he would never use; after all love was not involved, and there was a blunt, unvarnished Dutch word for the business concerned) was a sport in which he frequently indulged.

Certainly on an Orientalist, Japan exercised a special charm, an atmosphere which almost defies definition. This artistic, homogenous people, who lived their lives according to fixed rules of conduct and in a very idiosyncratic manner, had their very own culture, which diverged sharply from all others, even those of the neighbouring cultures of China and Korea. Japan had absorbed western influences selectively, without these actually impinging on its own civilization. The landscape, the houses, the gardens, the traditional costume, the aesthetic shop windows, all of these exerted an enormous attraction on romantically inclined foreigners such as Van Gulik. At that time Tokyo could still boast many mansions set in large gardens and an evening stroll through this sort of exclusive neighbourhood took on a fairy-tale atmosphere—the beautiful contours of the roofs were etched against a clear, starry sky in which a moon tinged with blue shed her brilliance. The more prosaically minded also recalled the stench of the open sewers and rotting fish.

In his autobiographical account, Robert wrote that after his afternoon lessons in Japanese he would dine somewhere in the city at a small Japanese or Chinese eating-house and then spend the whole evening reading in the gloomy bungalow assigned to him in the Legation compound. It was sparsely furnished with a few rickety bits and pieces left behind by his predecessor. He devoured modern Japanese books and magazines. This will certainly often have been exactly what happened, because he read and worked until deep into the night, but in this 'biography'—probably he thought it not important to this purpose—in his pocket diary the convivial twenty-five-year-old meticulously noted down many hours devoted to playing billiards, visiting or being visited by his many friends, congenial drinks and dinner parties, often followed by dancing or 'going to the girls'.

After the first few months his life in the office began to improve.

> I discovered to my relief that in Leiden I had after all received a sound grounding in Japanese, the main problem was to establish a link between theory and practice. I began to prepare for the Minister brief notes on the Japanese press-reactions, and he took me off accounts and ordered me to submit daily reports on the Japanese press on a daily basis. I came into contact with junior colleagues of other diplomatic missions and we explored together the night-life of this teeming city. I avoided international cocktail parties, etc. for I felt I had such a tremendous lot to learn that I could not afford to spend time on anything but my Japanese studies.

The latter turned out better than expected... 'Japanese studies' was interpreted in the widest possible sense, and certainly Robert van Gulik (and many of his colleagues as well) always loathed the sort of cocktail party which served no purpose other than to be 'seen'. Moreover, in his own words, he did not need 'to waste' his precious time 'gathering political information on the diplomatic circuit, in which as interpreter (a position which he gladly used as an excuse if too many demands were placed upon him!) he was put in a separate category, where he enjoyed the company of the other scholars of Japanese. The few foreign diplomats who knew him in this period thought he was an odd man out, a first-class Chinese scholar, a savant of stature, but also a 'foreign Chinese', who thought and acted in an Oriental manner.

In his Japanese studies Robert managed to unite the useful and the pleasurable:

> 24-8-1935: [Saturday] 1.30 took the Sakura express to Atami [a seaside resort with hot springs]. From there by car to Imaiso with Shizu[ko]. Walked along the beach, ate. x.

The next day:

> Swam in the sea and bathed. To Shimoda in the afternoon. Saw the grave of Townsend Harris [the first American consul in Japan] and

that of Okichi [Okichi was the housekeeper/concubine assigned to
T.H. by the Japanese authorities, who remained faithful to him and
was later revered in Japan]. Back at the hotel swam and bathed.
Played billiards in the evening. x.

And also on Monday:

[…] swam and bathed. Wandered beside the sea after lunch. x.

They returned to Tokyo the next day. On the following day,
Wednesday, in the evening he went to Yokohama with the far more
senior Theo Rocqué (with whom he often explored the nightlife and
whose love of the arts, above all for the late nineteenth-century Dutch
author Couperus, he shared) but, instead of going to K.1 (where
Shizuko and others worked), for a change they visited the Star again.
Robert put a x alongside 'Ruriko'.

This pattern continued until there was more certainty in Robert's
life. There were two reasons for this, a permanent relationship and
his own home.

His pocket diary reveals that in the middle of September he was
invited to an Indonesian lunch 'with Nanako and Fumiko' by his
faithful friend De Visser. This had obviously been arranged. Nanako
was Arie de Visser's steady girlfriend and she had a good friend, Iriye
Fumiko, who seemed to be (or thought she was) a suitable partner for
Robert Van Gulik. They hit it off very quickly, because later on the
same day he took her to a restaurant in Asakusa, and three days later
we read in his pocket diary:

At 2 o'clock took the measurements for sheets and the like with F.,
played billiards at Yamada with De Visser and had a drink at the
Blue Ribbon, after that at De V.'s house at 8 o'clock with F. And N.

Recorded in the back of the 1935 diary is a note of the 'most
important events':

7 March: PhD defence
3 May: left the Netherlands
23 May: arrival in Tokyo
29 September: moved into own home in the Legation compound.

Presumably the 'gloomy bungalow' he spoke of earlier had
been temporary accommodation. Now he had his own house (next
door to his colleague Snellen) and, for the time being, a permanent

companion. Although he did not forgo the company of his friends, drinks, playing billiards, bookshops and antiquarian book-sellers, we now find him much more at home:

> Worked at home, lunch at home, dinner at home, worked at home in the afternoon, worked at home in the evening, Jap. dinner at home with Nanako, F. and de V.

Very occasionally an 'x' still appears against 'Shizu[ko]', and twice against another Japanese girl's name.

Writing about his housemate Fumiko, Van Gulik said:

> Most of my bachelor diplomatic acquaintances took Japanese girlfriends along to restaurants and cinemas [Van Gulik was to do this later himself]. This was un-Japanese because Japanese men keep their mistresses at home and, when going out amuse themselves with the talent they find on the premises; moreover, these girls belonged to the "modern set", dressed in western clothes and had at least a smattering of English. Then I met IRIYE Fumiko, who though mostly wearing Western dress spoke no English at all, and she came to stay with me. At first all went well, for she was an attractive, cheerful girl, and of exactly my age.
>
> However, her aim was to become "westernized" as quickly as possible, and dreamt of becoming a film-star in Japanese American-style pictures; she despised everything Chinese. I, on the contrary, wanted to learn about Japan and the Japanese and [...] revered everything Chinese. [Fumiko] also could not get along at all with old Fuku-san, the incredibly ancient implausibly garrulous Japanese woman who kept the house clean, and she took no interest in the household.
>
> I tried to reason things out with Fumiko, as I was rather fond of her, but my Japanese was inadequate; so we agreed to disagree, and after three months she left, and I lost sight of her completely. I hope she did well, for she was a decent girl. She was the first oriental woman I lived with, and through her I got an inkling of the inner tensions and the emotional strain that the western impact causes Asiatics—a problem till this day still insufficiently realized or acknowledged by most Western observers.

5-12-1935: Ate at home with Fumiko and terminated relationship.

10-12-1935: 3-4 Abo. Made out a receipt for F. [with Abo's advice and help]. Half past 8 Fumiko, 100 yen and receipt.

Shortly afterwards some sort of financial arrangement was made with his nightclub girlfriend, Shizuko, who had apparently wanted some compensation for the services which she had provided. Although Robert enjoyed life to the full, he was not someone to squander his money. We see that he only drew small amounts out of the bank, and often he says that he was late paying his tutor. But now the sum involved was a fairly considerable one for that time:

> 13-12-1935: Abo and Shizuko came at 4 o'clock. The problem of S. discussed. Gave 350 Yen. Dined with her. 8 o'clock skating in Shibaura.

Now somebody who was to stay far longer than Fumiko arrived in his life. At first we find only a brief reference to this in the pocket diary:

> 16-12-1935: Okaya-san coming [her full name was Okaya Katsuyo, or Kachan for short], 2-4 Abo, 4-6 Narita [his two Japanese tutors], to the Tokyo Club, had a drink. Worked at home.

She is mentioned again on 23 December:

> 6 o'clock had a Chinese dinner with Kat(s)u in Sampuku. After that did some shopping in the Ginza.

And the next day:

> Did shopping in town with Katsuyo. 5 o'clock visited the Mulder family and celebrated Christmas.

In his autobiographical sketch he wrote:

> After that [after Fumiko], I met Okaya Katsuyo (shortened to Kachan), who stayed with me through my first seven years in Japan.
> Having finished elementary school only, Kachan had little knowledge and was not well informed, but she already possessed that intuitive wisdom the Orient has bestowed throughout the centuries on its women. She knew only Japanese and beyond a faint curiosity, she had no interest in anything western, but she had the traditional old Japanese respect for things Chinese [this respect lingered on among the Japanese in general, despite the vicious anti-Chinese government campaign before and during the Pacific War, and should not be underrated today—1994]. A devout believer in Shintō and of the Pure Land School of Buddhism

[whose doctrine taught that by vows and invoking the name of Amitābha—Japanese; Amida- Buddha, the devout can attain the 'Pure Land' or Paradise], she was Japanese through and through and possessed all the sterling qualities of Japanese womanhood, foremost among them loyalty, modesty and thriftiness. Though barely twenty when she came to my house, she was wise in the ways of Japanese life, treated Fuku-san with deference, and the old woman grew very fond of her. Together they bought a few simple but tasteful things that made my bungalow more comfortable, and thus there was established a pattern of home-life in which I was very happy; all through those seven years I can't remember a single quarrel, not even a hard word.

Through Kachan I gained an insight the subtle, unwritten rules that traditionally govern the complicated Japanese social pattern, and also into the Japanese way of life. She told me, for instance, that in order to enjoy occasional stays in a completely Japanese surroundings, one has to wear Japanese dress. I said that I didn't dream of making myself ridiculous, for I had often noted the contemptuous amusement with which the Japanese look at tourists and other foreigners who put on a kimono. But she bought me a complete outfit, she patiently instructed me in the intricate pattern of behaviour that goes with Japanese dress: how to walk, how to sit, what attitudes and gestures to adopt, etc. Thereafter I found indeed that the Japanese didn't give me a second look when occasionally I adopted Japanese dress on trips up country or downtown. I also learned from her that the greatest difficulty in speaking correct Japanese does not lie in idiom or grammar, but in choosing the style of speaking appropriate for each social contact and each separate occasion.

Kachan had a passion for Japanese historical films and for the classical Japanese stage, and there we went at least once every week. Apart from that, she never asked me for anything. New kimono I had practically to force on her, it was only after repeated urging that she agreed to me engaging a teacher for her in flower-arrangement; she insisted on wearing, during the daytime, inside and outside the house a white maid's apron, and dressed up only when we went out together, or at night when I was working in my ever-expanding library and she was sitting in her corner doing needle work or reading a novel. I was profoundly shocked when, soon after she had come to the house, she defined her position, with the utmost calm and using the traditional Sino-Japanese term, as that of "the maidservant who enjoys the master's favours". However, I had to admit that she was right—at least according to the standards of the Far East, and after all it was there we were living. In the nearly seven years she lived with me there were other Japanese and Chinese women, but she always retained her position of "first lady"—*nei-jên;* "she who rules the within".

Every westerner arriving in the orient has of course to adjust himself, but—contrary to what one would expect—this process is more difficult for the orientalist than for the non-expert; for whereas the latter has to digest only one world, i.e., the new one he is confronted with in the east, the former has to assimilate this new world with the mental picture he had formed of it during his previous years of study. In my case this period of assimilation and coordination of theory and practice, lasted nearly six months, then suddenly ended in the brief space of a few days. Through a conjunction of circumstances I can not only fix the exact date, but also submit a few snapshots then taken. During those few days Japan—and implicitly China—suddenly ceased to be for me an object of study and observation; it was as if, while observing a remote scene through a strong telescope, I suddenly found myself as if by magic transplanted into the very midst of that scene. It all happened during the New Year's holidays 1935-36, when I had taken Kachan for a trip up country, first to a seaside village, then to the hot springs resort of Odawara. Back in Tokyo I wrote my experience down and I append a rough English translation to this record. It meant for me the second turning point in my life; various problems I had been puzzling about for a long time became crystal-clear all at once, and I arrived at what might be called a personal equation with the orient. Thereafter I saw China and Japan so to speak from within and could read

Pl. 7.   With Kachan at the hot springs at Odawara, January 1936.

Chinese and Japanese texts without mentally "translating" them. Did auto-suggestion play a role then? I rather think it was one of those "sudden revelations" mentioned in Zen.

His pocket diary contains only a few bare facts:

31-12-1935: 3.10 from Tokyo Station to Yoshino in Izu [a peninsula southwest of Tokyo], 6 p.m. arrived in Yoshino, dinner and bath, heard the New Year chimes at midnight.

1-1-1936: Walked in the woods around Yoshino and visited the small Nichiren Temple [Nichiren was the founder of the only truly Japanese Buddhist sect]. At 9 a.m. sent a telegram to the Minister to explain inability to attend [New Year's] Reception.

2-1-1936: Went to Shūzenji by car. Met the priest Mokurai in the temple. Accompanied him to the Arae Inn, lunched with the owner, Aibara, and penned aphorisms. To the abbot with Mokurai. Returned to Yoshino at 6.

3-1-1936: By car from Yoshino to Yumoto via Mishima, where [I] visited the deer park and attended a Shintō feast. At 2 lunch in Yumoto. Then visited the Sōunji [a well-known Rinzai Zen temple]. Bought some souvenirs.

4-1-1936: In the morning, strolled to the waterfall and through the village. Half past three, long hike through the mountains.

5-1-1936: 11.55 left Odawara for Tokyo, lunch at Café Parisien at half past 1. Changed clothes at home. Took tea with the Mulders at 4. In the evening worked at home.

There is no mention of the exceptional incident which had befallen him at Odawara, which had subjected him to an overwhelming experience of the Eastern philosophy of the impermanence of all things. Nevertheless, he did write about it later in his unpublished essay *The Hot Springs at Odawara,* a shortened version of which appeared in *Elseviers Geïllustreed Maandschrift,* vol. 42, Amsterdam 1936 (later also in *Per Diplomatieke Koerier,* Amsterdam).

Robert van Gulik had been introduced to Buddhism at an early age through his studies of Chinese, Japanese and Tibetan. The concept of the impermanence of things and of an illusionary world was also known in ancient Greece and Rome, and is even found in

Christianity, but Buddhism, above all other religions, emphasizes its importance: 'Everything we see and experience is an illusion of our mind'. Certainly Robert's study would have made him especially susceptible to this doctrine, which also appealed to him as an artist and connoisseur of the arts.

Now Kachan, a devout Buddhist girl, had come into his life, and, after having visited a few small Buddhist temples and spoken with the priests, they had spent their first long weekend in the romantic atmosphere of a thermal spa. Earlier, Robert had practised writing (Buddhist) maxims in characters, and now he took it up again.

In *The Hot Springs at Odawara*, Van Gulik records how he and Kachan enjoyed the time they had spent in a traditional Japanese inn—the elegant interior, the exquisite food, the blissful hot bath, all accompanied by the gentle murmur of the hot springs.

The last day it rained, and in a trice a spa could seem dreary; but this was not the only reason Robert felt suddenly overwhelmed by sadness and despondency. It was one of those inexplicable changes of mood. Everything seemed futile, all perishes, nothing is permanent. He recalled some lines of verse written by the famous poet Bashō when he visited the site of an ancient battle:

> *The summer grass, the summer grass…*
> *All that remains of a warrior's dream.*

As they ate their evening rice, Kachan chatted gaily about everything they had seen together. He listened to her and answered, but all the while the words of Bashō's poem echoed in the back of his mind, reminding him of the impermanence of all things. He was sitting there with this very dear Japanese girl. How long would she remain with him? When would he grow old and ugly and become infirm? How long did he have to live? The pain of the farewell from Nellie returned: 'An old wound caused by the parting from a loved one began to smart again, old doubts long thought conquered suddenly resurfaced', Robert writes in this essay about the hot springs at Odawara.

Robert was confronted by a painful conclusion,

No, nothing will remain. Not our names which will become empty sounds and will only recall a personality who was not us to those who come. Not our words not our deeds, because as soon as our words are spoken, deeds done, they become extrinsic to us, cold and distant, and they take on their own life, go their own way, without a single backward glance.

The poet says it all: our hopes, our dreams, everything will disappear as soon as inimical fate decrees that this will be so. All that remains is the summer grass, which will sprout afresh each spring.

Then we are engulfed by the piercing awareness of our own impotence, the impossibility of ever finding stability, and of grasping some part of this fleeting beauty for ourselves.

The day they left was shrouded in a cold, thick mist. The floor mats felt clammy, and a chill breeze heralded the approach of the autumn. But then, in an instant, writes Robert, in this now hostile environment, he became aware of a 'calm, modest companion', whose loyalty never failed him: the murmur of the springs. He had forgotten their presence, precisely because they were so ubiquitous.

In a flash all his more trifling worries seemed unimportant and a broader perspective opened up before him. 'Why do we always want to possess and hold on [to things]?', he asked himself. He remembered an ancient Chinese painting of a monkey clinging to a overhanging branch as its questing hand reached for the reflection of the moon in the water below:

> Is this painting not a speaking image of our yearning, our striving to possess and cling on to? The reflection entices into the murky waters, while the elusive moon continues to shine just as far away as ever.

He now knew with certainty—and consequently finally felt completely at home in the world of China and Japan—that, as he writes himself, 'permanent possession is only possible by renouncing everything', by total abandonment. 'The many impressions of joy and beauty gathered during this shared trip derived their meaning purely and simply from the fact that it was their transience, and that alone, which aroused my longings for that which we never shall acquire, but from which none the less we shall never be free.'

Is this an indication that he was also something of a mystic, a trait which he had seen in his father and grandfather? Absolutely, but this quality seldom broke through the surface. It remained a hidden source. What was obvious to anyone who became better acquainted with him was that because of his profound knowledge of their cultures and ideas into which he had thrown himself completely, he really could see China and Japan *from the inside out*.

The poetical side of his nature found expression in his calligraphy and other forms of Chinese art, and every so often—after all he did

remain a Western man—in a few poems written in Dutch, like these
unpublished verses which he wrote during his Tokyo period:

Spring Morning in Shiba Park

The gentle delicacy of the early spring morning...
Where the winding paths meander ever farther
Under the petals of the cherry blossom
Which are blown hither and thither by the morning breeze:
Paths of blossom which lead to temples
Whose scarlet gates shimmer through the green.

Now all colours glow with a peculiar clarity
The unreal harbingers of the coming season.

The rising path often slows the footsteps
And stops them by a standing stone lantern.
Three leaves form a circle: a famed blazon
That elicits reveries of days long past,
When he—or she—still lived, who made this
Pious offering to the gods, or to the park,
When yet the temple roof was still unweathered
And the lawn spread more widely, ever more untamed.

But then as now, the dew glistened on the new-sprung grass
And a divine voice broke the morning calm:
The subconscious awaits the temple gong.

Autumn Morning in Shiba Park

A sudden wind scatters the light mist,
Sluggishly the withered trees shrug off the yellowed leaves.
The glance leads farther: this hill
Was unknown, over there for the first time
Under the moss of years, stones reveal
A pious inscription, an epitaph.

Remembrance haunts he who wanted to be forgotten,
The mourning of a life lost

In this season all bright colours vanish.
Over the gentler tints of muted red and yellow
The greyness of the dawn hangs heavy.
Did autumn seem so miserable to him
Who once built these temples here
Or did this season bring him satisfaction?

The satiation of melancholy and empty waiting
Which might perhaps still silence the final sorrow?

This is the lesson of these autumnal Tokugawa[1] graves:
Nothing remains, not even the richest graves.
...The passer-by shivers in the morning chill.

During these first six months in Japan, by dint of intensive daily study, Van Gulik consolidated the sound basis he had built up in Leiden and even earlier by acquiring a formidable knowledge of the Japanese language and of Japanese life.

While he was busy doing this, at the Legation he was forced to familiarize himself with the increasingly ominous political situation in Japan, and its economic ties and its relations with the Dutch East Indies. But then, as later, when necessary, he was able to keep his different spheres of interest completely separate. In contrast to most, if not indeed all, diplomats, after office hours he distanced himself from all the concerns to do with his work and he would never lie awake troubled by political situations or tricky diplomatic problems. Consequently, he rarely paid any attention to these matters, either in his autobiographical notes or in his diary. These belonged to the world of the Legation: he did not at any time underestimate its importance and he loyally made his contribution to it, but it was not his personal world. Art and scholarship, the humanities were what dominated his life and to its end he was able to make important contributions to these areas.

Throughout his life Van Gulik was a systematic worker. Now that he could speak and read Japanese fluently, he decided that the time had come to devote more time to Sinology, including his spoken Chinese which was still rather unsatisfactory, his fluency in particular.

He paid a visit to the Chinese ambassador Hsü Shih-ying, 'a frail old gentleman, a perfect example of a refined Chinese scholar, who had already become famous during the last years of the Ch'ing dynasty'. In response to a subtly formulated suggestion from Robert van Gulik, the ambassador appointed one of his staff to give him Chinese lessons (the spoken language, literature and calligraphy). The man chosen was the Third Secretary, Sun Ti, a master of Chinese and

---

[1]   The shōguns who ruled Japan from 1603 to 1867. The graves of six Tokugawa shōguns are located in the grounds of the Zōjōjo temple in Shiba, Tokyo.

Japanese literature. He was also a fine painter and calligrapher, and became Robert's best Chinese friend. The Counsellor of the Embassy, Wang P'êng-shêng, was an expert on the Japanese economy. Later, in Chungking, he was to play an important role in Robert's life.

His pocket diary reveals that Robert now devoted whole afternoons to his Chinese studies with Sun. Someone who taught him two to three hours of Mongolian was also a regular visitor. Occasionally, 'for good measure,' he added yet another to his store of languages, if he happened to need it to assist his studies or if it

Pl. 8. In the garden of the Chinese embassy, Tokyo 1936 (centre: Ambassador Hsü Shih-ying; second from right: Chargé d'Affaires Wang P'êng-shêng).

fitted in with his travel plans. At a slightly later date, the name of Kim, who taught him Korean, crops up constantly in his diary. The goal behind this choice was to be sent on an offical mission to Korea, a hope which was fulfilled on a number of occasions. Contacts with American, English, French and German scholars of Chinese began to occur more frequently.

Shortly after his arrival in Tokyo, he had left his card at several cultural institutions. He presented a copy of his thesis to the Maison Franco-Japonaise and the Deutscher Verein. He began to attend lectures at the Ostasiatishche Gesellschaft more often and even gave an address there himself:

26-2-1936: Half past four O.A.G. [Ostasiatische Gesellschaft]. Gave a lecture (Interpretation of Mandalas), 12 people present. [*Mandalas* are symbolic diagrams which represent the universe and are used in Buddhist rituals and meditation.]

Army incident, at half past five in the morning Takahashi, Watanable, etc. murdered. After lecture to the Tokyo Club, to Fabius [a Dutch journalist], went on together to the Imperial Hotel.

This was a very laconic reference to the tragic series of assassinations committed on a number of prominent politicians by fanatical junior officers, and the attempt by the latter to stage a coup d'état!

The notorious '26 February Incident' was far more than just a storm in a teacup. It was not the first time politicians had been murdered by extremist officers, but this time the centre of Tokyo was occupied by a thousand men of the first division and attacks were made on a number of prominent, moderate advisers to the Emperor. Three of them, including the prime minister, escaped but the other three were killed, namely: Takahashi, the Minister of Finance, Saitō, Keeper of the Great Seal and Watanabe, the Inspector-General of Military Training.

The coup d'état failed. The rebels who were quickly encircled by loyal troops, the majority of them naval ratings, surrendered after three days. The government gave them two hours to commit *harakiri*. They refused, because they were counting on being tried in a civil court which they could have used as a forum in which to air their views. Instead, they were court-martialled and some of them were condemned to death and executed.

Van Gulik recorded several events tersely, without any comment, without being upset by the incident. He imperturbably pursued his cultural activities and his social life with his friends. These incidents were a matter for the Legation, the place where the political situation was studied and discussed and, beyond this context, they were non-existent as far as he was concerned. During these tumultuous days the pocket diary only notes the following.

27-2-1936: Narita [teacher] coming.

28-2: De Visser to lunch, afterwards played billiards together in Toranomon [part of the business district of Tokyo]. Drove to the Sanno Hotel with Muller, Van Rechteren [First Secretary of the Legation] and Snellen [Secretary-Interpreter]. Afterwards past the guards to the Imperial Hotel.

29-2: Worked at home. De Visser came at 7, Allen at half past. Ate pea soup and listened to the gramophone with De Visser. Afterwards to Saiseriya [restaurant]. End of the military incident. Martial law in the city lifted at 4.30.

In his work at the Legation in this period, which he considered to be far less important than his studies, he was seriously hampered by his deep-seated antipathy to Minister Pabst. He acknowledged the latter's competence and his knowledge of Japanese history, but was exceptionally irritated by the way in which this 'martinet' treated him. The fact that Pabst was a homosexual and Van Gulik was a real ladies' man is not likely to have played an important role. The animosity was unquestionably entirely reciprocal. Pabst viewed Van Gulik as a scholar who was of no use to him, a lazybones, an egotist, and, as a civil servant a good-for-nothing who did not give a damn, as he was completely absorbed in his studies and his pleasures. Pabst was a dyed-in-the-wool militarist and Robert was very quick to take offence. Pabst was a stranger to tact and at times he could be pretty coarse. Once when he was giving a dinner and he thought the guests had outstayed their welcome, he said to the highest ranking lady present, who was supposed to give the signal to leave: 'I'm sorry Madam, I cannot offer you a bed for the night.'

A contemporary, who once happened to be standing talking to Van Gulik and Chancellor Witmans in the Chancellery very early on in Van Gulik's posting there, recalled the ambassador entering and remarking in a waspish tone: 'I say, Van Gulik, don't you have anything else better to do but to stand around chatting?' Van Gulik slunk off, giving the impression that at that time he was still intimidated by Pabst. When Pabst was absent, his position was filled by the First Secretary of the Legation, Van Roijen (Dr J.H. van Roijen had succeeded W.C. Count of Rechteren Limpurg M.LL. as Legation Secretary) in his capacity as Chargé d'Affaires. At such times, Van Gulik came out of his shell and was prepared to do everything within his power to assist him.

The *incompatibilité d'humeur* between Pabst and Van Gulik was also expressed in minor provocations. Their houses, as were those of Van Roijen and Secretary-Interpeter Snellen, were located in the Legation compound. One day Robert happened to walk home from Pabst's across the grass. The next day a board was placed on the lawn announcing in Japanese: 'Do not walk on the grass.' Van Gulik was furious and failed to turn up at the office for a few days, giving a 'cold' as his excuse. He sent a letter, which he had delivered by his friend Mulder (the banker), to the ambassador to inform him. Later, when Van Roijen came to see him at home he was treated to the following tirade: 'That bastard! That board was intended for me, that's why he had it written in Japanese.' In spite of everything, the diplomat Van Roijen was able to convince him that he could not continue to harbour a grudge and the next day he was back at work in the Chancellery.

Sometime earlier, Van Gulik, who had fallen under the spell of Eastern superstitions, had had his house 'cleansed' by a Japanese priest who exorcised the evil spirits. He had this done because he thought that several of the previous inhabitants had died a violent death. 'I hope that there's a window open in Pabst's house', he had remarked to Van Roijen, 'so that the demons can get in.'

Despite these troubles, as Van Gulik walked through the compound of the Legation, the gardeners continued to bow to him with more than usual deference. As custom decreed, they wore a smock on which their function in the Legation was announced in *kanji* (the Chinese characters used to write Japanese). Van Gulik argued that the designation used was too humble for the important position they occupied (a similar comparison would be between gardener and horticulturalist) and he came up with a new, more respectful name in fine characters. The gardeners were delighted with their new smocks and acknowledged their admiration of and respect for this learned scholar of Japanese, who had such a wonderful grasp of their culture.

The longer he remained in Japan, the more Van Gulik's contempt for Pabst grew. Professor C.R. Boxer, who was friends with both men, said that Van Gulik could never understand why Pabst, who had lived in Japan for nearly twenty years, collected Japanese art and was certainly knowledgeable about it, had never made any attempt to learn the language of that country. He read no Japanese and knew no more than a few brief expressions, such as 'good evening', in the colloquial language.

In retrospect, Van Gulik's contacts at this time with the well-informed German, Sorge, whom he used to meet occasionally for coffee, lunch or dinner are intriguing. He will not have had the slightest suspicion that, after a career working for the Komiterm in China, Richard Sorge, a prominent German journalist as well as correspondent for the Dutch paper, the *Algemeen Handelsblad*, was the head of a highly successful

Soviet espionage network in Japan.[2] Also the 'second man at the embassy' in the Legation, Dr Van Roijen, must never have harboured any suspicion at all about him. He often lunched with Sorge at the Tokyo Club and thought it strange that, before sitting down at table, Sorge always checked behind the curtains.

In a newspaper interview long after the war, Van Gulik said: 'We had no idea where Japan would attack, in the North or in the South. The only one who did was the German master spy Richard Sorge, who was working for the Russians. We knew this man well. He was a great

Pl. 9. Strolling in the Ginza with Frank Hawley.

friend of the German Minister. Undoubtedly that he was immensely clever. We never imagined that he worked for the Russians.'

Robert's best friend among the foreigners was the Englishman Frank Hawley, an outstanding Japanese scholar and polished stylist, who often assisted him with his work and frequently went out with him in the evenings. A Dutch student who had Japanese lessons with Hawley at the time recounted the latter had great affection and respect for Van Gulik, and was impressed by his qualities as a scholar of both Japan and China, but was amused by his exceptional interest in the weaker sex, to whom Hawley himself was certainly by no means averse. His appearance was remarkable as he was more than two metres tall, and had a well-rounded belly. Later, Van Gulik wrote that he wore his hair rather long and he sauntered rather than walked. They were both very original, unconventional types of scholars.

Robert's energy knew no bounds. Not only was he constantly busy deepening his knowledge, he was also expanding the scope

---

2   Sorge and his Japanese fellow-spy Ozaki Hotsumi were arrested in autumn
       1941 and executed in November 1944.

of his work. Unquestionably his ideal striving was to be like the classical Chinese scholar-civil servant, and he was well on the way to achieving his goal; however he still lacked several attributes. Playing the seven-string Chinese lute—the *ku-ch'in*—was part of the package, so he studied the Chinese literature about this instrument and scoured the antiquarian bookshops, never passing up an opportunity to learn something more about it. Among the informants he consulted before he went about buying such a lute (in Peking) was his new Chinese teacher and friend, Sun.

The writing table of the classical scholar-civil servant was always graced by seals, brushes, inkstones and various sorts of rice paper. His master's thesis, *Mi Fu On Inkstones*, was now revised using additional data and in 1938 was published in book form in Peking by Henri Vetch. His English friend Frank Hawley helped with the English of his text, just as he would do later with the language of many other English texts. Van Gulik trained himself in the art of carving of seals, which had to be done using the archaic seal characters, a specialized form of calligraphy. He also practised calligraphy with the brush, occasionally in the company of a friend such as the Chinese scholar Dr W.R.B. (Bill) Acker, and the finished results grew steadily more exquisite. He practised by copying classical and Buddhist aphorisms. He even had the temerity to write such an aphorism for the Chinese ambassador, who was about to retire from his post.

28-6-1936: Wrote aphorism for Chin.[ese] ambassador.

30-6-1936: Purchased seal and worked on it.

Now Van Gulik succeeded in finding a pretext for what could be called an 'official trip' to Peking, which he would—as so often— devote completely to his studies and his other hobbies. After he had fetched his travel permit from the Ministry of War (foreigners in Japan were forbidden to travel without such a document), Robert left for China on 5 September. By 10 September he was in Peking, the city of which all scholars of China dream, where for the first time he beheld the ancient imperial city!

After conversations at the Legation with the Minister and with Abell and the Chinese scholar De Josselin de Jong, as well of course with Chinese friends and with friends of friends, he immediately set off to eat Chinese food. Straight afterwards he went to Liulich'ang, the quarter famous for its antiques and antiquarian bookshops. Other days—on the evidence of his pocket diary—he visited the office of the Panch'en Lama (second only to the Dalai Lama as the highest authority in Tibet) and the Chinese Language School, where he consulted some Tibetan books. He met various Tibetans and talked to them. He also took lute lessons from the Chinese grand master, Yeh Shih-mêng, to whom he dedicated his lute book, and bought a beautiful antique *ch'in* (lute), which ever afterwards would always accompany him wherever he went, and visited more booksellers, sometimes alone, sometimes with a group of other people. He enjoyed Peking duck and other delicacies with friends, and in the evening he experienced the charms of the Chinese beauties in the tea houses in the famous quarter outside the central southern gate of the Tartar city, *Ch'ien-mên wai*.

He was responsive to the atmosphere of a city and the country and it was fortunate that his first visit to Peking was in the autumn. The clear light and the dry, cool air of the northern Chinese autumn have a particular charm. The scarlet gates of the houses and palaces, the golden yellow of the roof tiles of the Old Palace (the Forbidden City), the red and gold triumphal arches, the azure Temple of Heaven were sharply etched against the sky. The colourful markets bustled with life, and it was a delight to listen to the fine, distinctive, guttural

Pl. 10. With Chinese lute teacher at the Dutch embassy in Peking 1941.

sounds of the North Chinese Peking dialect. Caravans of heavily laden camels arrived from Mongolia, entering through one of the old city gates. It was as if time had stood still there. Robert would take a rickshaw through the narrow, grey *hutungs*, the myriad of small alleys with which Peking abounded, to the house of a Chinese scholar to whom he had an introduction. They would stop in front of a red gate embossed with bronze and the rickshaw coolie would announce in a loud voice that 'the great Lord Kao' had arrived. They would be received with bows and tea would be served, but the conversation would be halting and confined to generalities, until the subject of calligraphy arose and both gentlemen would seize their brushes. Thereafter, this 'Chinese' Dutchman would be completely accepted, indeed he was not just a Chinese, he was a worthy dignitary, a mandarin.

Alas this 'official trip' drew to a close. After a last lute lesson and a final visit to the bookshop, where he settled his account, he took his leave. He departed on 30 September and was back in Tokyo on 4 October.

Although the visit to Peking had certainly not been a holiday, Van Gulik immediately picked up the threads of the hectic pattern of life he had mapped out for himself. He had become fascinated by the Chinese lute and he bought a tuning pipe in a music shop, had a special *ch'in* table constructed and practised on his own antique instrument. In Tokyo he now also took lute lessons from a Chinese lute master. He read classical texts about the lute, discussed it and other ancient Chinese musical instruments with a host of specialists, and accumulated so much knowledge that he wrote two books about it: *The Lore of the Chinese Lute* and *Hsi K'ang and his Poetical Essay on the Lute,* both still standard classics.

In the latter 'poetical essay', the poet Hsi K'ang gives instructions about how to play the lute:

> '[The lute should be played] in a lofty-ceilinged building, either in a spacious hall or in a room dedicated to this purpose, on a winter evening when the light is translucent and a cloudless moon spreads her light, clad in rustling new garments to which the scent still clings: then the instrument feels cool and the strings are properly tuned. When the heart is at peace and the hands are skilful, any touch with the fingers will respond to one's thoughts.

A song is sung to the accompaniment of the music of the strings:

Pl. 11. Van Gulik, in Japanese attire, playing the lute.

*Borne aloft in the drifting sky, I come to rest on the Island of the
Blessed;
I am overwhelmed by a desire to be a companion of the Immortal Who
Rides the Wind;
Drinking nectar, I gird myself with the morning mists;
Floating aimlessly, I approach the bournes of heaven;
Melting into the universe, absolute freedom is my reward.*

Just as in his other academic work, he set about this project
meticulously and conscientiously. He scoured antiquarian booksellers
in Japan, Peking and Mukden for ancient works about the *ku-ch'in*
(antique lute). For months he spent every afternoon in Tokyo at
the *Naikaku-bunko*—the Cabinet Library, where he had discovered
important old works. Finally, when he had enough to commit to paper,
he had his first, second and third drafts (sometimes even more) read
critically by friendly scholars whom he asked for their comments.
The complete English text of the manuscript was as ever corrected
by his friend Frank Hawley. He delivered a lecture entitled 'On Three
Antique Lutes' to the Asiatic Society of Japan (of which he was an
active board member). He devoted time to the role of the Chinese lute
in Japan in a lecture which he gave in Nagasaki: 'Chinese Literary
Music and Its Introduction into Japan'.

Van Gulik, as did other classical Chinese scholars, considered the seven-stringed lute to be more than just a musical instrument, in a large measure it was also an antique work of art, a quintessential element in the study of a learned man. He reminds us that, by way of comparison, on account of its refined lines, a bronze sacrificial vessel dating from before the Han dynasty,[3] displayed on a ebony stand, enhanced the antiquarian atmosphere of a library. At the same time, the archaic inscription on the underside of the relic provided the fortunate owner with the material for dating and establishing the origin of his work of art.

A writhing translucent jade dragon, laid on the writing table, likewise served a dual purpose, as a support the wet writing brush rested on it and it also served as a topic of conversation about the use of jade by the Ancients for the scholar and his friends.

According to Van Gulik this humanistic quality displayed by the Chinese literati made them remarkably reminiscent of the classical scholars of the European Middle Ages. After all, the old humanist liked to surround himself with marble busts and bronze statues and, as he did his best to date them by their stylistic characteristics, he liked to stroke their graceful forms. Or else, he was fond of rolling out old palimpsests out on his heavy writing table in order to admire the powerful letters on the greyish-blue parchment, while he tried to discover copyist's errors as he looked for variant readings. The Chinese scholar will likewise have cared for his treasures lovingly as he pondered the proper interpretation of inscriptions and conjured up the past in his thoughts, endeavouring to discover the significance the object might have had in the period in which it was made.

Van Gulik came to the conclusion that the Chinese lute was rarely ever played now. Not because the music of the lute was unimportant, quite the contrary, in the opinion of many its music was the apogee of Chinese music. The problem was to play the lute expertly required years of study and an accomplished teacher. Few scholars had either the time or the motivation to devote to this art, moreover good teachers were relatively few and far between. (In an article 'The *Qin* and the Chinese Literati'—*Qin* is an alternative way (*p.y.*) of writing the transliteration of *ch'in*, pronounced 'chin'—in the journal

---

[3]   The golden age of bronze covered the years 1500-600 BCE (Shang and Western Chou). If the Eastern Chou and Ch'in are included this would extend to the Han (206 BCE).

Orientations, November 1981, J.C.Y. Watt argues that the *ch'in* lost its popularity because scholars monopolized the instrument and, in the late Ch'ing, became so precious as to play each note as a separate unit, losing sight of the melodic line as a result).

Although, as Van Gulik discovered, the pleasure of playing the lute was reserved to a small, privileged circle, the appreciation of the instrument as an antique lay within the reach of every scholar. Possession of a valuable instrument which had once belonged to a famous man, who had embellished it with inscriptions, could even inspire its present owner to change the name of his study so as to call it after the lute.

Robert had studied all the technical details. He knew exactly which sort of lute was made from what sort of wood, which varnish was used, which sort of silk was needed for the strings, how thick they should be, in which position the player should sit, and what the various fingering techniques were. He became such an expert that his pocket diary soon gives evidence he was repairing the lutes of his Chinese friend Sun and of the American Chinese scholar Bill Acker.

His intense interest and great skill in the technical side of things were expressed in all sorts of ways. In writing his calligraphy, he expended enormous care in finding the ink-stone as well as the brush and paper. A beautiful scroll painting could cast him into transports of delights, but as far as he was concerned the way in which it was mounted, taking account of the right proportions and using the most appropriate silk, was almost as important. Van Gulik wrote learned treatises on these sorts of subjects. He was constantly realizing that layout of a book—searching for the type face, its internal division, the illustrations, the cover and all the rest—gave him almost as much pleasure as writing it did. He was an artist on one single terrain, but he was perhaps even more an artisan, a craftsman in the highest sense of the word—and then in wide-ranging areas. Science, art and craftsmanship all required total dedication. He had the greatest contempt for shoddy workmanship or second-rate presentation.

It is also amusing that he even applied this 'technical' attitude to the sexual terrain. Speaking about his many explorations into Japanese and Chinese night life, he once said: 'She doesn't have to be very beautiful. A good technique is much more important.' He silenced a whore in the port city of Yokohama (Van Gulik was anything but fastidious in this area), who immediately began to moan and groan 'passionately' before anything had really happened by remarking irritably: 'Keep that pretence for your sailors; I prefer to see what you really can do'.

The next day he would make his appearance at the imperial palace in morning dress and top hat with other diplomats for some sort of official ceremony; he would attend the opening of Parliament in white tie and tails or he would be called upon to defend Dutch interests at the *Gaimushō*, the Ministry of Foreign Affairs. Life was full of variety, in fact he was leading various lives, and transferring from the one to the other did not cause him the slightest difficulty, perhaps because he could always return to his permanent home base, culture.

At the end of April 1937, Robert made another short visit to Peking, but he had little to say about it in his diary.

Shortly after he had returned to Tokyo, he and his Chinese friend Sun suddenly conceived a plan to compile a biographical dictionary. Later we read that he had been working on it, but its precise nature and if anything ever came of it is uncertain. Probably it was a biographical dictionary of Chinese artists (painters? poets? connoisseurs of the lute?). There is a strong possibility that the manuscript, finished or not, was later destroyed with many other of Van Gulik's possessions in a bombardment.

He also enjoyed more light-hearted books, provided their quality was good enough. He was a fan of English detective novels and also put together a large collection of naughty limericks, from which many friends derived great enjoyment over many years. An entry in his diary recalls this: 'Gave Mulder a limerick book'.

Van Gulik spent nearly every afternoon either studying in a library or having someone come to give him a lesson or to work with him, usually from four to six (or sometimes later). He continued to work a great deal with Sun, but Sun was replaced as his permanent tutor by Kuan, who was followed in his turn by Chao. He took lessons in Chinese language, calligraphy and other subjects. Sometimes they assisted him with the translation of Chinese texts. Certainly one of them will have helped him with the writing of the foreword to the Chinese lute book, or will at least have corrected it. In the meantime, it seems he had learned enough Mongolian as he thought fit. Now an Indian called Sandiljayana appeared some afternoons to practise Sanskrit and later Hindi with him. After a while, he took up his Korean lessons again.

He commenced 1938 with a severe bout of 'flu, which he quickly shook off with the help of Dr Wittenberg. This skilled physician who was of German Jewish origin treated many of the foreign diplomats. Even the members of the German Legation, Nazi or not, consulted him, but in the evening after dark, so as not to be conspicuous. 'I don't give a damn', said Wittenberg, 'but I send them a bill for double the fee!'

Robert put the finishing touches to his *Lore of the Chinese Lute* and took the manuscript to Kraus, at the Roman Catholic Sophia University, who was going to publish it in *Monumenta Nipponica*, a journal which Van Gulik had helped to found. He also kept in regular touch with Father Roggendorf of the same university, an extraordinarily tall, incredibly thin man, who always made a comical contrast when he went out walking with his equally tall but more sturdily built and somewhat rotund fellow Orientalists, Van Gulik and Hawley.

As well as dealing with serious matters during the day, there were plenty of visits to the Star, Sunshine, Kijo (or Kiyō) hotels-cum-nightclubs, accompanied by notes of all sorts of Japanese girls' names. This is the first year in which his pocket diary repeatedly mentions some establishment or other plus the note: 'watched nude dancing'.

The pocket diary also reveals that now there were also smaller discomforts: 'at home on account of earache, at home because of foot, inflammation of the nose, spectacles broken, collected wallet from the police station'. But these were just trivial incidents along the way in the midst of much more pleasurable activities.

He was not the only Western bachelor who lived for the day in the Far East, but everything he did had an extra dimension. His energy was incredible; his days and nights were crammed so full that one is left standing amazed that he did not suffer from some sort of physical dip more often.

Except for a bit of swimming or rowing in the summer, he avoided any sport in the open air. In the winter he skated. Indoors he played a lot of billiards and he stepped up his performance of the already mentioned nocturnal 'indoor' sports. He ate often and copiously, with a preference for Chinese, and he liked to discover new dishes. Opposite the Legation was a barracks, where Japanese soldiers who had been guilty of plundering in China sometimes sold pieces of art and other items. There Van Gulik dug out a very special Chinese cookery book which he purchased immediately.

He reasoned that the Chinese would no longer have any use for the book and it would have been a pity to leave it in the hands of the Japanese. He took the book to the chef of a Chinese restaurant whom he had befriended and instructed him in the making of a number of rare dishes. Later he invited Van Roijen to eat there who declared that it had been delicious.

Van Gulik's interest in culinary arts led him to acquire great personal skill in this field. He prepared Chinese, Japanese and Indonesian meals for his friends and occasionally he served them something exceptional. Prof. Boxer remembered the head of a wild boar prepared in the way Kublai Khan would have eaten it—it was one of the favourite dishes of the thirteenth-century Mongol conqueror of China. Naturally Robert served it with Mongolian wine, namely *arak*. He could also serve up a dinner prepared in the style of the Tokugawa period, or for his *Rangakusha* (Japanese scholars of Dutch) friends, a meal such as that the Nagasaki painter Shiba Kōkan would have eaten at the end of the eighteenth century.

Although Robert was a moderate drinker, he was a chain-smoker and was to remain so for the rest of his life. In his own notes, Van Gulik says that he enjoyed a glass in good company, but seldom alone, and that he had never been drunk.

> Tobacco is my vice. Although I can go for months without a drop of alcohol, one hour without a cigarette or pipe unsettles me. I began to smoke when I was seven, hence there must have been some genetic factor at play as well. Father smoked twenty-five small cigarettes a day and a few pipes until he died of a heart attack at the age of eighty-three years. During the years we spent in Batavia Father was in the habit of smoking one cigar before he took his siesta, so that I and the son of Father's Javanese groom would squat down every day under the window of his bedroom and wait until Father threw the butt of the cigar outside. We collected it, dried it, rolled the tobacco in maize leaves and so provided ourselves with all we needed to smoke. Now I have to pay for this mischief with a chronic cough and all sorts of nasal ailments. I have never ever succeeded in ridding myself of this addiction.

In 1938, he began work on a book about mounting Chinese and Japanese scroll paintings ('a beautiful but badly mounted painting is even worse than a beautiful woman who dresses atrociously' he said once). He was also busy with an article about 'Kuei-ku-tze, the Philosopher of the Ghost Vale', intended to be the introduction to his complete translation of this work attributed to this father of Chinese diplomacy (around the third century BCE). The article was published in the Dutch journal *China*, vol. xiii (1938), but the manuscript of the translation was lost during the war and he never got round to making a new translation.

The amount of work at the Chancellery was growing (before the war it was pretty quiet in most Dutch chancelleries; after all the Netherlands was a neutral country). Sometimes Robert had to work there in the afternoon, and somewhere in fact he notes surprisingly:

23-8-1938: wrote a political report in the morning.

One of his contemporaries, Gerard Dissevelt, a civil servant at the Bureau for East Asian Affairs in Batavia and later also a diplomat, remembered the excellent reports about the political situation in Japan and Japanese foreign policy (although now well enough known, at that time usually misjudged by the West) which Robert wrote at this period. They often caused his colleagues to sigh: 'This time let's hope that The Hague pays attention to it'. These reports were consistently little gems of profound knowledge, showing decisive insight and a level-headed sense of reality. That Pabst had now begun to appreciate his scholar more is shown by the fact that he had these reports issued under Van Gulik's own name.

Tension did indeed rise among the Japanese population, especially after the large-scale Japanese military actions in North China commenced, in the wake of what was known as the China Incident in July 1937. Japanese troops had opened fire on Chinese soldiers at the Marco Polo Bridge, a vital railhead a few miles to the southwest of Peking (an event used by Japan as a pretext for greater expansion, considered by many historians to mark the beginning of the Second Sino-Japanese War, 1937-1945) and the conflict had erupted into a full-scale war. The Japanese were already a people who felt a continuous obligation to exert themselves to the utmost, and this sense of commitment was now compounded by an even heavier sense of responsibility. The *Kobubō* (Civil Defence) organized processions of women to encourage young men to join the services. There was great waving of flags and patriotic slogans were to be heard everywhere. Despite all this, in wider circles people were upset by what was happening and did not want to go to war, but no one, or almost no one, dared to speak out against what was happening.

The authorities in what by then could be called a police state kept foreigners under even stricter surveillance. Hence, if such a foreigner happened to speak good Japanese, it was not long before he would hear: '*Supai darō*? You must be a spy? (*supai* = spy)

Generally speaking, diplomats had to confine their contacts to Japanese at the Ministry of Foreign Affairs or at the court, and those parties were too afraid to say much. If there were other contacts, the Japanese involved lost no time in breaking them when the police arrived to threaten them. If you wanted to go on a journey, permission had to be granted first, and you were constantly followed. If you took photographs and had the films developed, suddenly the negatives had been 'mislaid'. Van Roijen, among whose tasks was the economic work at the Legation, observed how closed the Japanese were in that area, whatever you wanted was regarded as espionage.

The fact that Van Gulik was able to build up and maintain contacts in the wider circles of Japanese society, that for many months he was even able to work every afternoon in the Cabinet Library, usually almost impossible for foreigners to access, is a testimony to his diplomatic gifts and his formidable knowledge of Chinese culture, for which, even during the war, there was still a deep admiration in Japan.

Robert's day-to-day routine was seriously disrupted in the first months of the new year, 1939, by a female affair which threw him more off balance than usual, followed by a protracted illness. On 5 January, Robert ate frogs' legs in a Japanese restaurant called Minenoya, where he met a girl called Miyoko, with whom he lost no time in making a date. A few days later: 'Spoke to Miyoko', followed by: 'to bank and the electrical goods shop, bought a radiator and took it to Minenoya [the restaurant where it seems Miyoko worked and perhaps also lived], apart from this worked at home'. The next day (13/1) 'to Minenoya, where [I] met Miyoko'. He was now seeing her almost every day and on 21 January they went by train to Yumoto, where they strolled to the waterfall and stayed overnight.

On 27 he visited her, and he rented an apartment for her: 'viewed apartment'; the 30th '7-8 o'clock inspected M's room in Shuwasō'; 31st 'half-past three to bank, 4 o'clock to Mitsukoshi [department store] where met M. Bought kimono and handbag together. Accompanied M. to her room, where ate Chinese, half-past eight went home and did more work.' The next evening he again visited her in her new apartment, and the next day, 2 February, at three o'clock he went to withdraw money from the bank and then bought a gas stove, which he personally carried to Miyoko's apartment. She apparently felt the cold. The next day he purchased a small table for her.

What course did the romance take after this? What did his permanent partner, Kachan, think about it all? Notes in his pocket diary show that although Robert visited Miyoko virtually every day, he never remained with her for long. They often went out to dine, after which he would spend a short time with her, or he would take tea with her in the afternoons between 4 and 5. If he had knocked at her door twice without raising any response, he sent Kachan there:

> 21-2-1939: 2-4 did some shopping in the town, 5 o'clock sent K. to fetch M., drank some tea at home first, then ate Chinese food. Worked after that while K. and M. played cards.

A domestic scene: the scholar seated peacefully at his writing table studies ancient books and manuscripts, perhaps he writes some fine characters or he carves archaic characters on a seal stone, while both young ladies played cards. Did Kachan see Robert's latest acquisition as a rival? If she did, she was wise enough not to show it. Her preferred tactic, which seldom succeeded, was to draw Miyoko into her household—a sort of ménage à trois—and by doing so bind her permanent partner even more to hearth and home.

As a matter of fact, later in Chungking, Robert once remarked to Barkman, 'It is all far more exciting with two women at the same time and there are more possibilities.' Did these two, as he expressed it then, 'warm his bed for him'? Whatever the case might have been, the sphere was then (still) good, because the next day both the girls go to the *kabuki*—one of the forms of traditional Japanese theatre.

Perhaps it was around about this time that Jonkheer D. (Roon) van den Brandeler, then employed with the Java-China-Japan Line in Shanghai (later assistant-military attaché in Chungking), came to Japan to ski and was invited by Van Gulik to have a meal with him one evening. Later Van Roon said that Robert had two charming Japanese girls who served them a superb Japanese meal. 'As I was leaving, one of them said something to Robert in Japanese, at which he turned to me and said: "They're now going off to warm my bed together. Can you understand Roon, I have been so spoiled that I shall never ever be able to make an ordinary Western marriage in which love and friendship play an important role?"'

On the evening just mentioned, when Kachan and Miyoko went to the *kabuki*, Robert attended a lecture with Frank Hawley, after which they had a Japanese meal and went off to drink beer somewhere. This was followed by a visit to the Sembai nightclub, 'where Kikuko'(girl's name), and finally: 'half-past eleven home, where found Kachan and Miyoko.'

This Miyoko must have been a very special courtesan who was chary with her favours. One afternoon, Robert even took Van Roijen to visit Miyoko in order to parade her proudly before him. They drank some tea. This was again followed by short visits to Miyoko, 'took tea with M and talked'. Finally:

8-3-1939 spent the night with M.

9-3 11 o'clock left Miyoko to go home, where I worked for the rest of the day.

In the back of his pocket diary he noted, possibly inspired by Miyoko, short Japanese songs and poems, most of them erotic ditties, more useful for obtaining knowledge of Japanese terms than beautiful, such as this:

> *Haru no yo ni / shippori nururu / toko no naka / suzu hahā suzu hahā / umekigoe / hana wo tsumarase / shiorashii / kogoe de sasayaku / mutsu-goto mo. / Makura futatsu ni / mi wa hitotsu.*

In translation:[4]

> *In the bed,*
> *Where in the spring night*
> *We make love*
>   *O la la!, o la la!*
> *Our moaning*
> *Makes us gasp for breath,*
> *[but there are] also words of love*
> *Which we whisper tenderly…*
> *On two pillows*
> *We are one body.*

Now Robert fell seriously ill. He suffered a sudden, throbbing

---

4   The author is very grateful to Prof. Dr F. Vos for the explanation of this and other passages. Moaning makes the lovers breathless (a 'blocked nose'). In view of the fact that *suzu* means a small bell, hence 'acorn' and hence 'penis', while *hāhā* is an exclamation of admiration, one is tempted to translate *suzu hāhā* (here rendered freely as 'o la la') as 'O what a monster!'

pain in his throat and a few days later it turned out to be scarlet fever. On 16 March, he was admitted to the isolation ward of St Luke's English hospital, and was only discharged six weeks later, 29 April to be precise.

After he had had his hair cut—this is mentioned in his pocket diary—and tidied up at home, the next day he wanted to see Miyoko. She does not come to him, he goes to her:

> 30-4: at 4 in the afternoon to M., where talked with her and her sister until 5 o'clock. After that worked at home.

Apparently something was wrong. Perhaps, in the meantime, she had found another boyfriend, or Kachan had plotted against her, or perhaps, during his long, lonely confinement in hospital Robert has given this relationship a good deal of thought and concluded that it would be better to end it:

> 3-5: 7 o'clock Koike Miyoko came, relationship terminated.

A trip to Shanghai (29 July-14 August) gave him the opportunity to make contacts with Chinese scholars and the large publishing house Commercial Press, to shop (in Japan a great many items were not longer available, while in Shanghai literally everything was), not to mention to participate in the intensive night life in Chinese and Russian houses (brothels). This ensured that during the day he was reinvigorated to take up his intellectual and creative activities.

Having a break from his residence in Japan by making a trip to China was always a bracing experience. Remarkably, in contrast to Japan which was waging the war, in this period in China where the war actually raged, there was still relatively little to see of this. The Chinese, who were cheerful by nature, gifted with boundless stamina and a sense of humour, had a different way of dealing with the tension caused by war and occupation, showing themselves to be anything but hostile towards Westerners.

Normal, carefree life went ahead as usual in Shanghai and Peking, almost as if there was nothing the matter. This country, with its centuries-old civilization, had experienced so many disasters, none of which had had any lasting impact, that this present war was considered a temporary aberration which would soon be over and from which China would survive. This was the attitude of most Chinese, certainly the older people.

However, this should not be interpreted to mean that the Chinese population was indifferent to the Japanese invasion. Quite the opposite in fact; after the Marco Polo Incident and the fall of Peking and Tientsin, followed by Shanghai and Nanking, the Chinese closed ranks behind their national government in an unprecedented show of unity and wave of patriotism. In the initial period, Japan had often been able to manipulate the dissension among the Chinese. At that time, the flight of the national government from Nanking to set up headquarters in Chungking, deeper into the hinterland after a brief residence in Hankou, had demonstrated the absolute military superiority of the invasion armies.

As it withdrew, the Chinese government adopted a scorched earth policy, and entire factories, military installations and universities withdrew to escape grasp of the Japanese. In 1938, when Hankou and Canton had fallen into enemy hands, the Chinese sense of realism and of the necessity to bow to the inevitable had begun to prevail among large groups of people: in March 1940 no-one less than Wang Ch'ing-wei, a Kuomintang veteran and rival of Chiang Kai-shek, became head of the Chinese 'government' in Nanking which collaborated with the Japanese. Only later, in the nineteen forties would the Chinese population be moulded into an organized resistance through its bitter experiences under the invader.

Even though, on the evidence of his pocket diary, the visit to Shanghai was difficult to claim to be an official trip, armed with his profound knowledge of the country and its people, Van Gulik will certainly have had talks and acquired impressions which will have provided him with material for a report to Foreign Affairs. Evidence of this is found in a very rare note in his pocket diary, on 29 August: 'compiled a political report'.

He wrote book reviews for *Monumenta Serica* published by the Catholic University in Peking, including one of the new edition (Peking 1939) of the well-known *China under the Empress Dowager* by J.O.P. Bland and E. Backhouse. In this, Van Gulik reveals some of his political opinions. He identifies two sorts of revolution, one top-down, the other bottom-up. In contrast to Japan, where revolution (the Meiji Reforms) had been imposed from the top, in China the dowager empress had thwarted all urgently required reforms so that in the end they had to be implemented by young revolutionaries who had no experience in government. Consequently, Van Gulik thought, this revolution from the bottom-up had 'a catastrophic and subversive character'.

Robert made another attempt to acquire a second permanent girlfriend; after all, from a 'technical' point of view, this was more interesting. However, he was anxious to safeguard against problems and hence he made a contract with the girl. The first was with a certain Harumi on 25 September (with whom the relationship had already been terminated five days later) and later, in April 1940, with Haruko, but this pleasure was also relatively short-lived:

22-6-1940: Lunch at home, then to Kamakura [where he had rented a summer house]. 5 o'clock sent Haruko packing, K. (Kachan) arrived at half-past five.

26-6-1940: 4 o'clock to Kamakura. Matter of Haruko. H. dismissed.

Van Gulik's contracts with these girls had also been signed by their fathers. They stated that 'Miss X. would enter Van Gulik's household and render all the services that he, the master, might desire of her', in other words a pretty broad description. Nothing is known about whether there was any clause about giving notice and a silver handshake.

Whatever the case, he noted a Japanese proverb in his pocket diary:

Sake do doku yori	Worse than the poison of strong drink
Nebusoku yori mo	worse than lack of sleep
Honemi ni kotaeru aibusoku	[is] a lack of sex.[5]

From the end of 1939, the name Hosono frequently occurs. If Sun Ti was his best Chinese friend, and Frank Hawley his best English friend, Hosono was the Japanese who was closest to him:

My best Japanese friend was the Chinese scholar, poet, tea-master and art critic Hosono Endai. Even though he was in his sixties by then, he was still remarkably active and he could consume amazing quantities of *sake*—Japanese rice wine. Hosono was acquainted with prominent politicians and famous actors, well-known novelists and notorious courtesans, and had a real nose for the best restaurants and antiquarian booksellers. Respected by the right-wing as much as by the moderate groups, he was the last of the 'learned Ancients', who had exerted considerable power

---

5   Literally: a lack of sex, more than poison and sleeplessness penetrates through bone to the marrow.

Pl. 12. Hosono Endai.

behind the scenes since the days of the Tokugawa Shogunate. He died a few years ago [Van Gulik wrote this in 1964] at the respectable age of 93, living out his last days on *sake* and salt fish...

Writing about his own activities in this period Van Gulik remarks:

As far as my scientific work was concerned, I had decided that above all I wanted to remain a Chinese scholar and would use Japanese data to further my Chinese studies. The upshot was that I concentrated on modern Japanese. Consequently I set aside classical Japanese language and literature, as well as all purely Japanese topics such as for instance *Shintō*. What I did study was the history of Chinese-Japanese [cultural] relations and Chinese studies in Japan. With the exception of two years during the second period I spent in Japan [1948-1951], I have abided by this policy, and this is reflected in my publications.

Gradually I also succeeded in coordinating my official duties with my scientific hobbies. Through the second of these activities I considerably broadened the circle of my Chinese and Japanese friends, and these included notorious extreme-nationalist leaders who directed the aggressive plans of the Japanese military clique from behind the scenes. I was one of the very few Westerners who, because of our common interest in all things Chinese [it seems paradoxical, but these extremists really did have a great knowledge of and an admiration for Chinese *culture*], had regular contact with Tōyama Mitsuru, Okawa Shūmei and other leaders of the Black Dragon Society [an extreme right-wing, ultra- nationalist society], and of other societies which were responsible for Japanese aggression in China.

Okawa's name occurs in his pocket diary on a few occasions, but Tōyama does not. There is no reason to doubt what Van Gulik says about his valuable contacts in these circles, but had he wanted to gild the lily a little by also mentioning Tōyama? Robert never had the slightest difficulty in advertising himself and he enjoyed, as he put it, contributing to the creation of a legend around his name. Certainly he had met these powerful ultra-nationalists—regularly too—even more frequently than was noted in his diary. Tōyama played a crucial role in two extremist organizations, whose goal was the expansion of Japan. They were the *Genyōsha*[6] (the Dark Ocean Society) and the *Kokuryukai*[7] (the Black Dragon Society). The British Minister in Tokyo, Sir Robert Craigie, described Tōyama as 'an elderly mystic and as an almost legendary figure whose eyes beamed through horn-rimmed spectacles and whose patriarchal beard seemed to bespeak benevolence. Donning in his early days the cloak of ardent parliamentarianism, he devoted most of his life to stiffening, by his own peculiar methods, the foreign policy of Japan. This organizer of zealots and terrorists prided himself on the influence he had exerted in bringing about most of Japan's foreign wars. ...In later years he appeared to have retired altogether from the cloak and dagger business.' (Sir Robert Craigie, *Behind the Japanese Mask*, p. 159)

---

[6]   Named after the strait between Korea and the Japanese island of Kyushu. The goal of this organization was the occupation of Korea.

[7]   Named after the border river between Russia and Northeastern China, the Amur, which is call the Black Dragon River in Chinese and Japanese. The goal of this organization was Manchuria.

Then came the tenth of May 1940:

The news of the German occupation of the Netherlands came as a tremendous shock, and because Japan collaborated closely with Germany, Dutch-Japanese relations were affected by it.

The pocket diary mentions:

10-5-1940: 1-3 Chao [Chinese teacher]; 4 o'clock journalist arrived to say that Germany has invaded Holland. To the office, then to Tokyo Club, etc. 7 o'clock to Reuchlin's where listened to the radio with the Minister.

Again the following evenings:

10-11 o'clock listened to the radio at Reuchlin's.

On 8 May Van Gulik had delivered a lecture for the German Club and afterwards had dined with German scholars. Probably the lecture had been about the Javanese *wayang*, because on 11 June the pocket diary says that he went to the *Deutsche Verein*, 'where I picked up the *wayang* puppets'.

The situation in East Asia was rapidly deteriorating, nobody doubted any more that the Japanese militarists were planning a major attack, the only question was when and where: on Russia in the north, or the Netherlands East Indies in the south. I decided to send my entire collection, now expanded to some 8,000 books, scrolls and art-objects, assembled in Japan, Korea, and Occupied China, to Batavia, for greater safety. During the war, the forty boxes stored in a godown on the way to Tanjong Priok were burned during the bombings and a total loss.

Every day there were cables from our Government in exile in London and from Batavia, and I regularly worked in the chancery till late in the night, coding and decoding messages. I maintained contact with the intelligence officers of the Allied diplomatic missions, and also with men from the British Ministry of Economic Warfare—excellent people who during the war did many marvellous stunts that deserve to be written up in detail some day; they managed, for instance, to have rubber smuggled out of the Japanese occupied Netherl[ands] East Indies.

The political situation in Japan worsened for the Allies. Impressed by Hitler's successes in Europe, the Japanese militarists and the proponents of a totalitarian regime succeeded in expanding their influence. At the end of July 1940, a pro-German cabinet was formed under Prince Konoye as prime minister and Matsuoka as minister of foreign affairs. In relation to the occupation of the Netherlands by Germany, voices asserting that Japan should ensure that the Dutch East Indies did not fall into German hands in the near future were raised; in other words it would be better that they should be placed under a Japanese administration. At the end of September, Japan concluded the Tripartite Pact with Germany and Italy, with the purpose of keeping the United States out of the war. In Japan anti-Allied, especially anti-British, feeling was mounting. A number of British citizens were arrested.

Van Gulik, who kept his finger on the pulse of what was happening in Japan, even in extremist circles, happened to hear that, in imitation of Hitler's admired and friendly Germany, plans were afoot among the more junior officers and the right-wing elements to launch an anti-Semitic campaign. The ultimate goal would be a total boycott of Jews, their continued persecution and eventually their potential expulsion from the country. This disturbed Van Gulik so much he personally approached an influential Japanese, a certain Tetsuma Hashimoto, about it. After the war, in 1974, the president of the Jewish Community in Japan, Rabbi Marvin Tokayer, drew Van Gulik's son Peter's attention to the episode, which is described in the postwar autobiography of the said Tetsuma Hashimoto.

Hashimoto says that in June 1940 he had received a brush-written letter in perfect Japanese from a Mr Van Gulik, first secretary of the Dutch Legation in Tokyo, in which he requested an interview. After telephone contact, Hashimoto visited him at the Legation, because at that time his house [in Japanese style] was still 'not suitable for [receiving] foreign guests'.

A search through Van Gulik's agenda for confirmation of this event reveals only the note:

27-5-1940: 56 Hashimoto.

They had barely made each other's acquaintance, according to Hashimoto's story, when Van Gulik said: 'Allow me to recite a poem by the Meiji Emperor.' To the astonishment of his visitor he did so in fluent Japanese. It soon became apparent that Van Gulik had quoted this poem, which counselled humanity, to put pressure on Hashimoto. 'Raising his voice', Hashimoto said, 'he asked me: "Why are the Jews being boycotted by the Japanese people, to whom such a sacred imperial exhortation had been addressed?"' His rather impassioned face made me want to laugh, but I replied to him calmly that we were not boycotting the Jews. "You are boycotting them," he said once again raising his voice.'

Van Gulik repeated his accusation a couple of times (which does not seem surprising, in view of the fact that the reports of impending anti-Semitic actions were disturbing; besides he was a young, impetuous diplomat and moreover Japan was an ally of Germany, which had occupied the Netherlands only shortly before), whereupon Hashimoto explained to him that the dangers which an anti-Jewish witch hunt would be unleashed were very real, but he had already taken this matter up with the various ministries responsible and all had assured him that they would oppose it. Van Gulik accepted this explanation and thanked him.

In his story, Hashimoto also mentions that, because of Van Gulik's 'abnormally emotional' attitude, he had drawn the conclusion that both he and his wife 'were either perhaps of Jewish descent or were closely involved with the Jews.' This chapter in his book is entitled: *The Anti-Semitic Movement in Japan during the Last World War Nipped in the Bud*.

Although Robert van Gulik had to work more, putting in longer hours at the office after 10 May 1940, the pattern of his life, divided between study and pleasure, was barely disrupted. He was able to divide his time so systematically that even a quarter of an hour was seldom wasted. His article about Kuei-ku-tze was now finished ('Kuei-ku-tze, the Philosopher of the Ghost Vale') and he also completed his book about Hsi K'ang (*Hsi K'ang and his Poetical Essay on the Lute*). He also pressed on with his book about the Chinese monk Tung-Kao, which he would later publish in Chinese. He used the material he had assembled about this monk as the basis for lectures he gave. In December 1940, he spent two days almost entirely at Sophia University to 'stamp books' (probably he stamped his Chinese name in the lute books).

Afterwards, on 19 December 1940, Van Gulik was granted a month's sick leave, for which there were apparently no serious medical indications because he used it to take a trip to Peking, where he arrived on 26th. Once again he embarked on a very busy programme. He took lute lessons with Lute Master Kuan and delivered a lecture on the monk Tung-Kao, at a Chinese university. In Peking he met various Chinese and foreign scholars. He visited bookshops and antique shops with Minister Flaes (who also enjoyed fame as a writer under the pseudonym Terborgh) and with De Josselin de Jong and Abell. He paid only one visit to the tea houses of *Ch'ien-mên wai*.

After he returned to Tokyo, he gave a lecture about Tung-Kao to the Women's Club and again flung himself into work on all sorts of projects, including his book about mounting scrolls. The Legation demanded even more of his time and sometimes he even had to work on Sundays.

In March 1941, Japanese Foreign Minister Matsuoka visited Moscow, Berlin and Rome. In Moscow he signed a Soviet-Japanese neutrality pact. By the beginning of July, Japan had put its navy onto a state of full alert, an example speedily followed by the army, and that same month Japanese troops entered the south of Indochina (for which permission had been exacted from the weak French Vichy government). This gave Japan an important naval base, which formed a threat to the Malay Peninsula.

In response, the United States, Britain and the Dutch Indies government announced a complete embargo on all exports to Japan. This reduced Japanese petroleum imports to one-tenth of what they had formerly been, which was regarded in Japan itself to pose such a threat as to be declared internally a *casus belli*. American-Japanese talks in Washington turned out to be worse than useless and international tension mounted steadily, albeit the American government did not believe that Japan would take the risk of attacking its country and Japanese military power was hugely underestimated in the West. Meanwhile, in Japan food supplies began to run short during the summer and autumn of 1941.

These were ominous developments, and the danger of a war in Asia began to present a real threat. The question was whether Japan would confine its attack to the Dutch East Indies to secure essential oil supplies, or whether it would also attack the United States and England in a bid to seize control of sea and air space in the South Pacific, as a prelude to the occupation of the regions on which it had set its sights.

The last chance to avoid war seemed to arise in November, when Japan offered to withdraw its troops from southern Indochina in exchange for the lifting of the oil embargo and a guarantee of United States abstention from intervention in China. Washington's reply was a ten-point programme which necessitated Japan to withdraw all of its armed forces from Indochina and China (including Manchuria). As far as Japan was concerned, this signalled the end of negotiations and the military was given the green light to carry out the plan that it had drawn up earlier to attack Pearl Harbour.

Van Gulik bought paint brushes, attended the antique auctions at the Bijutsu Club, which still holds art fairs in the centre of Tokyo, played the lute and billiards, and suddenly discovered that he was having more contact with allied colleagues, engaged in matters other than Chinese studies. For instance, we often come across the name Smith-Hutton (the American naval attaché). The apparently imperturbable, to the outside world at least, way in which Robert van Gulik continued his normal activities, contrasted sharply with the tension which was mounting daily, sweeping everyone in its wake. Portents of impending catastrophe were multiplying on all sides.

By now Van Gulik had been promoted to interpreter, second class, which meant a salary rise to a net income of 330.05 guilders a month.

In his recommendation for promotion dated 20 March 1941 his chief, Pabst, could not pass up the opportunity to remark: 'Of course the precarious state of his health has frequently hindered his capacity for work and stopped him from using his comprehensive knowledge to the fullest extent, however a more sensible lifestyle might offer hope of a lasting recovery.'

At the ministry, a note was placed alongside this final remark: 'What does this mean?', a question which nobody could answer.

Van Gulik was not insensitive to criticism and therefore shortly afterwards, on 9 July 1941, he produced a masterly memorandum on the extreme right-wing parties in Japan, in which he was able to display his astonishing knowledge of this subject, some of which had been obtained first hand. Pabst did dispatch the report in Van Gulik's name.

The memorandum dealt at length with all aspects of the extreme nationalist parties, which were divided into four categories: secret political societies, semi-economic organizations, semi-cultural organizations and modern mass associations.

The first category included the 'Dark Ocean Society' of Tōyama Mitsuru (the 'elderly mystic') and its sister-societies, among them the 'Society of the Black Dragon'. The second category was composed of a group especially interesting to the Netherlands and the Dutch East Indies, the enormous and heavily subsidized (by the Japanese navy) 'Research Bureau for the East Asian Economy', of which Dr

Okawa Shūmei, whose name Van Gulik had mentioned earlier, was the real leader. Van Gulik knew him well and often spoke with him. He considered him 'a highly gifted but extremely dangerous zealot, completely obsessed by a mystic belief in the sacred mission of Japan to control Asia'.

Apparently Okawa showed a great interest in the Dutch Indies. He had an encyclopaedic knowledge of its colonial history and lauded Dutch achievements in their colonies. Even while doing so, he expressed to Van Gulik his 'sincere regret that the Dutch had to disappear from there'. 'Nothing can be done about it' he declared. 'The Dutch East Indies are destined for Japan.'

These are just a few of the passages from Van Gulik's weighty report about the extreme right-wing organizations then active in Japan.

A month and a half later, another matter cropped up which would have been no more than risible were it not for the fact that it sheds some light on the tragedy of two intelligent people who made each other's life a misery at a distant post.

Van Gulik submitted a remarkable request. He suddenly asked for three months' sick leave, to be spent in the Dutch East Indies at no cost to the State Treasury; in other words at his own expense. To it, he appended a letter from Dr Wittenberg which stated that he was overworked and exhausted. He was also suffering from a stomach ulcer and should take things more easily, a change of air 'now and then' was advisable (in the department a note was added to this latter: 'in other words, the weekends'.)

Understandably this request clashed with Pabst's plans, being especially inconvenient to him just at that moment, but it is a sign of his narrow-minded, bullying nature that he demanded Van Gulik should personally bear the costs of the long telegram in which this leave was requested, and to which General Pabst appended a negative recommendation. The telegram was sent on 21 August 1941, but Van Gulik did not have the ghost of a chance of it actually being granted, because Pabst had added to it, at Van Gulik's own expense: 'In my opinion, Van Gulik's ailments are the fruits an intemperate lifestyle and his lack of will-power to live more healthily. Consequently, no benefit can be expected from any time spent in the Dutch East Indies'. In the department in London a note of assent was placed beside this last comment plus an unanswered (at least not in a written form) question from the minister to the secretary-general: 'Are you acquainted with Van Gulik? Do you think it likely that he will leave Japan in view of the situation there?'

It is almost incredible that, on 23 August, each man was sitting in Tokyo furiously typing a long letter to the minster intent on explaining his own point of view at great length.

Pabst:

'In due course, Dr Van Gulik may become a fine oriental scholar, all his work and effort is completely directed towards this goal, consequently he considers the usual work expected of a civil servant in the interpreting service a necessary evil. Knowledge of Japanese is useful for, indeed indispensable to, studying trade, industry and the like, not to mention economic affairs, but Dr Van Gulik will not make much of a success of it; he can't concentrate on figures [...]. I have needed to supervise him constantly, it has been obvious that his thoughts—perhaps unconsciously—are often occupied elsewhere. In my opinion, the necessity of having to tackle work which is not compatible with his personal interests, fills him with a certain aversion, which he has not always been able to overcome.

I think that what has just been mentioned should be first on the agenda, because aversion to his work makes him all the more sensitive to any symptoms of illness.

In my telegram, I mentioned an intemperate lifestyle, by which I mean excessive eating and smoking and no exercise in the fresh air. He has not shown enough strength of mind to adopt a healthy lifestyle, but instead, day in, day out, sits in a smoke-filled room with his nose stuck in a book [...]. What he expects to gain from spending any time in the Indies is completely beyond my comprehension.

I have told him I have, for instance, no objection to him taking a fortnight's leave in the mountains and that he can divide his working day up to suit his state of health, but all to no avail. Nor indeed would it be of any great help; he would also spend the fourteen days' leave in the mountains in a closed room, hunched over his Chinese books, even though he has been warned that he should take care of his eyes. [...]'

Apparently Van Gulik had long been a thorn in Pabst's side, and the ill-feeling was fully reciprocated. As early as 11 August, in a letter to Acting Secretary-General Van Bylandt, the Minister had reacted enthusiastically to the former's suggestion that in future people appointed to the interpreting service should be more practically

orientated, which would obviate the need for a full university study.
Pabst reported that:

> 'over eighteen years [he] had observed that in very many
> instances this university study produced scholars or pseudo-
> scholars, disinclined, unwilling even, to do the practical work.
> One remarkable example of this is Dr Van Gulik [...]. He is subject
> to moods during which he shows great promise and works
> effectively, but this frame of mind is followed by others when he
> is inattentive to his work, totally absorbed in some or other East
> Asian topic which has no real connection with his work at all.'

Also on 23 August, Van Gulik wrote a long letter addressed
personally to Minister Van Kleffens, striving to refute all Pabst's
arguments, which he proceeded to do, as might have been expected
of him, robustly. For instance, he points out that if his ambition had
been centred on an academic career, he would not have accepted his
present position. When he did so, he had other opportunities open
to him to become a member of a university department, either in
the Netherlands or in China. The reason he spends so many hours
endeavouring to improve his knowledge of Chinese and Japanese
culture is purely a matter of personal taste, and the same could be
said of bridge, dancing and other hobbies. However, whereas the
latter pastimes are simply forms of amusement, his academic hobbies
benefit the service:

> 'The fact I have made my name as a Japanese scholar has had a
> beneficial effect on the status of this post in the eyes of the Japanese.
> Moreover, especially during the past few years, above all after the
> outbreak of the war with China, my Chinese studies have been of
> the utmost importance in building up my Japanese connections.
> Indeed, although unofficial contact with prominent Japanese is
> growing more difficult by the day, and official dealings are virtually
> worthless, completely by chance these studies have helped me to
> establish friendly relationships not only with the China experts in
> the Japanese government but also with many extreme right-wing,
> patriotic leading figures in Japan. Without these contacts, I would
> not, for instance, have been able to compile the [recent] report
> about the extreme patriotic leading figures in Japan.'

Van Gulik goes on to state that he has spent his leaves in China
in order to form a picture of Japanese political and economic aims on

the mainland. He had presented a report in this vein to the Minister in Peking, Baron (Godert Willem) de Vos van Steenwijk, who had said that it was a valuable supplement to the reports compiled by his Legation and insisted that he should pass them on to the government through his chief in Tokyo. However, Pabst had put them to one side with the comment that this—the Japanese in North China—was not a topic which concerned Van Gulik. Furthermore, the fact that the results of his work were mostly conspicuous by their absence from the reports from Tokyo was, 'because Mr Pabst had elected that only very rarely would he give me the opportunity to write an independent report.'

And so it dragged on. He also reported that Pabst had never helped him to come into contact with well-informed people in Tokyo. In six and a half years, the Minister had never invited him to a dinner with foreign diplomats (the sole exception being when the Chinese ambassador was present and Van Gulik had to act as interpreter). Finally, he claimed that the reason he had been able to make the connections which were essential to his work had been through the good offices of the Legation secretaries, Van Roijen and Reuchlin, plus his personal activities in academic and cultural fields.

Van Gulik assumes that 'in general terms, Your Excellency [Minister Van Kleffens] will already have been informed of the relationship between the chief and his staff at this post by other sources'. All he wanted to add was '[to give] the assurance that I think that I have never failed to maintain an entirely correct attitude towards Mr Pabst. Even though at the slightest opportunity, Mr Pabst has been in the habit of telling me off, often fleshed out with cursing and other unseemly additions, I have never allowed myself to be tempted into giving an ill-considered response, and therefore at the moment the working relationship at the chancellery is normal.'

In conclusion, Van Gulik asks if, should the requested leave not be granted, he be transferred as soon as the tenure of his office permits 'to another post beyond Mr Pabst's jurisdiction'.

What happened to this cry from the heart? The letters had only just been sent when a telegram dated 22/8 arrived from London: 'Please inform Van Gulik that under the present circumstances everyone who is able to do so should remain at his post. A fortnight's leave is feasible, longer on medical grounds.'

A disappointment for Van Gulik. In the continued absence of an answer to his lengthy letter to Minister Van Kleffens, he wondered with increasing bitterness if the ministry had elected to throw all its weight behind Pabst. Nevertheless, at the ministry it was a known fact that 'Pabst was usually at odds with his staff' and was unsatisfactory as head of mission in all sorts of ways.[8]

In hindsight, Van Gulik was fortunate. The refusal of Pabst and Van Kleffens to grant him the long leave which he wanted to spend in the Dutch East Indies saved him from internment in a Japanese prison camp. However, Van Gulik did not know this at the time. Curiously enough, the Dutch East Indies seemed such a safe haven to this Japan specialist that not only did he want to spend his furlough there, he actually sent his art collection to the colony. He asked piteously why he encountered so much opposition and in a philosophizing mood wrote in Chinese characters in the back of his diary a Chinese (Zen?) saying which he must have read somewhere or other:

> Yü chih ch'üan shih hsin,
> Hsü tê sung fêng i.

For which perhaps the best translation is:

> If you want to study the very heart of the landscape,
> Then you should grasp the intention of the wind in the pine
> trees (you should become one with the wind).

The tension in the political situation continued to build up. Belligerent banners appeared and there were ubiquitous processions. With mounting frequency it was openly being written and said that Japan should take the Dutch East Indies 'under its protection' against the United States and England. In the chancellery, Van Gulik was 'frittering away' (as he saw it) a great deal of his precious time encoding and decoding telegrams in cipher. There was still no reaction to his letter.

Finally it did arrive from London after a very long delay. It gave Minister Van Kleffens the chance to respond sympathetically, dated 1-12-1941:

'Dear Mr Van Gulik,

Your letter of 23 August reached me only recently.

The summer months are now but a memory, and I can only hope that this season will afford your health some respite.

---

[8]   See A.E. Kersten, *Buitenlandse Zaken in Ballingschap*, A.W. Sijthoff, Alphen aan de Rijn, 1981, in particular pp 193-198.

As far as your request for a transfer is concerned, I am unable to give it my consideration just now. At this moment, your knowledge and professional skills can be used nowhere better than in Tokyo; the national interest necessitates that you remain there until the threatening situation in the Pacific has somewhat improved. You know as well as I that there is not one single portent at the moment which gives any hope of this. Therefore you must prepare yourself to remain in Tokyo, unless war should break out in the Pacific or tensions should ease markedly.

In the above, I do not mean to indicate in any way that I have no understanding of the difficulties you are encountering in your work. In fact, the opposite is true, nevertheless circumstances dictate that at this moment I cannot allow your objections to prevail too heavily.

I am delighted to hear that you still maintain a completely correct attitude towards your chief. Actually, I had expected nothing less and trust that you will be able to manage to keep it up, even if this might cost a great deal of effort on many occasions.

The costs of telegram no. ... from General Pabst have been incorrectly charged to your account by His Excellency; you will be reimbursed by the Accounts Department.'

Unfortunately this ministerial reply, which as it turned out did not acquiesce in Van Gulick's wish, but might have given him some satisfaction at least, was never sent! In the dossier there is a note, "Should this letter not be sent now?' However, a little farther on: 'Tokyo can no longer be contacted.' The links for written correspondence had already been broken. Later there is another note, 'This dossier can now be set aside. Our first task is to get our people in Japan out, then we can see what can be done.'

In Tokyo Van Gulik noted in his pocket diary:

8-12-1941: *Outbreak of war*. In the evening listened to the radio at Reuchlin's [house].

The next day they ventured out to buy medicine at the pharmacy and at home Van Gulik was busy packing his possessions. In the evening, 'again at Reuchlin's to listen to the radio with others'.

10-12: 9 o'clock visited the city for the last time with Reuchlin, Kanda [bookshops]. Burning the archives at the office.

3 o'clock Minister handed over declaration of war at the *Gaimushō* [Ministry of Foreign Affairs];

In the evening the police came to the house to look for a radio.

11-12: Legation under police surveillance. In the morning consulted with the police about what steps should be taken.

Besides these short annotations in his pocket dairy, Van Gulik also wrote the following about the situation.

The early morning papers of 9 December 1941 carried banner headlines about the attack on Pearl Harbour; and war was on. The Japanese confiscated all the telecommunications apparatus from the enemy diplomatic missions, and we were sequestered in our various compounds, pending the arrangement of a diplomatic exchange.

The negotiations for this exchange were to drag on until July 1942, and for the entire time the allied diplomats were confined within their respective compounds. Foreign visitors were not permitted, with the exception in the Dutch case of the Swedish Minister, Bagge, because neutral Sweden was taking care of Dutch interests.

Japanese suspicions of westerners now began to assume grotesque forms. Mrs Reuchlin had been admitted to hospital to give birth to a baby, and when the police rifled through her luggage, they found a postcard with a photo of the famous *sumō* wrestler Futabayama sent by friends of hers. This aroused grave suspicions and she had trouble explaining to the otherwise perfectly correct policeman that she did not have the slightest connection with that mountain of flesh.

Like all other concerned, I passed those months in a fool's paradise: we had seen the Doolittle's planes bombing Tokyo and thought that the Americans and British were closing in on Japan and and that Japan would be defeated in a year or so. Japanese news about their great victories we dismissed as so much propaganda.

Since we were treated quite well, the Japanese military police seeing to it that we got everything we wanted, we assumed that our compatriots in Japan would also be treated decently. We organized a regular routine in the compound, with fixed hours for common physical exercise, fixed nights for bridge and poker etc. I devoted most of our spare time to writing the first draft of a larger book on the connoisseurship of Chinese pictorial art, and of my work on the Ming priest Tung-Kao, mentioned above.

It might have been that the Dutch Legation was luckier in its guards than the other diplomatic missions, but here one does get the impression that by way of an exception, Van Gulik, is being rather too modest about his role. His gift of being able to identify completely with the Japanese way of thinking and customs meant that, whenever he had to confer with the military police officers about his own interests and those of his colleagues, he usually succeeded in convincing them. This made life in the Legation easier and naturally he also benefited from it personally.

In January 1942, he (once again) developed stomach problems and he asked the guards to summon Dr Wittenberg, which was totally against the rules. Initially he was unsuccessful but, after a few days had passed, permission was granted and he was allowed to go to Seibo Hospital to have X-rays taken.

On 24-1-1942 he noted: 'Minister died early this morning'.

A contemporary once remarked that Minister Pabst thereby performed the diplomatic corps a great service, because it would have been very difficult for the Japanese to have refused an official memorial service in church, and this gave the allied diplomats, until then kept incommunicado from each other, the chance to exchange ideas. The Reuchlins and the staff members of the Dutch Legation (with the exception of Van Gulik, detained by his stomach problems) attended the service, at which they were joined by the other chiefs of mission: not only those of the Allies but also their counterparts of the Axis Powers, as well as of the neutral countries led by the Dean, M. Arsène-Henry, the Minister of the Vichy government.

Robert's illness was short-lived. Accompanied by the same guard who had gone with him to the hospital as escort, Van Gulik and Reuchlin were able to visit the bookshops and antiquarians in Kanda one more time. He had new shirts delivered to him at home, his Japanese billiards teacher was allowed to visit, and on 26-3-1942 he was even able to order lute strings from Peking, a fortnight after the note:

10-3-1942: The Dutch Indies surrenders.

After months of poker and bridge, dining with each other and strolling around the Legation grounds, in July at long last a departure date finally hove in sight:

22-7-1942: in the afternoon billiard table dismantled, 9 o'clock poker in the *honkan* [the main building, i.e. the Minister's residence]; won 16.60 [guilders].

23-7: Ericson comes [from the Swedish Legation], packed in the afternoon, in the evening put the finishing touches to the book about mounting.

26-7: Billiard table packed, winter clothes packed.

28-7: Nakajima came to say good-bye, 5 o'clock went into the city with Reuchlin and Yamanaka to do shopping (medicines, suitcase).

29-7: rest of the luggage in tea chests fetched, 7 o'clock final dinner with Reuchlin, chatted afterwards until 10 o'clock. Back home packed the last suitcases.

30-7: 9 o'clock to Tokyo Station in three cars; 10:15 with the boat train to Yokohama, where embarked on the *Tatsuta Maru* around 12 noon. Spoke with Hawley and Morris, 7 o'clock sailed from Yokohama.

When it became known that the exchange would take place on the steamer *Tatsuta Maru*, but we could take only one suitcase, I crammed into it those two manuscripts [Chinese painting and Tung-Kao], and also a few small Chinese books chosen at random, so as to have at least some Chinese reading at hand in the uncertain days to come. Among those was a small size, lithograph edition of an 18th century crime-novel, describing the exploits in detection of the T'ang statesman and master-detective Ti Jen-chieh; it was only one year thereafter that I opened this book.

This work, the *Wu Tse-t'ien sse-ta-ch'i-an* (Four Important and Curious Cases in the Time of the Empress Wu) would later provide the inspiration for Van Gulik's famous—Chinese detective stories, the Judge Dee novels. In 1949 in Tokyo Van Gulik published a translation of the book[9]—at least that part of it in which, while a district magistrate, Ti Jen-chieh solves crimes: the murder of two silk merchants, the poisoning of a bride on her wedding night and the mystery of the 'chaste' widow who turns out to have murdered her husband. He gave it the title *Dee Goong An*, Three Murder Cases Solved by Judge Dee.

The last day I put Kachan's affairs in order. I had already in the first months of our acquaintanceship opened a bank account in

---

[9]   See W.L. Idema, 'Het mysterie van de gehalveerde Rechter Tieroman', in *Hollands Maandblad*, No. 318/319 (1974), p. 58-66.

her name, where I put a monthly amount, and now I added my savings, so that she would have a small capital for starting a shop in her native village. Our parting was all the more poignant because she wanted it according to the traditional rules: strictly formal, and outwardly completely dispassionate. The last picture of her I retain in my visual memory is of her standing in the doorstep of the empty bungalow, making her last bow while I entered the car that was to take me to Yokohama and the ship.

It was 30 July 1942, and that same day I got a second severe shock. For the first time we heard the war news from a neutral source, the Swiss representatives on board, and discovered that everything the Japanese had been telling us about their astounding military successes and the great victories of their German allies had been perfectly true. Allied nationals who had been imprisoned by the Japanese after Pearl Harbour, among them my friend Frank Hawley, told us about the disgraceful way they had been treated; combined with what I had seen myself in the Japanese-occupied areas of China, it added up to a very grim picture indeed.

The *Tatsuta Maru* touched Shanghai to pick up allied diplomats there, including our Embassy staff from Peking, then Saigon and occupied Singapore, then we made for Lourenço Marques in Portuguese Southeast Africa. Thus we said good-bye to the Far East and Southeast Asia, little realizing that at the same time we said good-bye to a period in history: that the days that the white man meant something special in those lands were, for better or for worse, definitely past.

Chapter 6

SECRET AGENT IN AFRICA
August 1942-January 1943

While this exchange of Japanese and Allied diplomats was being effected under neutral supervision, the war in Europe, North Africa and the Pacific was in full swing.

In June 1942, General Rommel secured a great victory which made a profound impression everywhere. The British Desert Army had lost all the terrain it had captured in Libya and Cyrenaica. Its losses had been heavy (more than 50,000 men dead or made prisoners-of-war) and it had been driven back over a distance of 400 miles to the Egyptian frontier, close to where it had launched its advance at Mersa Matruh.

In the Pacific, the Japanese had won tremendous victories in December 1941 and in the first three months of 1942. They had destroyed the Allied Far Eastern Fleets and had inflicted such heavy losses on the British fleet in the Bay of Bengal and the Indian Ocean that it had been driven out of these waters. Japan now had Hong Kong, Siam, the Malay Peninsula and almost the whole of the Dutch East Indies in its grasp. Ceylon was under threat; India and Australia were in danger. Later, in May 1942, an American victory in the Battle of the Coral Sea would prove to be the turning point in the naval war in the Pacific, but the danger had not yet been averted.

After their losses around Ceylon, the British were seriously worried about the establishment of a Japanese naval base either in Ceylon itself or just opposite on the East African coast or in the island of Madagascar. In the latter case they could choose to achieve their goal either by force or by wresting permission for their move from the weak Vichy government, repeating what they had done in Indochina. Japanese submarines were already operating in the zone; a base in Madagascar combined with one in Ceylon could have disastrous consequences for shipping throughout the whole of the Indian ocean and the seas around the Arabian Peninsula. Sea traffic around the Cape would also be imperilled, and attacks on the east coast of Africa could emerge as a real threat. The response of the British government was to decide to be one step ahead of the Japanese; in May 1942 British units landed in Madagascar and occupied Port Diego Suarez; the rest of the island where the Vichy troops did put up some resistance fell into their hands at the end of October.[10]

> We had an eerie crossing on the brightly illuminated exchange ship, steaming peacefully through the black war-time world, and on August 27 arrived at Lourenço Marques. The Netherlands minister to South-Africa [Jhr Van Lennep] came on board with our instructions from the Government in exile in London: I was placed at the disposal of the Headquarters of the Allied Forces for special duties and was to stay in Lourenço Marques pending the arrival of detailed instructions. Since "special duties" were mentioned, I thought I had better not stay in the luxurious Polana Hotel on the bay where the other diplomats went; I knew that it was the centre of espionage, and I have always hated luxury hotels anyway—they are of a deadly uniformity the whole world over. So I took a room in the first Portuguese boarding house I saw, a small building with a long balcony overlooking the quay. The enormously fat landlady spoke only Portuguese and I proposed that she give me lessons. She winked and introduced me to three girl-boarders; they proved to work as hostesses at the Casino: two rather faded French girls and the third a rather nice mulatto girl with enormous black eyes. Since they slept till noon and had to be in the Casino at seven, we had the afternoons for our Portuguese sessions—held on the balcony, drinking beer and eating the delicious fried shrimps, while one of the touts played the guitar—a rather nice fellow who wept copiously when he sang sad songs about Portugal. At night friends from London came (agents of the British Secret Intelligence Agency, his new temporary instructors) and gave me the war-picture: Rommel was renewing his offensive at Al-Alamein, the Jap navy wanted a submarine basis in Pétain-administered Madagascar. The enemy master-plan was a pincer-movement, the Japs landing on the E. Coast of Africa, and the Germans taking Egypt and then closing in on the Allied basis in Mombasa where the British warships, having been bombed out of Ceylon, were lying packed as sardines in a tin. They told me my task was to travel all along the east coast, helping the local authorities (who of course knew nothing about Japan) to

---

[10] See *i.a.* Winston S. Churchill, *The Second World War* (London, 1951), Vol. IV, Chapter XIII, pp. 197-212.

devise measures against the infiltration of Japanese agents; I also had an official job for my own Government, viz. to have a look into the difficulties our Dutch interests on the East Coast (which were considerable) were having because of war time regulations. Before I set out, however, they (the agents of British Intelligence) wanted to go over with me the whole Far Eastern picture. On this we spent night after night, again consuming large quantities of beer and shrimps, and I was amazed to discover, under their experienced guidance, how much I knew of matters relevant to the war effort: apart from the Japanese political structure, also such technical matters as for instance the location of Japanese industrial plants in Manchuria, the kind of Chinese labour they employed there and its attitude to their Jap masters, the distribution of Japanese and Chinese puppet troops in North China, their means of transport, the degree of loyalty of sundry Chinese warlords, etc. During one month my routine was: in the mornings reading up on Africa in the surprisingly well-stocked municipal library, including African history, in particular Prince Youssouf Kamal's voluminous work on ancient African cartography with many references to old contacts with China [the recently appointed secret agent-scholar could not resist the temptation—always the Sinologist first]. I also tried to learn Swahili, the lingua franca of the East Coast; alternated with delightful boat trips up the Limpopo River where I saw for the first time hippopotami, crocodiles and other wild animals in their natural state. In the afternoons our language and musical sessions on the balcony, and at night the technical gatherings followed by visits to the Casino where I was treated as a member of their staff. On Sept. 23 my London friends left, and I embarked on the SS *Tilawa* bound for Dar-es-Salam, after a noisy farewell party with my girlfriends of the balcony: they had been good company, my only objection being their free use of obscene language—never once had I heard one of their Chinese or Japanese sisters use an indecent word, though heaven knows how well their colloquial is provided with those. At sea I saw the first signs of Japanese presence: we were pursued by a Jap submarine, but escaped their torpedoes by frantic zigzagging. On October 3 we arrived in Dar-es-Salam, and the next day on the—at that time!—enchanting clove-island of Zanzibar, a perfect dream, straight from the Arabian Nights. The Govt. Secretary Dutton was a level-headed and efficient man, and we soon found that the Jap agents were Indians recruited from the Azad Hind forces in Singapore, brought by Jap submarines to S.

Arabia, and from there they crossed in *dhows* (Arab sailing boats) to the east coast of Africa. I stayed with our (honorary) consul, a young bachelor who lived in a huge old Arab house and had many friends among the Arab plantation owners who threw splendid moonlight dinners for us in the true Arab manner, seated on thick carpets on their terraces and eating with our bare hands. The women, a mixture of Swahili and Arab, impressed us very much.

Van Gulik also told his friends how enchanted his sojourn on Zanzibar had been. He used every day, every single hour, to learn as much as he could and to enjoy himself.

6-10-1942: 2.45-3.45 lunch at club with [the honorary consul] Egberts, 2-3 Garidi [who gave him Arabic lessons] came, rested 3-4, 4-6 trip with Egberts. Persian bath, clove plantations and coconut groves, 7-8 spoke to Bartlett at the club, dined alone, 9.30-11 strolled through the bazaar with Garidi. [The Persian bathhouse is marked with two small x's and the names of two girls].

There was plenty to do in Zanzibar, not forgetting the cultural level. Nearly every day he went to the museum to study artefacts, books and old manuscripts. He browsed in bookshops and antique dealers. There were innumerable excursions, swimming in the sea, an Arab tea party with Egberts and 'both sheiks', a reception at the palace with the sultan and, the same day:

13 October 11 o'clock returned home [from the reception], 12 o'clock to the *shamba* (garden) of the sheik with Saleh, Natham etc., where [enjoyed] Indo-Arabian lunch. Afterwards viewed the *shamba*, 5 o'clock took tea there. Swahili boy sang Arab songs, half-past 5 to Z'bar and back via Dunga [palace ruins], 6-7 drank beer with the crew of the *Donau* [the boat which would later take him from Zanzibar to Mobasa], work at home in the evening.

The British Club also housed in an old-style Arab building had a fine reference library, and there I read up on Islam and Arabic, practising a little Arabic calligraphy (as far as I know, apart from Chinese and Japanese, Arabic is the only living script still thought of as highly as painting).

His pocket diary also bears witness to his interest in cinema: in Lourenço Marques he saw *Northwest Passage*, *You Will Find It Out* and *Four Just Men*; in Zanzibar *The Feminine Touch*.

None of this would have been possible had Robert van Gulik not been able to prolong his stay on this wonderful island. He managed this by visiting a doctor on 8 October, who advised him 'to take a few days' rest', whereupon he immediately wrote a letter to Winkelman, the Consul-General in Mombasa, to inform him that his arrival there would be somewhat delayed. Mombasa did not appeal to him.

> From Zanzibar I went to Mombasa [on 19 October] where our Consul-General briefed me on the Dutch economic position, while Dutch intelligence officers [among them Lieut. Brouwer] serving with the British Navy briefed me on the general situation in East Africa. In my spare time I visited the old trade centres along the coast where I found many traces of Chinese contacts, and I was fascinated by the deserted medieval town of Gedi. From Mombasa [by train] to Nairobi [where he visited various bookshops, bought a lion skin and worked on Hindustani], Kampala [where X-rays were taken of his abdomen and appendix, in the evening the cinema: *The Man from Dakota*] and Entebbe: many days of consultations with Dutch traders. Personally I thoroughly enjoyed trips around Mount Kenya where I spent several nights in a hunter's hut up in a tree in the jungle, not for shooting the animals but for observing them at their watering places; witnessed a magnificent fight between a lion and a rhino. And I picked up much information on African beliefs and customs that brought to mind what Prof. Uhlenbeck had taught me on anthropology. I collected a chestful of primitive wood carving, that was lost somewhere in transit. Memorable was a trip with a Nile-inspector to Murchison Falls.

Van Gulik's intelligence friends in London passed on news of the latest offensive of the German General Rommel and his Afrika Corps near Al-Alamein on 30 August 1942. This had been preceded by dramatic developments. After Rommel's sensational and alarming victory in June, Churchill had flown to Cairo in person to make some changes in the British Middle East Military Command (afterwards he flew to Moscow for his first meeting with Stalin). General Auchinleck was replaced as Commander-in-Chief Middle East by General Alexander, and General Montgomery took over command of the Eighth Army from General Ritchie. This army was reinforced and planning and training were intensified. The result of these changes and hard work was that the British were able to beat off the new offensive launched by Rommel within a few days.

Fewer than two months later, on 23 October, the British had reached the stage at which they could mount an offensive against Rommel in the area around Al-Alamein. They won a victory on 4 November and, after having inflicted heavy casualties on them, drove off the German and Italian troops. The tide in North Africa had turned in favour of the Allies.

The British success near Al-Alamein was the prelude to Torch, the large-scale Allied offensive against Vichy French North Africa under the American general, Eisenhower. It was launched on 8 November 1942 with huge landings on the coast of North Africa. Casablanca and Oran fell into Allied hands, followed by Tunisia and Libya in December 1942.

The original plan was that Dr Van Gulik would fly from Central Africa to Cairo, but instead he was asked by his friends in London to make his way there by boat along the Nile so as to find out more about what game an Egyptian princess was playing. The reason behind this request was the political situation in Egypt.

During the Second World War this country was completely subjugated to British influence. However, the relationship between the autocratic Egyptian court and the British government was poor, or at its best 'an uneasy alliance'. In the 1920s and 1930s, King Farouk's father, Fu'ād, was already scheming to strengthen his position, first with the British, then with the Wafd Party, the representative of a nascent nationalism. The most prominent Wafd politician, An-Nahhās, who had already been prime minister a couple of times, was dismissed by the young King Farouk as soon as the latter attained his majority.

Nevertheless, at the beginning of 1942 as the German forces were preparing to invade Egypt, the British forced Farouk to re-appoint An-Nahhās, whom they found more acceptable, as prime minister, an office which he held until 1944.

This British interference strengthened both King Farouk's anti-British sentiments and his antipathy to An-Nahhās. Moreover, it also damaged the nationalist image of the Wafd Party. Given this situation, it is not surprising that the British were following the doings of the Egyptian royal family with considerable suspicion and were apprehensive of pro-German intrigues.

I got word that Princess Kerime Halim, the divorced wife of Prince Yussuf Kamal [whose book about ancient African cartography Van

Gulik had studied in Lourenço Marques], was travelling by Nile
boat back to Cairo, together with her suite. Now the Allies doubted
the Egyptian Court, which was riddled with enemy agents, and
they ordered me to board the Nile boat and try to find out exactly
why the princess had left for the south and what her ideas were
about the situation in Egypt. So I discarded my martial attire and
took on the role of a young Dutch diplomat again. The voyage by
Nile boat was quite an experience, and I found that the Princess
and her suite were only badly frightened people who had [neither]
the inclination nor the capacity of concocting subversive plans. I
was struck, however, by the fact they all spoke Turkish amongst
each other, and positively despised the Egyptian population.

Van Gulik had no difficulty in winning the trust of the Egyptian
princess and her entourage. The young Dutch diplomat, so recently
arrived from China and Japan, about which he could tell such spell-
binding stories, was far removed from the multitudinous intrigues of
the Middle East. He was a charming man and impressively erudite.
He had a considerable knowledge of Islam, knew a little Arabic and
Swahili, and had learned a great deal about Africa from the book her
ex-husband, Prince Yussuf Kamal, had written. The princess, petite,
slender, a little more curvaceous than the Japanese women Van Gulik
had known, with very large dark eyes brimming with expression,
showed her Dutch travelling companion, as much as she could in
the presence of her entourage, that she was really taken with him.
They had animated conversations with each other and consequently
during the voyage she did not suffer a moment's boredom. Later, Van
Gulik would be invited to her home in Cairo.

On 13 and 14 November, Robert and some English friends
explored the Nile and one of its tributaries in a rowing boat.
Afterwards they drove by car to Juba, where he bought a ticket
for the boat trip to Khartoum. Naturally, in his pocket diary he
makes no mention of either his secret mission or of his animated
conversations with the seductively beautiful Egyptian princess. It
contains no more than a few place names and notes such as, 'saw
elephants' or 'land flat, saw crocodiles'. From 14 to 21 November he
journeyed to Khartoum on the *Rejāf*.

After a brief stay at Khartoum I went to Cairo [by train as far as Wadi
Khalfa, after that on the Nile boat *Sudan*], breaking my journey
for three days in Luxor to visit the Egyptian antiquities. I saw the

Valley of the Kings under exceptionally favourable circumstance, for I and a British major suffering from shell-shock were the only visitors, and there were no Arab guides to pester us.

Then on to Cairo [by train, arrived 30 November], where our Minister [A.W.C. Baron van Bentinck van Schoonheten, then Minister and acting *chargé d'affaires*] allocated me an office in the Legation to work out my reports. Cairo was in a festive mood, for Rommel had been defeated [4 November], and every night there was something on. In my spare time I visited the El-Ashram University and other Arabic sights [institutes] in Cairo and Alexandria. I also continued my studies of Islam which had begun to fascinate me.

Later, when I was Director of the Africa and Middle East Section in the F.O. and then as Minister in Lebanon and Syria, the work done in Africa proved very useful background information.

In Lourenço Marques Van Gulik had been informed that, after this African interlude, his ultimate destination would be Ceylon, where he would be assigned to the staff of the Commander of the Forces in the East, Vice-Admiral C.E.L. Helfrich. The London archives of the Ministry of Foreign Affairs reveal that, at the beginning of 1942, there had been a discussion with Admiral Furstner and Van Mook [Acting Governor-General of the East Indies in Exile] about how the skills of Interpreter First Class Van Gulik could best be deployed and that indeed a decision had been made to send him to Colombo. There, as well as being on hand to give advice, he would be able to do useful work on breaking Japanese codes.

However, when Foreign Affairs made enquires at the Naval Ministry (Rear-Admiral Termijtelen), it turned out that nobody there knew anything about it. At the request of Foreign Affairs, the Navy still sent a telegram informing it of Van Gulik's arrival.

Meanwhile, in a personal letter to his friend from Tokyo days, Jonkheer O. Reuchlin, head of diplomatic affairs in the Ministry in London, Van Gulik expressed dissatisfaction with his posting to Ceylon, urging that he be appointed to the Chinese wartime capital Chungking. Reading between the lines, what was really at stake was a private plan of Robert's (one of which Reuchlin alone knew) to be assigned a brief detachment to Allied Headquarters in New Delhi to advise on the sort of psychological warfare tactics to be used against Japan. During his visit to Zanzibar, he had launched a campaign with the British Chief Secretary Eric Dutton to convince him of the soundness of the plan.

Who could picture Van Gulik's surprise when, the day after his arrival in Cairo, Bentinck showed him the following telegram:

For Van Gulik due to arrive in Cairo around 25 November.
'You have been appointed to work in Mombasa with Brouwer. Request you travel there directly after your leave. Lt Brouwer and the Minister for the Navy have been informed of this telegram. 1116-0845 Nether. Navy.'

He was to be assigned neither to Chungking nor to Delhi, not even to the less attractive job with the Eastern Command in Ceylon, but to *Mombasa!* This beggared belief. Van Gulik immediately dashed off an urgent letter to his friend Reuchlin, who certainly was aware that his dearest wish was to go to China (Chungking). He explained to his friend that he had just been to Mombasa and had familiarized himself with the situation there, 'a God-forsaken spot where all one sees are soldiers, black people and third-rate Indians and Arabs, absolutely devoid of culture.' Actually, it was a well-thought-out plan devised by Brouwer personally, not by the admiral, to send him there. However, in view of the fact that the work Brouwer did was exclusively naval, to which Van Gulik was completely unsuited, the latter thought that his 'seven years' experience in Tokyo and China would be absolutely useless' there. He devised a crafty solution by proposing that Reuchlin inform the Navy that he should first be given permission to go to Bombay to see whether his luggage ('all that is left of my earthly possessions') had been sent there and to make sure it was safely stowed. In Bombay, where he need not remain longer than a fortnight, he could 'make contact with the English authorities in Delhi. If indeed they should set me to work there (and after all my preparatory work I had good reason to think that this would be so), I shall forward a proposal to this end to London through our Foreign Affairs.'

He added, 'I hope, my dear Reuchlin, that you won't hold my bitterness against me. However, I must confess that my first secondment to Colombo, without as much as a by your leave, and now once again this sudden switch from Colombo to Mombasa, all apparently sanctioned by the F.O., have pained me deeply[...] For the sake of our time together in Tokyo, take your time to look through these matters calmly, and at the very least try to give Kleffens a better picture of me and my work. *De profundis oro ad te* [From the depths I beseech you]!'

Reuchlin's reaction to this appeal was positive, and Van Gulik had his way. Foreign Affairs asked the Navy to part with Van Gulik once again, because his services were required for diplomatic work in China. Cairo received a signal that Van Gulik should not proceed to his new destination (Mombasa) but should await instructions. The Navy acquiesced and Cairo received the telegram: 'In consultation with the Navy, Van Gulik to return to the interpreting service. He is to be assigned to Chunking with the personal title of Secretary to the Legation.'

This had just been arranged when the Dutch military mission in London received a request from the British War Office asking it to trace a certain Dr Van Gulik, last employed in the Dutch Legation in Tokyo, on its behalf: 'In view of his knowledge of Japanese, our authorities would be pleased to make use of his services in India. We have understood that he was recently living in Nairobi, but his present whereabouts are unknown to us.' The Dutch authorities acquiesced in this request and so Van Gulik's plan ran like clockwork. Ultimately he went neither to Colombo nor Mombasa, but to Delhi and thence to China.

While all this was being played out somewhere else, Van Gulik remained tranquilly in Cairo, awaiting further developments:

> Since our Minister Baron Van Bentinck had his hands full with other work, I took the contacts with Dutch soldiers and sailors in the Allied forces from him, helping them to straighten out their manifold troubles. Now for the first time I received news about my family in occupied Holland and learned to my relief that Father and Mother were comparatively safe in *Severen*, and that my brother Piet, the gynaecologist in Amsterdam, was doing good work in the underground, helping Jews to escape from Holland.

His travelling companion on the Nile boat, Princess Halim, invited him to come to visit her, and when her ex-husband heard from her and from her secretary, who had accompanied her on her travels, what an exceptionally multi-faceted and pleasant travelling companion she had had, she also issued Van Gulik an invitation:

> 5-12-1942: half-past four visited Princess Halim at her home in Maadi, half an hour by car from Cairo.

> 7-12-1942: half-past one large lunch with Prince Yussuf Kamal.

> 8-12-1942: went to Prince Yussuf's palace, looked at his library.

10-12-1942: half-past 12 to Prince Yussuf Kamal, where lunched with secretary and an Arab lady, given a book as a present.

During the one and a half months he spent in Cairo, Van Gulik had again succeeded in extracting the maximum benefit from the time at his disposal. His daily diaries give an amazing picture of his incredible number of activities: work at the Legation, contacts with Dutch and British colleagues and with the British Secret Service, and first and foremost with professors, both foreign and Egyptian: scholars of Arabic and Islam, art connoisseurs, archaeologists and, of course, Chinese scholars.

They showed him rare collections which were never shown to tourists, guided him around museums and mosques and took him to visit historical monuments. Even though every hour, indeed every quarter of an hour was filled, he remained calm and was seldom tired. In the evenings he had long, informative talks with these scholars, usually quite informally, after dinner or with a cool drink on the terrace under the palm trees. Between morning visits, there was always time for a cup of coffee in a cosy café, or in the afternoons a cup of tea. Almost every day there was an opportunity for a drink, and once in a while for billiards. In Cairo, more frivolous matters rarely intruded. On two occasions a visit to a cabaret with friends, 'where saw dancing', an American film (*How Green Was My Valley*) and a Russian war film (*In the Rear of the Enemy*).

On Boxing Day Van Gulik travelled by car to Suez and Port Taufik to board a Dutch cargo boat and two tankers on which he distributed Christmas presents. He spent the night on the cargo boat, where he got on splendidly with the crew. When he was just being a Dutchman among other Dutch people, he knew how to strike the right note and he shed the image of the scholar or the diplomat. In fact, he was wonderfully clever at deflating all bragging. He was inquisitive, interested in the work of these people and in their personal lives. People soon realized that this interest was genuine and that he wanted to delve below the surface of matters; while enjoying a glass of beer tongues would loosen and everything was very relaxed; the respect he aroused in people only grew as a consequence. His time in Egypt was coming to an end.

When my work in Cairo was finished, I was ordered to New Delhi and left Cairo on Jan. 14 [1943] by plane.

Chapter 7

CHUNGKING
1943-1946

DELHI INTERLUDE ON THE WAY TO CHINA

Before taking up his post at the embassy in Chungking, the 'wartime capital' of China, Dr Van Gulik continued to be 'on loan' to the British Intelligence Service and, as an eminent authority on Japan, he was briefly despatched to New Delhi for a short period because the British wanted to pick his brains about the sort of psychological warfare to be used against Japan. In his talks with Major Dutton, Chief Secretary of Zanzibar, he had dropped some hints, whereupon 'on his own initiative', Dutton had written to the British Colonial Secretary, Leo Amery.

During his last fortnight in Egypt he made a short trip to Alexandria, where he visited the Asian market and a number of bookshops, admired the catacombs and Pompey's Pillar, attended the *Tribunal Mixte* in the company of the Dutch judge Arnold Struycken, strolled in the Park of Antoniades and the rose garden, had drinks with Dutch airmen, dined out and saw a few films: *Ringside Maisy*, *Appointment with Love*, *The Invisible Agent*.

In those days, the journey from Alexandria to Delhi was not a trip to be taken lightly; it took Robert twelve days, partly by flying-boat and the rest in a small three-seater plane belonging to Tata Airlines. He did, however, have an interesting travelling companion, Professor Joseph Needham, who was on his way back to Chungking where he was posted to the British Embassy. Needham, with whom he had many long conversations, was *the* Western authority in the field of Chinese natural sciences.

> 14-1-1943: left hotel at 4.30, departed from Nile at 7 a.m. on a flying-boat, at 9 landed on the Dead Sea, where we rested for fifteen minutes and had some tea. Flew on to a lake near Baghdad, another 4 hours to Basra, where put up at the Airways Hotel Shat-el-Arab. Dinner there at 8 with Air Commodore Warburton and another air force officer, and early to bed.

19-1-1943 [in Karachi]: After breakfast talked until 11, afterwards went shopping with Needham, then lunch in the Chinese restaurant Apollo with Head and Needham. Afterwards returned to hotel, where talked with Needham, at 7 went with him and a hotel man attended a Sikh *Mandar* [*mantar*—a session of sacred chanting] and visited a Rāmā temple.

When my work in Cairo was finished, I was ordered to New Delhi, and left Cairo on January the 14th by plane. While the situation in North-Africa had improved, India was fervently preparing for a Japanese invasion, and General Wavell had established in Delhi a large centre for anti-Japanese psychological warfare; also the Ministry of Economic Warfare had a large office there, a fine body of men, and there was plenty of work to do. As to Wavell, I agree with Somerset Maugham that most statesmen prove a disappointment when one actually meets them, but General Wavell was an exception. I greatly admired his utter simplicity, his quick intellect, and his broad interest. After a business meeting he often took me apart for long talks about Chinese poetry, a subject he was particularly interested in.

Like Van Gulik, Wavell was actually very modest, with a tendency towards taciturnity—when he did speak it was very slowly and deliberately (Robert stuttered a little now and then) and also seldom wore his emotions on his sleeve. Field-Marshal Wavell was a truly exceptional man. In August 1942, in his capacity as Chief of the General Staff, he had accompanied his prime minister, Churchill, on his first visit to Stalin in Moscow. He spoke Russian and Churchill said that he harboured literary ambitions. He had summarized the message which Churchill had for Stalin in the form of a poem, each verse of which ended with the line, 'No Second Front in 1942'. 'It was', wrote Sir Winston Churchill in the *Second World War*, 'like carrying a large lump of ice to the North Pole.'

The head of the centre for anti-Japanese psychological warfare in Delhi, D-Division (later called Force 456), was the gifted and extraordinarily inventive British journalist and writer Peter Fleming. The Japanese were fed information in all sorts of ingenious ways or were sold it for large sums of money through double agents. This was to entice them either to undertake or to abandon actions which would hasten their defeat. Whereas Peter Fleming was operationally active, Robert van Gulik's role in this sphere was an advisory one. Unlike Van Gulik, Fleming was not a scholar, but both had an great sense of humour and both were thoroughly conversant with the mentality of the Chinese and Japanese. Understandably, Van Gulik betrayed nothing of his secret activities in Delhi and Chungking, but it is plausible that he would have also met Fleming in Chungking during the latter's visits to that city. Later, Mrs Van Gulik remembered that her husband occasionally mentioned the name, but could not recall ever having met Fleming personally.

In the course of his work, one year prior to Robert's arrival in Chungking, with the consent of the Chinese authorities, Fleming who was in the Chinese war capital with a MOST SECRET document—the forged minutes of a meeting of the Joint Military Council—passed this on to the Japanese. Fleming assumed that, sooner or later, when the Allied strategy had been played out differently to the plan described in this document, suspicions would be aroused about the authenticity of the minutes, but not before it would have ruffled some feathers among the higher echelons.

> I do not think (he wrote about this operation Purple Whale) it will be easy for the Japanese Service Chiefs to begin to suspect. The idea of using (e.g.) the personality of the Deputy C-in-C in a forgery—a forgery which depicts us as bickering with our Allies—is entirely alien to their mentality. We have a number of senior officers on our side who would be virtually incapable of seeing the point of Purple Whale if it was explained to them; it is safe to assume that their counterparts exist in Tokyo.[11]
>
> This was my first visit to India, I travelled widely in small military planes, and in spare moments visited the Ajanta Caves and other old Buddhist sites important for sinologues. I also met a number of Indian Sanskrit scholars which revived my interest in Indian literature. Finally I passed three weeks in Calcutta, where I had the advantage of long conversations on Later Buddhism and Tibetan Lamaism with our great Dutch scholar Johan van Manen, many years secretary of the Asiatic Society.

On his journey on to China, Van Gulik spent some time in Calcutta. In the meantime, he had been transferred back to the Dutch Foreign Service and appointed first secretary to the embassy in Chungking for where he was expected to leave as soon as possible. However, he was in no hurry and, as had happened more than once

---

[11]   Hart-Davis, Duff: *Peter Fleming: A Biography.* Oxford: Oxford University Press 1987, pp 273-274.

before, his ailments came to his aid. The Consul in Calcutta sent a signal to Foreign Affairs on 1-3-1943: 'Van Gulik here ill severe sinus infection departure Chungking delayed by two weeks.'

On the 15th March 1943, I boarded the plane that took me over "the hump" (the foothills of the Himalayas), which would bring me back to China.

CHUNGKING, MARCH 1943 – MAY 1946

Chungking, China's wartime-capital, was a gray city of barracks and sheds, having been flattened several times by the regular Japanese bombing-attacks. Yet it was a cheerful city. Chinese of all parts of China and foreigners from all parts of the world being brought closely together by the shared hardship and danger. The Embassy had been evacuated to the mountains south of the city, a room on the top-floor of the ramshackle "Victory House". Hsü Shih-ying, whom I had known as Chinese ambassador in Tokyo, now occupied a high position in the National Government, and his Counsellor Wang P'êng-shêng now turned out to be a general, and he was chief of Foreign Intelligence. Through our old friendship in Tokyo I could work together with him closely, and profited immensely by his amazing knowledge of what was going on in occupied China, where he maintained a network of excellent secret agents; he also was very well informed about the situation in the Japanese-occupied Netherl[ands]. E. Indies.

In scholarly and artistic fields, my years in Chungking were of incalculable benefit for my studies: all the best Chinese scholars and artists from all the great cultural centers in China had flocked together there, and since there were practically no opportunities for other amusements, the main relaxations were daily tea-gatherings and interminable talks about all aspects of Chinese culture one could imagine. I became a member of a number of literary associations, chief among them the *T'ien-feng-ch'in-shê* ("Heavenly Wind Lute Association"), which was joined by such eminent scholars as the aged Yü Yu-jen (...), and colourful characters such as the 'Christian general' Fêng Yü-hsiang. We had close contacts with the local Szechuanese gentry, and when there were no Jap planes coming, spent delightful weekends at their country houses in the outskirts of Chungking. Now for the first time I completely shared the Chinese way of life—and liked it immensely.

A Belgian diplomat with whom he was friendly, Robert Rothschild, who was working there in the same period, has given a good, more detailed description of this wartime capital:

> Chungking, that dirty but wonderful city, was an ancient stronghold, situated at the confluence of two great rivers, the Yangtze and the Chialing (*p.y.* Jialing), which flowed down from the glaciers in the Tibetan plateau and the Himalayas. The reason for its thousand-year-old importance was that it was a transit harbour for the rich provinces of Szechuan and the plateaus of the Himalayan region. Fifty million inhabitants brought their produce: rice, cattle, silk, musk and fur, here to exchange them for textiles, petroleum and the all-important tools which came from the coast.
>
> Of the old city, devastated by bombardments, only the quarter of the southern bank and the ancient, reinforced walls on the northern bank survived; overshadowed by pagoda roofs they still retained its medieval character with their massive stones and their gates. The main gate, Tung Yüan Men, gave access to the ancient imperial route which ended 1,500 km farther on in Peiping [Beijing]. Within the walls, the backbone was formed by two asphalted roads, off which sprawled hundreds of winding alleys along which the inhabitants had rebuilt their dwellings, destroyed by enemy bombardment, from bamboo and stamped earth.
>
> Many alleys were so narrow that two people could not pass through them side by side. They swarmed with wretched, cheerful, noisy humanity; half-naked children played and fought there with each other; pigs with almost black bristles [which were put on a leash on the street, as were cats; both were greatly desired as opponents of the plague of rats], dogs which never barked, and scrawny chickens scratched for their food among the garbage in the gutters. Mothers, with breasts bared, nursed their babies or let them defecate; innumerable coolies in brief cotton shorts, their torsos dripping with sweat, a filthy piece of cloth wound around their heads, carried heavy loads suspended from a carrying pole over their shoulders at a trot [often singing or humming].
>
> Each of the different sorts of peddlers—the hawker of textiles, the seller of iron, the peddler of food—had his own advertising jingle. You soon learned to move out of the way of the night soil carrier, who collected this valuable product every day.
>
> As evening fell, the darkness was punctuated by thousands of candles and oil lamps which offered feeble illumination in the

small shops which remained open until late in the evening. A strong odour prevailed: a mixture of a farmer's market, incense and damp decay. Often as I strolled around, my mind turned to the narrow streets of medieval Paris, described in the novels of Victor Hugo.[12]

By this time, both the nationalist Kuomintang Government (since 1938) and the Chinese Communist Party (after its Long March in 1934-1935) had been driven to remote corners of the country. Their United Front against the Japanese enemy soon revealed that it was nothing more than a sham. Neither dictatorship was prepared to allow itself to be swallowed up by the other and mutual distrust was rife. Nevertheless, the Communists did hold out some chances for co-operation, which were dismissed out of hand by the intransigent arch-conservative Chiang Kai-shek.

When Van Gulik arrived in Chungking at the beginning of 1942, China, which had initially carried on the struggle against Japan alone, had been allied with the Western powers for more than a year. In January 1943, the treaties with the United States and Great Britain had been amended and these countries had ceded their privileges in China. As a consequence of waging a war against the common enemy, the American presence in Free China was massive—far greater than it had ever been before. American aid was immense and was a source of enormous moral support to the Chinese.

The failure of this aid to have any really decisive influence on the course of the war, as China had expected, is attributable to a number of factors: the Japanese occupation of Burma had cut off the supply route via the Burma Road, leaving only the air route from India to Kunming; the prioritization by Allies of victory over Germany; and, by this time, the centre of the war against Japan had increasingly moved to the Pacific. Consequently, China was relegated to secondary importance as a theatre of war. Over and above this, the rampant inflation, aided and abetted by the incompetence and corruption under the authoritarian regime in Free China made it extremely difficult to render effective help.

In Van Gulik's own autobiography and his diaries, he pays no attention to the political, economic or military situations in which China was embroiled. Certainly these topics did interest Robert— both personally and in his capacity as a diplomat—but they did not

---

[12]   From: Robert Rothschild, *La chute de Chiang Kai-shek*, Paris 1972, pp. 12-13.

affect him deeply, or if they did at least to a much lesser degree than his studies and his mingling with the Chinese intellectual and artistic community. Once again the (few) official reports which he wrote here and at other posts consistently reveal his lucid insight, often astutely formulated, into the complicated internal political developments in the country to which he was posted. After the outbreak of the war, as he admitted himself, he had lived in a 'fool's paradise' in Japan because it was generally expected that a Japanese defeat was imminent. During the time he spent in Africa and India, he had been confronted with the reality of the situation which still seemed far from bright for the Western Allies. Although this made him a more serious person, he did not feel under any pressure to surrender his philosophical attitude. Cultural interests and study were paramount, as well as his serious work as a diplomat (with a preference for secret intelligence work) occupied the lion's share of his attention. There are few mentions of sexual escapades in this period.

A month after he came to Chungking, Ambassador Lovink, who presented his credentials on 23 April, arrived. The latter was a man of boundless energy but none the less of a sympathetic nature, with a love of sports, the epitome of a healthy outdoors-man—almost the complete opposite of Van Gulik, who spent his time tucked away in dark rooms smoking and studying. However, there was one matter on which they were in complete agreement—their burning desire that 'the Indies' should be returned to Dutch hands once again, and that any influence, whether from the United States, England, Japan or China was to be completely excluded. The contacts which Van Gulik had already struck up in Chinese society in Chungking were of inestimable value to the embassy, and Lovink was entirely aware of just how valuable they were. Robert's fame had preceded him; immediately after his arrival he not only found a number of staunch friends in high positions, he also made many new ones. Even in Republican China, the majority of politicians and senior civil servants were also scholars, and Van Gulik's fame was such that many 'already looked up to (*chiu-yang*)' him. This was the Chinese phrase which was always used when introductions were made and, in his case, it was not just empty words. On shared visits together to bookshops, antique shops and exhibitions of paintings, during dinners and while playing the lute, he was able very unobtrusively to gather all kinds of political, sometimes top secret, information or to foster specific Dutch interests. He knew everybody of any importance.

9-5-1943: painted fan in the morning, 3.30 visited Prof. Shen Chien-shih, returned home 6, bathed, dinner with an Indian man, 9-10 Mr and Mrs Wu dropped in for a chat, then worked.

12-5-1943: 9.30-11 Sun came to work on Tung Kao manuscript; [he was helping Robert with the book which he was writing about the Chinese monk], 12.30 Wang Shih-chieh [Minister of Information, later of Foreign Affairs] and [Prof.] Ma Hêng [great scholar and calligrapher, former director of the Old Palace Museum in Peking] came to lunch, remained to chat until 3, 4 p.m. Visited Yeh Ch'iu-yüan [another famous scholar and calligrapher; he and his wife were particularly hospitable people and became Van Gulik's great friends; they later emigrated to the US] and talked until 6. Bought an ink stone. Half-past seven dined alone.

18-5-1943: Wang Shih-chieh came to look at Chinese scrolls [including some in Van Gulik's calligraphy].

In his short biography of Van Gulik (*Ho-lan Kao Lo-p'ei*—The Dutchman Van Gulik), the Chinese ambassador and scholar Chen Chih-mai has this to say about his lute-playing: 'When I first knew him, he was already a master of this instrument [the classical Chinese *ch'in*]. He was in the habit of taking the lute, a rather cumbersome object, along to various social occasions in Chungking and it was his custom to play various melodies on it after dinner to entertain his friends. I remember one of these occasions very well, a hot summer evening, when we were all at dinner in a house which was precariously situated at the top of a slope of the bank of the Chialing River. After we had all had our portion—and perhaps more than our fair share—of food and drink, Dr Van Gulik began to play an old song in which in the Chinese tradition "the music echoes the water which flows gently down from the slopes of the high mountains". It was a romantic occasion. Romantic in the traditional Chinese sense, so very dear to Dr Van Gulik's heart, which we all enjoyed immensely. How could we not be captivated by this young man from Europe, whose physical characteristics were anything but Chinese, as he played us this song which has survived in the Chinese soul for two thousand years? In the years which followed, Dr Van Gulik gave many lute concerts to packed halls in the wartime capital to raise money for charitable purposes. This was his contribution to the Chinese war effort; his music became part of his diplomacy.'

Chen Chih-mai also admired his literary style which was '...so classical that few contemporary Chinese writers would have dared to attempt it'. He added that Van Gulik was an arch-conservative in his views on literary Chinese. He refused to write the vernacular (*pai-hua*), which had been used in China as a written language for decades, he did not even punctuate what he wrote in the modern manner. Naturally, later he would be a fierce opponent of the simplification of the Chinese characters which was introduced in the People's Republic.

Van Gulik visited Fu Tan University, where he delivered a lecture in Chinese about the monk Tung-Kao. Afterwards, at the request of the professors, he embellished several scrolls with his highly appreciated calligraphy and then lunched with them after a short interruption (an air-raid alarm).

He set up his library as best he could, as he was still accommodated in Victory House, where he was in charge of the liaison office of the embassy until the chancellery could be established again in the city and Robert could then assigned his own house. He played the lute and painted, every now and again diving into an air-raid shelter when the alarm sounded. By that time the heavy bombardments were in fact over, but the uncertainty and danger still continued to leave their impression on the city. He was in close contact with the military attaché, Colonel Everard, and with the latter's colleagues at other embassies. He got on famously with Ambassador Lovink and the councillors, Jan van den Berg and Count De Marchand et d'Ansembourg. As a result of his secret-service activities in Africa and Delhi, he has a few special contacts at the British Embassy, among them Findlay, Andrew and Crawford, not to mention such China specialists as Prof. Needham and John Blofeld, with whom he occasionally played Chinese chess.

At this time somebody appears in his life whose name will crop up frequently: her family name was Shui, her given name Shih-fang.

25-6-1943: 2 o'clock Miss Shui came to chat
26-6-1943: 1-2 Miss Shui
29-6-1943: 1-2 Miss Shui
30-6-1943: 7-8 Miss Shui

Robert took Chinese lessons with Miss Shui whom he had met at a reception. He takes her to the theatre and dines with her; they also go to see a film, *One Night of Love*. It is not long before she is being mentioned in the diary as Shih-fang (her personal name) or simply SF. They dined together with the scholar Yeh Ch'iu-yüan, who has been mentioned earlier, and his wife, who confirmed what he had already discovered; namely that not only was she a girl from a good family, but that she had also enjoyed a thorough classical upbringing. Later they were very frequent visitors to the Yehs. Shih-fang often accompanied Robert to such cultural happenings as art exhibitions. Chinese painting and calligraphy were lifelong passions of his.

Pl. 13. Shui Shih-fang, Van Gulik's wife, Chungking, 1943.

8-8-1943: 3 o'clock Wang Shih-chieh sent his car; visited his home and took tea and looked at paintings.

29-8-1943: 9 o'clock Bill Acker came [the gifted Chinese-lute-playing, hard-drinking American sinologist, with whom he had been friends since Tokyo days], wrote Chinese until 12 o'clock and sang [Bill sang American songs and Robert hummed along], 12 o'clock Shih-fang arrived, lunched with her and Bill at the Chukiang [Pearl River] Restaurant [Cantonese], afterwards bought paint brushes together and visited antique shops etc.. In the evening with her and Bill to a musical evening at the British Embassy.

1-9-1943: 8.30 to British Embassy to fetch petrol, 9 o'clock picked up Shih-fang, together by car to Kao-lo-shan [a mountain resort], arrived there 10 o'clock and visited Chang Shou-chien [banker and husband of Shih-fang's sixth sister, Shih-lin], talked until 11. From 11-12 climbed the mountain with Shih-fang and paid a visit to Yün-lin-sze [a temple], 1 o'clock lunch at his house with Mr Chang, 3 o'clock returned to Chungking by car, 4-7 chatted to Shih-fang at home, 7 o'clock dined on Chinese food together, 8 o'clock took Shih-fang home, after that worked at home.

By now they were seeing each other almost every day.

11.9.1943: Engagement announced

The next day they went by palanquin to the embassy residence on the mountainside on the other side of the river, where Robert introduced his fiancée to some of his closest colleagues. After tea they returned to the city on foot. Two days later:

> 14-9: Wang P'êng-shêng's car arrived at 6 o'clock, fetched Shih-fang, picked up Bill [Acker] and others. At Wang's a 'moon-viewing' party was held on the occasion of the *chung-ch'iu chieh* [mid-autumn festival].

Drinking wine and reciting poetry when the moon is full is a time-honoured, well-loved Chinese form of recreation. On another occasion Robert noted, 'My friend Yang Ta-chün played the *p'i-p'a* by moonlight while I played the lute [the *p'i-p'a* is another type of lute with four strings]. Shih-fang recalled that these were delightful evenings. In another place he says that, to mark the occasion of his engagement, he renamed his study *Yin-yüeh-an* (Hut for Singing to the Moon).

In his pocket diary Van Gulik now noted his beloved *waka* (five-line verse) which he remembered from his time in Japan:

Kumo harete	Even when the clouds have cleared away,
Nochi no hikari to	think not
Omou na yo.	that day has broken.
Motoyori sora ni	The heavens are still illuminated
Ariake no tsuki.	by the glow of the dawn moon.

In the summer of 1943 I met a secretary of the Ministry of Social Affairs, a 22 year old girl from Peking called Shui Shih-fang. She had left Peking with a large group of other students shortly after the arrival of the Japanese, fled to Changsha, from there to the south, crossed over to Hanoi, and thus reached Kunming, in the S.E. of Free China. There she had enrolled in the refugee-university, thence had gone to Chengtu in the NW of Free China and taken her MA in Social History at the University there. We fell in love, and I asked her to marry me. I was 33 then. I felt the time had come to settle down and establish a family. And although I had met attractive Western girls in Cairo and Alexandria, it had become clear to me that there were slender chances that I would make a western wife permanently happy, nor she me; the best chance of mutual happiness lay in a marriage with an Asiatic woman, preferably a Chinese.

In a series of conversations with Carl Barkman, Shih-fang told her own story:

Entire universities had fled from Peking when the Japanese occupied the city. With twenty female students from Ch'ing-hua University, most members of the YWCA (Young Women's Christian Association), and a few male fellows from the YMCA, I set off on an odyssey. My father had given me some money from which I could live for a very long time, but after my university studies, first in Kunming and later in Chengtu, this had been used up, and I had to look for a job. I found this in the Ministry of Social Affairs in Chungking. At that time the salaries were so low and the inflation so high, most of us earned extra by giving Chinese lessons to foreigners.

During a party at the British Embassy, one of my girlfriends—her name was Liu Mo-hsien—introduced me to a Dutch diplomat who spoke fluent Chinese, which made a deep impression on me. He was a burly man, very pleasant, with good, 'Chinese' manners. He wanted to improve his Chinese even more and I gave him lessons. Then I discovered that not only he was well versed in Chinese classical literature, he also wrote splendid characters. As a calligrapher he could compete with the best Chinese. He also played the classical lute beautifully.

We fell in love with each other and decided to marry. Robert asked: "Shall we marry in church?" and I had had exactly the same thought. We asked the Rev. Chang Hai-sung to conduct the marriage service; he was the uncle of the girl who had introduced Robert and me. Our witnesses were Wang Shih-chieh, the Minister of Foreign Affairs, who was an intimate friend of Robert's, and the wife of Wang P'êng-shêng, a married couple with whom we were also very close friends (he had already become very well acquainted with my husband in Tokyo, and in Chungking, as Head of the Foreign Information Service, he was able to help us to convey my father's consent to the marriage from Peking to Chungking via the 'underground'.

After the wedding ceremony we gave a dinner at the 'People's Foreign Relations Association', followed by a reception at home.

Count D'Ansembourg gave an exceedingly gracious speech in English (Ambassador Lovink was then absent from Chungking), whose text I have preserved and in which he said among other things:

"From all the circumstances surrounding this wedding we realise we are gathering here in a time of war. The marriage is celebrated in the war capital of China—on the part of the bridegroom none of his relatives are here—on the part of the bride, we miss her parents who would have been glad to be here with us.

Nevertheless, we celebrate, were it only because a festival of love makes us forget for a moment that a war is on. But there is more—it is good to realize that the war will not be going on forever.

War is based on hatred and envy; peace on harmony and love. War is only a passing phase in our life and in the life of nations, because love is the stronger and more lasting element in life.

Peaceful people and peaceful nations will therefore continue to exist and people and nations bent on aggression shall perish— it is love which sustains human beings and also nations. Venus is stronger than Mars.

I have known Dr van Gulik and his wife for a comparatively short time. But of one thing I have been able to convince myself— the bride has all the charms of her country and she is very well suited to her husband, who as a scholar and diplomat has no other ambition in life than to promote the cause of humanity and good relations amongst nations.

It is fortunate he has been able to make such a good choice and find a partner for life whose character guarantees that she will understand her husband's work, moreover will appreciate it and be of great help to him. On such a sound foundation of mutual love and understanding permanent happiness and a harmonious life can be built."

Robert had moved into a proper house only shortly before, and he had furnished it almost completely by himself: on 5 December, with the help of coolies and the car from the military desk, he moved from Victory House to Kuo Fu Lu 295. Together we bought a dinner service, chose beds and chests-of-drawers and suchlike, while Robert had purchased a lute table and bookshelves by himself and had employed a cook.

Shih-fang was an almost classic Chinese beauty, an affectionate personality with a cheerful nature. She had a great sense of humour and an infectious laugh. From the point of view of his ideal of the scholar-civil servant, in Robert's eyes the fact that she also was the scion of a very good family of mandarins was an added blessing. He gave her the literary name: *I ch'in* (Lovely Zither).

When I came to know my future wife better during our betrothal, I found that all the elements that might lead to a happy married life were there: we came from the same social level, her father having been a diplomat under the Chinese Empire already, and scion of an old Peking mandarin-family; SF had received an old-style Chinese education, yet had a genuine interest in western things—but never so deep as to want to become westernised. She was interested in foreign things in the same manner as we are interested in a foreign book. So she did not suffer in a way from the tensions and doubts of many young oriental women confronted with the impact of the west.

Now [1965] that we have been married 21 years, I can say that our marriage has been an unqualified success. SF has adapted herself very well to western life, speaks Dutch, English and French, and has proved an excellent diplomat's wife. Yet she remains convinced that there is no better way of living than in completely Chinese surroundings and that there is no better culture than that of China, and this conviction has given her a great self-assurance that has been an unfailing source of strength in all the tribulations in a diplomat's life.

The Netherlands Foreign Office at once gave permission for the marriage, but there were great difficulties on the side of SF's family. Her old father being in occupied Peking, the head of the clan in Free China was an old uncle, a banker—a most conservative, old fashioned gentleman who profoundly despised everything foreign. He thought SF's marriage to me a terrible misalliance, and a blemish on the family. When the Netherlands Ambassador urged him personally to give his consent, he stalled matters by saying he had no authority to do so without written consent of SF's father. It was then that my friend, General Wang P'êng-shêng, came to the rescue: he had one of his secret agents contact Dr Shui in Peking! In the incredibly brief space of two weeks a brief note from Dr Shui was smuggled through the Japanese lines to Chungking: he had no objections!

Dr Shui Chün-shao, born in 1878, was a high-ranking civil servant of the old school. Under the Empire, besides holding various posts in China itself, he had occupied diplomatic posts in France and Germany. He had also held high office in the railways under the Republic; later he had been minister/consul-general in Leningrad and mayor of Tientsin. He died in 1963.

In the good years he had lived in great pomp. As minister he journeyed to Russia on his own special train consisting of more than twenty carriages, in which he transported not only his household staff but also twenty-five kitchen personnel. On his arrival in Leningrad, he was received on the platform with all the honours required by protocol. His first question to the welcoming committee was: 'Where can I play mah-jong here?'

> On 18th of December 1943 we were married in the Grace Community Church in Chungking, passed a few days in a hot-spring resort, Nan-wên-ch'üan, then flew by military plane to India, for a continued honeymoon and official business trip; besides contacting the Netherlands and British intelligence agencies in Calcutta and Delhi, we made some fine excursions to the Taj Mahal and other sites, and I came to like India very much.

> Shih-fang: The years in Chungking were the happiest of my life. Our honeymoon to India was marvellous. The Taj Mahal... glorious! But later Robert and I were not so fond of the Indians (in as far as one can generalize). He thought them too gloomy, often arrogant, and lacking a highly developed sense of humour.

Once Robert remarked to colleagues: 'All those sorrowful, staring eyes! What a difference with China: [where there was] always a laugh and an alert expression.'

The difference in national character also struck Peter Fleming (*op. cit.*), likewise a fairly frequent traveller from Kunming to Calcutta: on the airfield of Chungking he crouched down under the wing of a Dakota in the pouring rain:

> ...[he] shared a tremendous, absolutely foolish joke with the groundstaff coolies... and realized again with pleasure how great a gulf there is between India and China.
>
> The streets of the two cities provided as vivid a comment as you can find in Asia. Garbage, corruption, poverty, crowds, noise and a steamy climate were common to both. But is was hard, almost, to believe that the Bengalis and the Chinese were members of the same race. The brown men dressed in white looked listless, sullen, foolish, ineffective, miserable; the yellow men dressed in blue, swarming up and down the tortuous, dark grey alleys clinging to the scarred buffs above the Yangtse and the Kialang, looked exactly the opposite of all these epithets. You felt as if you had landed on another planet—more inconvenient, more expensive, if anything

a slightly smellier planet than the you had left this morning, but a planet (and this was what struck you more forcibly than anything) with a sense of humour.[13]

Robert wrote later:

Despite the fact that Dr Shui in Peking had given his blessing to our marriage, SF's family in Free China remained aloof. The old uncle made—as I heard later—dire predictions: a Chinese woman married to a foreign devil could never have offspring. When on 30th December 1944 she bore me a nice boy of 8½ pounds, the attitude of the family changed completely: from then on they fully accepted me as one of their own. I had a small shack built in the compound of our Military Attaché's office, we furnished it with some simple local Chinese pieces, and called it 'Hermitage where One Sings to the Moon'. There hardly went by a day when we had no gathering there of Chinese writers and artists.

Late at night I continued my own studies, mainly the editing of my work on the Chinese monk Tung-Kao, mentioned above. I wrote the text in Chinese; Hsü Shih-ying and Wang P'êng-shêng added prefaces and the book was published in 1945 by the Shang-wu [Commercial Press] in Chungking under the title *Ming-ch'ao i-sêng tung-kao-ch'an-shih chi-k'an* [The Collected Works of the Ch'an (Zen) Master Tung-kao, a Loyal Monk of the Ming Period].

In his own preface, Van Gulik discloses that, although a man of exceptional literary and artistic talent and of noble character, this monk was unknown in China. In Japan, in contrast, he had acquired great fame and under the protection of Tokugawa Mitsukuni, Prince of Mito, he had founded a new sect of the Ch'an (Zen) School which still exists. Van Gulik first came across Tung-Kao's name in 1936, when he was commencing his research on the history of the Chinese lute in Japan. This monk was the man who had introduced it. This initial acquaintance stimulated his interest in other aspects of Tung-kao's life, so much so in fact that he made his custom to choose to spend his holidays in places which the monk had been accustomed to pass his time. This had given him the opportunity to assemble a large number of paintings, manuscripts and other materials relating to Tung-Kao in Kyoto, Nagasaki, Osaka and Mito which had a bearing on Tung-Kao.

---

13   Hart-Davis, Duff: *Peter Fleming: A Biography*. Oxford: Oxford University Press, 1987, p. 271,

The small lithograph edition of the anonymous Judge Dee novel I had dragged along with me in my hand-luggage all over Africa now lay on the shelves in my small cubby-hole of a library. One day I read it and found it rather interesting; but there were so many other literary and artistic activities I was occupied with that I soon forgot all about it.

My manuscript of *Chinese Pictorial Art* I discussed with a number of Chinese connoisseurs, and made many changes in it. I also experimented with various kinds of paper and silk used for the mounting and repairing of antique paintings, and it occurred to me that students of the subject should also have actual samples of these materials at their disposal. Now we had to stay in the air raid dugouts often for several hours, and since the light was bad there, one could not read. So I made it a habit to take a few rolls old Chinese and Japanese paper and silk with me when the air-raid warning had sounded and passed the time cutting them up myself in small squares. After I had a small booklet with explanations of these various samples printed, I pasted them in those. Thus, when many years later my large work on Chinese pictorial art was published in Rome, I could add to each of the 900 copies printed the small booklet with the actual samples. In my Preface I briefly mentioned this fact.

Willem Robert was born on 30 September 1944. The day before there had been an air-raid alarm and Robert and Shih-fang had had to spend some time in the government air-raid shelter.

Shih-fang recalled:

Three days after the birth there was another air-raid alarm and all patients had to go to the damp, primitive air-raid shelter of the hospital. There was great pushing and shoving and one had to walk over narrow planks to reach it. I thought it terrifying and hugged little Willem to me closely. The partially flooded air-raid shelter was inhabited by a whole horde of gigantic, hungry rats and I was terrified that they would attack my baby.

Despite everything, during the Chungking years she was never afraid that the Japanese would ever capture the city. Robert will certainly have considered this possibility, but he never spoke about such matters at home. He will not have wanted to worry his wife during her pregnancy or just after the birth of the baby.

In the middle of November 1944 there was a large-scale offensive which led to the whole length of the Peking-Canton railway falling into Japanese hands. The Chinese army had suffered a severe defeat and morale plummeted to zero. Corruption and inefficiency meant that the soldiers were not paid and had very little to eat, prompting General Fêng Yü-hsiang to exclaim: 'Our army is not a people's army. You cannot mobilize recruits and then let them starve.' The American general, Albert Coady Wedemeyer, who had succeeded Stilwell as Chief of Staff attached to Chiang Kai-shek not long before, began preparations for an eventual evacuation of his general staff either to Kunming or Chengtu. The outlook seemed extremely grim and the suppressed tension mounted, but outwardly life in the wartime capital, on the rim of a volcano, went on as usual. Diplomats, war correspondents and the American military filled their evenings drinking, dining and dancing (except for Van Gulik, who did dine out often but spent most of his time at his desk) and nobody betrayed any hint of anxiety.

'For the moment', the ambassador reported to the Foreign Office, 'there is no longer any direct danger, but if General Wedemeyer had not taken adequate measures, it would have been touch-and-go whether the Japanese might or might not have occupied Kweiyang with an army of no great significance. The embassy was not unduly concerned about the rapid collapse of Free China; nevertheless, the events of these last few weeks have revealed the trust shown in their government and in their military by the average Chinese is almost non-existent, consequently the most enormous apathy has taken hold everywhere and the action is already deemed lost, if the Japanese do no more than point their finger at Chungking and Kunming.'

The opinion of the embassy was that the Chinese contribution to the struggle against Japan and the defence of the American air force bases was virtually zero. The embassy also reported that, after assessing the prowess of the Kuomintang troops, the American military authorities had more faith in the determination and competence of the Communist armies to protect the American air bases. Were Chiang Kai-shek to raise the blockade against Yenan, which the Americans were urging him to do as this would release more soldiers to join battle against Japan, the Americans would be able to set up air bases closer to occupied North China and Manchuria. However, Chiang Kai-shek refused to countenance the idea. He also maintained a strict censorship on all reports from Communist Yenan. When a group of foreign journalists returned to

Chungking from Yenan with favourable reports, every word was suppressed by the censor.

Van Gulik was convinced that secret agreements had been made between Chiang Kai-shek's National Government and the Japanese. At the beginning of January 1945, he wrote to Van Roijen that, although of course it was impossible to lay hands on any evidence of such agreements, plenty of indications pointed in this direction:

> To mention just one example: when the Japanese were advancing ever closer to Kweiyang-Chungking at the end of last November-beginning of last December [1944], and had already begun to sow panic among the Chinese population, the high-ranking Chinese leaders remained as cool as cucumbers and did not lift a finger to send their possessions and families unobtrusively to some safer place. In other words, we have a distinct impression that, despite the fact everything seemed to indicate that Chungking was in serious danger, the most exalted persons *knew* that the Japanese would withdraw at a certain moment.

Van Gulik was thoroughly informed about the Chinese situation (at least that in Kuomintang China). His reports on it were both realistic and cynical. As so many others, he was also, rightly, highly critical of American policy because it did not take sufficient account of the specifically Chinese circumstances, but his suggestions about how the Chinese should be dealt with were not always as feasible as they might have been. In the letter he wrote to Van Roijen at the beginning of January 1945, he dwelt on the ambivalent attitude of the Chinese (Kuomintang) government:

> If the business is viewed from a completely Chinese perspective (almost unheard of on the American side), it seems that: just as we are, Chiang Kai-shek is convinced that sooner or later Japan will suffer a total defeat. However, this victory should cost China as little as possible, and yield the greatest number of benefits in the future. China should not feel in the least embarrassed about leaving the British and Americans to do so much of the fighting, after all the Chinese say: "What would have happened to us if Japan had opted for the British and American side on 8 December [1941]?" Moreover, C.K.S. has other, more pressing reasons for not having his troops fight against the Japanese; after the Japanese have been expelled from China, he *has to have* his own armies virtually intact, otherwise he will not be able to defend his central government

against the Chinese warlords and anti-C.K.S. factions in other parts of China. As such an enormous part of China is in Japanese hands, he cannot allow himself to antagonize the Japanese too much and, finally, after the war China is very eager to co-operate with a *weak* Japan [...] Therefore, propaganda-wise it is best for China to blow its own trumpet about its achievements in the war against Japan, the importance of the Chinese Front etc., and do its level best to promote itself as a member of the Big Four, so that after the war it can claim whatever there is the claim, and (if it succeeds!) become the leader of a *Chinese* 'co-prosperity sphere' in East Asia, but *in fact* to play a completely passive role as far as Japan was concerned, and to work with might and main to secure its own internal position. This is the Chinese stance.

Millions of dollars and significant military defeats on the American side could have been prevented if, two years ago, when they seriously launched their China Front, the Americans had held a frank, off-the-record talk with the Chungking leaders, had declared they could understand that China could not afford to offend the Japanese too deeply, and therefore wanted to know what precisely would be the Chungking contribution to the China-Front, naturally in public maintaining the pretence that China was delivering an all-out war effort. At that point, it would not have required much [effort] to have had the Chinese admit that, for example, they neither *could* nor *would* defend the advanced American air bases in China. On the other hand, they could give the Americans all the help they wanted by providing coolies for transport, building airfields etc., collaborating with an American landing on the Chinese coast, everything which could be explained to the Japanese as ceding to American pressure. Such a heart-to-heart talk never took place, loud slogans were crowed about the gallant ally and there were negotiations about completely *notional* factors. I think it was [American General Joseph W.] Stilwell's unforgivable mistake that he threw himself so completely into his North Burma Campaign, that he—who knew better—did not intervene then. The upshot has been that Japan has been able to capture fourteen air bases constructed by the Americans at great trouble and expense while suffering almost no losses [...] and, if they had wanted to deploy a sufficiently large force, could have driven the Americans out of China. Such an event would leave Chungking cold: the Japanese want to expel the Americans from China, but the survival of Chungking would be to their political advantage. Cut off from abroad on all sides by the Japanese, [for Japan] Chungking represents no danger at all, but is in fact absolutely essential as a) a barrier between the Japanese and the Chinese Communists in Yenan; b) a trump card against the puppet governments in Peking and Nanking; and finally c) potentially an ideal mediator when Japan is ready to enter into peace negotiations.

In the same letter to Dr Van Roijen, Van Gulik finally touches upon the topic which affected him (and Lovink) most deeply:

What impinges on us Dutch most directly are the plans now being laid in Chungking to make China the leader of all 'subjected' East Asian people after the war. I am writing this to you above all because I think that the situation, that is the political constellation of which it seems the Netherlands will be a part, is *extremely disturbing*. If we do not stand together closely, shoulder to shoulder, and adhere to one definite policy (especially our various propaganda services), we *shall never get the Dutch East Indies back*: at the most we can hope to have a place in the international commission responsible for training the Indonesians for self-government—a commission in which China will dominate! I know that our embassy in Washington does *not* share this belief! However, here in Chungking I am in constant touch with representatives of every possible American civil and military organization. The leaders are unanimous, the Netherlands should not expect the slightest support from America in its demand to have the Dutch East Indies back. [...] The only solution is: come out in defence of our own affairs. It is therefore I was so delighted to read that, in the liberated part of the Netherlands, [the government] is now busy forming an army specifically intended to help liberate the Dutch East Indies. If we can claim the lion's share in the war in the Dutch East Indies, we should have a reasonable chance of getting back what is our right.

His love of the Indies where he had enjoyed such a happy youth blinded him to the many changes which had occurred since then. He was and would remain a colonial, but one whose attention was predominantly concentrated on the Indonesians as people and on their history and culture. On the other hand, because of his family of 'sabre-rattlers', he was more interested in the military activities of the Dutch authorities than in civil government. He was a man of contradictions.

In China people did not dare celebrate the birth of a child until it was a month old, the full month (*man-yüeh*) feast. For Willem Robert this fell on 1 November. That day there was a fancy-dress ball at the house of the military attaché, Colonel Everard, which Robert attended in a Japanese kimono and Shih-fang in a beautiful, classical Chinese gown. Although Robert had a relatively high-pitched voice, he could do a marvellous imitation of the deep growl of a samurai. The Wang P'êng-shêngs and the Wang Shih-chiehs were present among forty or so other guests.

At Christmas little Willem (Wimpie) accompanied them to friends, where he saw his first Christmas tree. It was not long before his parents were taking him with them when they lunched with Chinese friends. Sometimes father paid visits on his own:

> 9-2-1945: 9.30 went to the north bank with Liang Tsai-p'ing and Yang Ta-Chün [who was also a painter besides being a lute-player], walked to Yang Shao-wu's estate, arrived there at 12.30, lunched and played lute and zither with Yang and the elderly gentleman, Shih Shao-fu. Dinner, talked and played music in the evening. Slept in the library.

> 10-2-1945: In the morning strolled in the park with [Yang] Ta-chün. Late lunch. Visited Pan T'ien-shou's school for the visual arts with Ta-chün; afterwards to Hsü P'ei-hung [renowned painter, whose galloping horses became very famous] in Academy. Returned to Chungking by boat with Chia-ling, dined at 5 o'clock in Peking Restaurant with Ta-chün, and went home where went to bed early.

The next day the whole community of scholars and artists in the city came to lunch at the Van Guliks', who by now were completely immersed in Chinese society and culture. The following months were filled with plenty of music, and Robert repaired Yang's *p'i-p'a*.

> 23-2-1945: 7.30 dinner with Wu Kuo-chêng, danced at Mr K'ang's home with Chinese artists, played the lute.

> 25-2-1945: 11 o'clock Yang Shao-wu and Yang Ta-chün came, drove together in car to Yang's house, where there was a large lunch in honour of the founding of the T'ien-fêng (Heavenly Breeze) Lute Club. Spent the afternoon with musicians, viewed the lantern feast after dinner.

General Wang P'êng-shêng, a large, well-built, jovial man, an old friend from Tokyo and now head of the foreign intelligence service, was also a frequent visitor. 'When he visited us,' Shih-fang said, 'they often spoke Japanese together; I could not understand it. Naturally they often had political secrets to discuss.' There was a group of Japan experts in Chungking, to which Robert van Gulik, Bill Acker and others with a position for allied intelligence services belonged; they met frequently and had regular contact with Wang P'êng-shêng.

At the end of 1944 and the beginning of 1945, there seemed to be some movement in domestic policy in China. The Communist mediator, General Chou En-lai, later prime minister of the People's Republic, who sometime earlier had already been in talks in Chungking with the Minister of Information of the Nationalist Government, Wang Shih-chieh, and with General Chang Chih-chung, Generalissimo Chiang Kai-shek's personal envoy, returned there in January and February 1945. Chou negotiated with Wang Shih-chieh and T.V. Soong in the presence of the American ambassador and mediator Patrick Hurley. Chou and Wang almost reached an agreement, but this was rejected by Chiang Kai-shek. The Communists were prepared to put their army under the command of the Generalissimo and to integrate their area into the rest of Free China under one national government, but it had to be a coalition government, in which they would have a reasonable representation, and they wanted guarantees of democratically elected local governments (that is to say, in the area under their control and in those of the guerrillas). Chiang Kai-shek did not want to go any farther than the setting up of a 'political consultative commission', in which the various parties would be represented but which would not have governmental powers. Chou En-lai returned to Yenan empty-handed.

Although various Western diplomats, like the Belgian *chargé d'affaires*, sought contact with Chou En-lai during his time in Chungking, Van Gulik made no attempt to do so. He was an arch-conservative, adored Old China and avoided any personal contact with Communist Chinese. Ambassador Lovink also wanted at all costs to avoid 'the Netherlands involving itself in these Chinese domestic matters'. Van Gulik's great friend (and witness at his wedding) Wang Shih-chieh kept him informed about the talks with Chou, albeit in a rather prejudiced fashion. As a consequence of the attitude adopted by Lovink and Van Gulik, the embassy received only second-hand information.

The ambassador in Washington suggested (but this was Van Gulik's own bright idea; he was a master in manipulating others to his own ends) that it would be useful were Van Gulik to come to the United States for a short time to help in Allied discussions about Japan. Lovink assented, and with some difficulty he managed to book a seat on an American military aircraft. Foreign Affairs sent a signal that this trip would have to count as *leave*. It would be paid by the government, but Van Gulik would have no allowance above and beyond his salary.

In a very detailed telegram Lovink set out why Washington was so keen to see him. He pointed out that in his Tokyo period, Van Gulik had been very friendly with a number of very important officials with whom it would be very useful to re-establish contact: Dr Ch. Fahs, Head of the Far Eastern Department of the Office of Strategic Services (the wartime intelligence service), Dr W.R.B. Acker, Head of the Japanese Section Office of War Information, Lt Cdr H. Smith-Hutton of the Section Japanese Intelligence of the Naval Staff, plus a few others. He went on to say that Van Gulik was grateful for their courtesy in granting him leave, but did not wish to leave his post during wartime, except on service or for urgent health reasons. Therefore he had cancelled his air trip.

Van Gulik did not forget a reprimand quickly. When he had requested unpaid sick leave in Tokyo, he was told by Pabst and Minister Van Kleffens—as indeed was their right—that, because of the war, he had to remain at his post. Now he played the ball back successfully, because Lovink's impressive summing up convinced Van Kleffens and it was now thought 'useful that Van Gulik should resume the said contacts again'. The government would pay the travel expenses and also provide an allowance of 15 dollars a day. Now Van Gulik was ready to go!

> In July 1945 the Japanese defeat became imminent, and I received orders from our government to proceed to Washington, to take part in Allied consultations about the future of Japan, and of the Netherl[ands] East Indies. I left Chungking on July 27 for Kunming, together with S.F. and our infant son; they would stay in Kunming to await my return there. In the plane towards the U.S. I heard the radio news of the Japanese surrender.
>
> All the decisions taken in Washington are well-known. I may add only that I was among those who strongly advocated that the Japanese Emperor would **not** be removed; I argued that the

Japanese had never been defeated before, and that the Emperor was the only central point they could rally to, thus preventing bloodshed or total chaos.

On Sept. 22 I came back to Kunming, had a couple of fine trips in the mountains there with S.F. and our son, on Sept. 30 flew back to Chungking.

Every single hour of that four-week visit to the United States, spread over Washington D.C., Boston and New York, was occupied. A truly incredible number of people and activities are recorded in the diaries. Taking pride of place was his official business, which entailed many contacts with the embassy (Loudon, Reuchlin, Van der Mandele, Boon and Van Boetzelaer) and the State Department, but just two days after he arrived he was holding discussions with prominent Chinese scholars (Hummel, Beal and Wu) in the Library of Congress, where he was even assigned a room in which he could occasionally work in peace. A couple of days later he visited old Chinese friends from Chungking, scholars and lute-players; he went to the Smithsonian Institution, the Freer gallery and the Carnegie Institute, talked to American Chinese scholars like Mortimer Graves and Creel. He even personally gave a Chinese dinner for friends, made a few excursions, visited every possible bookshop and also had a medical examination in the Bethesda Naval Hospital.

He went to Boston so as to visit the famous Harvard-Yenching Institute, where he worked on his manuscript, as well as the Peabody Museum. Professor Elisséeff came to visit him and at a dinner at the home of this renowned Japanese scholar he heard more about the Japanese surrender on the radio and he listened to Truman's speech.

He went on to New York, where the first item on his programme was a visit to the Hollandse Club, followed by discussions with the Netherlands Indies Commission. Once again he had talks with such other famous American scholars of China as Goodrich, Dubs and Wittfogel at Columbia University. Once again most of this official trip was devoted to Van Gulik's own studies.

On the return journey to China via Bermuda, the Azores, Casablanca, Tripoli, Cairo, Abadan, Karachi, Delhi and Calcutta (at that time travel by air was a pretty complicated business), he spent two days in the last city.

20-9-1945: arrived at Dumdum, the airfield of Calcutta at 8 o'clock, took a bus to the city, booked into the Great Eastern. Went to the consulate in the morning, rested at the hotel, lunched alone at the hotel at 2 o'clock, went shopping, slept in the hotel 3-6. Legget came, together to his house in Barakpur, dinner, looked at books, spoke to Brinkley and visited Jap. POWs [a mystery: did he interrogate these Japanese prisoners of war?], 12 o'clock home in the hotel.

In Kunming he found his wife and young son in good health. Her Chinese friends and Consul Wierink had taken good care of them. Nevertheless, although he was just back after eight weeks' absence, initially Robert did not have much time to devote to Shih-fang for he had received word that there was a general in Kunming who played the *chêng* (a zither with 13 to 16 strings) on a particularly fine specimen, and of course he had to hurry off there at once:

> 23-9-45: Went shopping with Shih-fang in the morning, then lunched with S.F. in Hou-tê-fu, 3 o'clock to Gen. Sun, and heard the *chêng*, and opium [another small mystery: did he smoke a pipe of opium or did they talk about it? Probably the former. Opium was produced on a large scale in Yünnan], 4-5 to Yünan University, did not find Hsü at home. Returned home in the rain and went to bed early after dinner in the hotel.

Two days later he visited General Sun Yung-an, whose *chêng* he photographed again.

The Van Guliks made another couple of exhilarating trips into the mountains and flew back to Chungking on 30 September.

> There came a very busy time now [in Chungking]. I was appointed member of the Allied War Crimes Commission [in fact the Committee on Facts and Evidence of the Commission which met in Chungking], and had to help out [the] ambassador with preparations for moving the Embassy to Nanking [to where, now the war was over, the capital would be relocated].

Actually the schedule was not too hectic, because reinforcements arrived at the embassy. The first was C.W. Baron Van Boetzelaer, who was to succeed Valck Lucassen. He was followed by H. Scheltema, C.D. Barkman and Dr J. Vixseboxse (the latter two, Chinese scholars), and—last but not least—the experienced Dr H.N. Boon, who would eventually take over the non-Sinological work from Van Gulik.

> 24-2-1946: 11 o'clock with Shih-fang, Barkman and Mulder [a Chinese scholar who would shortly afterwards become a lecturer

at a language institute in Peking] to city, saw exhibition of curios from/of Lü, lunch in Kuan Shêng Yüan. Home via booksellers.

2-3-1946: Barkman and Mulder came at 7, had a drink and dinner at Canton Restaurant.

12-3-1946: 5 o'clock with Barkman to Shen Yin-mo [eminent calligrapher and expert on old manuscripts], borrowed an ink-stone.

9-4-1946: Dinner at home for Lovink, Boon, Scheltema, Barkman and Vixseboxse.

Recalling this period, Carl Barkman noted the following:

'I really became properly acquainted with Robert van Gulik when I arrived in Chungking to work under him in January 1946. I and the other young Chinese scholars from Leiden had already met him and we had formed a certain [preconceived] picture of him. Indubitably he was an exceptionally gifted scholar, but he also had the name of being an eccentric. At any rate, as a scholar of Chinese he had strayed into somewhat eccentric paths. He had not been able to see eye-to-eye with Professor Duyvendak, whose student and admirer I was, and he went off to Utrecht to write his thesis on a curious topic, the horse cult in China and Japan. We were aware of the Sanskrit lessons he had taken with the great Uhlenbeck while still at grammar school and the *English-Blackfoot Vocabulary*, also not really a subject with which the average Chinese scholar occupied himself (but then again he was not an 'average Chinese scholar', as I would soon learn). He was interested in ink-stones and the Chinese lute. Whether he had as thorough a knowledge of Chinese history as we who were trained in Leiden might have been open to question, but his attention had been captured on such original topics that I could only look forward to a closer acquaintance.

'Although Van Gulik made me very welcome in Chungking, he waited to see which way the wind blew. I shared a dusty room in the chancellery with him, which could only be reached by an outside staircase. It was Van Gulik who guided my first steps on the diplomatic path and imparted the sinological work of the embassy to me. This consisted principally of looking for important articles and reports in the Chinese press, having these translated by the Chinese translators and checking their work afterwards. All the other translations, such as diplomatic notes, also had to be scrutinized. It was not long before, with his encouragement, I began to compile reports on political and economic matters for The Hague. Nevertheless, quantitatively speaking, I was not given much direction, at least not by Van Gulik. He gave me a very free rein to do my work, and, of course, I was very happy with this situation. Moreover, he seldom turned up at the chancellery before 11 o'clock and he devoted most of the day to his own work and interests.

'It was his custom to arrive in the mornings with a cheery, jovial greeting, the eternal cigarette in his mouth. He would show a momentary interest in my wellbeing and activities, and then would devote himself to getting on with his Chinese reading ("to wake up properly") with a gossipy tabloid which he esteemed highly. He smoked and coughed the whole day, one cigarette was lit from the smouldering butt of its predecessor, and he scattered the ash over the desk and his suit. None the less, whenever the occasion arose, it seemed that he was prepared to devote a large portion of his time to the Chinese scholars who were placed under his aegis (my colleague, Jan Vixseboxse, joined in March), and, from the point of view of quality, his leadership was of inestimable importance. It was possible to learn an incredible amount from him in a short time; he knew China and the Chinese inside out.

'Spoken Chinese is fairly easy to learn, but—as is well known—the written language is particularly difficult, and consequently most attention was paid to this aspect of the study. It so happened that Jan and I could read both classical and modern texts as well as being familiar with the special journalistic language, but we were not very fluent. Van Gulik told us this was what had happened to him in the same situation. Every morning, before office hours, an elderly, venerable Chinese tutor came to give us conversation lessons.

'Although for the last few years Jan Vixseboxse and I had been mainly concerned with the political history of the Far East, as mentioned, Robert van Gulik's interests were captured by completely different matters. They covered an extraordinarily wide field, and it did not take us long to discover what an enormous, profound knowledge he possessed of the everyday matters of life in ancient and modern China, to do with the man-in-the-street but especially the literati. Indeed he had consciously developed himself into a Chinese-style scholar-official. More than anything else such a mandarin was expected to have knowledge of the classical texts, and Van Gulik complied completely with this requirement.

'However, far more fascinating in his eyes than the predominantly dry classical literature were the other fields with which the literati immersed themselves: calligraphy, poetry, engraving seals, playing the lute, appreciating nature, painting, bronzes and porcelain. Nevertheless, first and foremost, besides being a scholar and art connoisseur, a mandarin was also an official; his official duties were also very important to Robert van Gulik, and he performed them conscientiously with great dedication, albeit in his very personal, original, sometimes eccentric, manner. He did not suffer fools gladly, but was usually too tactful to allow the person concerned to be aware of it; only if that person continued to behave himself in a particularly pompous manner, would he cut him down to size in a masterly fashion.

'He enjoyed the special ambiance in Chungking:

"Take a look at what the war has done, Barkman; politicians, scholars, poets and calligraphers have fled here from every part of China, and they have been joined by restaurateurs, cooks and beautiful women. Here you can enjoy everything China produces, especially Chinese cuisine."

'He took us to Szechuan, Peking, Hunan, Shanghai and Cantonese restaurants, and explained the dizzying multitude of specialities. His delightful Chinese wife Shih-fang, a typically Chinese beauty, gentle with an infectious laugh and a good sense of humour which completely matched Robert's, sometimes accompanied us. We rummaged around at the book market and in antique shops with him. Everywhere he went, he was able to strike just the right note and crack a joke, sometimes in the local dialect, with the person with whom he was conversing. His Chinese accent was not very good, but he had an enormous vocabulary; if there was ever any misunderstanding, he grabbed a pen or brush and wrote the words in his beautiful, clear Chinese handwriting, commanding respect.

'What I especially valued in him was that he immediately introduced me, the absolute new boy on the job, to a number of his friends, well-known scholars and artists. I was only to see one of them ever again, much later, in Peking in 1962 where he occupied a high position in the People's Republic, including being President of the Academy of Sciences. He was Kuo Mo-jo, the famous man of letters, historian, archaeologist and Marxist, who, after casting a significant look at Van Gulik's seals and antiquarian books in Chungking, recommended that I should also, indeed especially, study modern China. Nevertheless, at that time it was this old, in 1946 still largely untouched by modernization and Westernization, Chinese life which fascinated us most. This was one of the reasons that at the time we did not realize that the victory of the Chinese Communists was imminent and would be so all-encompassing. We were considered experts, but at that moment we could not have predicted such a development. We thought that what was going on was a bid for power between two totalitarian systems and that the real Communism, even in its more Chinese form, would not be able to take root in a China where the staunch family ties, the desire for personal property and the strongly developed regionalism would all be incompatible with Marxist-Leninist-Maoist ideology and practice. Even though in the short term our assessment was wrong, in the long term it was perhaps not entirely incorrect.

'One of the highlights of my time in Chungking was when Robert invited me to attend an evening of Chinese classical lute playing. He was the only non-Chinese member, indeed the secretary of the extremely select lute society of the 'Heavenly Wind'. With a laugh he said: "According to the strict rules which have applied in China for centuries, the lute cannot be played for a 'barbarian', but I have been given dispensation for you as a scholar of Chinese." He went on to explain that a club or 'spiritual society' as this one was formed not on the basis of social or geographical unity; one could only become a member if one had mastered this art and played the instrument in accordance with the strict rules.

'We went to a small reserved room in one of the most famous Szechuan restaurants and I met the members of the society, among whom was the well-known, colourful Christian General Fêng Yü-hsiang and such scholars as the elderly gentleman Yü Yu-jen. There were also of couple of remarkably beautiful ladies, not—I assumed—the spouses of the gentlemen present.

'A lute was tuned, and an elderly sage with a refined countenance and grey goatee began to conjure forth one soft tone after the other. This cliché is not truly inapposite here in as far as it seemed as if the instrument could only to be coaxed to produce a sound. With some difficulty, the listener caught the sound of very soft, high, rarefied note, then nothing, then another completely different, just as subtle note.

'It was impossible to identify a melody. Each note seemed to stand on its own and elicit its own mood, as do the separate words of a short poem. Sometimes the same note was played in another tone or different timbre. Initially, I felt as if I was listening to a microscopically tiny insect. A young woman began to sing, tenuously, on a high note, in a scale completely foreign to us. A cool sound, often poignant only to those who knew the text. Another lute echoed another voice, yet most of the pieces seemed to have been composed for the lute alone with no libretto. Van Gulik's lute also brought forth completely Chinese sounds, listened to attentively and respectfully by the connoisseurs. The atmosphere was almost sacred.

'Later we took our places at the table and food and wine were brought. Lively conversation broke out, toasts replete with literary or political word play were made, jokes and anecdotes told and there was much laughter. The Szechuanese waiters, who brought one refined dish after the other were—as were most here—simple peasant boys who were unable to follow the conversation and looked sheepish until a Szechuanese member of the club cracked a joke with them in their own dialect.

'After dinner one of the gentlemen seated himself at a long table on which a lengthy piece of paper had been unrolled. He drew back his sleeves, moistened his ink-stone with a little water, moistened his brush on it and began to make a series of elegant characters, which did service both as a poem and a painting, flow over it. Nor was this the end: other increasingly more difficult texts were penned and the challenges became more difficult. Other calligraphers, among them Van Gulik, took up the challenge. People sprang from one style, from one historical era to another; now playful and light-hearted now strict and stern, depending on the content of the text, the style and the period. Finally characters were dashed down with a certain controlled, conscious tempestuousness, no longer with a brush but with matchsticks or whatever one could lay one's hands on, and the miracle was that these creations, improvised as the wine flowed freely, were imbued with great beauty.

'The next day I asked Robert whether, even though in principle the lute might not be played for barbarians, it could be played in the presence of courtesans… He looked at me with an understanding smile: "A good question! I'll show you the rules." He pulled one of his own works out of the bookcase, one I had heard of but never seen: *The Lore of the Chinese Lute* (Tokyo, 1940). In it he showed me that the lute might *not* be played:

1. When there is wind or thunder, and in rainy weather
2. When there is a sun or moon eclipse of the sun or the moon
3. In a court room
4. At the market or in a shop
5. For a barbarian
6. For a vulgar person

7. For a merchant
8. For a courtesan
9. After inebriation
10. After having had sexual intercourse
11. In dishevelled and strange clothes
12. When being flushed and covered with transpiration
13. Not having washed one's hands and rinsed one's mouth
14. In loud and noisy surroundings.[14]

'In practice, Van Gulik claimed that Rule 8 should only be applied to the lowest rank of courtesans. Rule 9 was also taken with a pinch of salt.

'Later Robert was to tell the Secretary-General for Foreign Affairs, Baron S.J. van Tuyll van Serooskerken, that he had been rapped over the knuckles for immodesty at this lute club, when he—the only foreigner and not long a member—had asked the president at the end of an extraordinary meeting if he might be given a chance to express his gratitude for his admission to this exalted society. After some hesitation, this was allowed. However, after his brief speech in refined, polished Chinese, the president had addressed the company in more or less the following vein:

'"We have just had the opportunity to listen to the words of a stranger in our midst. We are struck by the fact that he, just as we Chinese, is a person who is able to frame his thoughts in words so that we are able understand him. Naturally, this does not alter the fact that in our eyes he is and will always remain a foreigner, albeit he will always be especially welcome." Van Gulik had taken this reprimand—he was too young and too short a time a member to take the floor—to heart.

'One of the many remarkable characteristics of Robert van Gulik was his gift for being able to work systematically under almost any circumstances and to make use every 'lost' minute: when he rested he did this consciously so that later he could resume his work refreshed. He lived with his Chinese wife and his small son, Wimpie, on the ground floor of the house of the military attaché, which was built on a hill. Above him lived a couple of young officials from our embassy, one of whom was I. Conditions were rather primitive.

---

14   Translation based on text from a 1969 book edition, *Monumenta Nipponica*, p. 61-62. For original text (in English) see p. 60, *The Lore of the Chinese Lute*. Tokyo: Sophia University, 1940 [reprinted Bangkok: Orchid Press, 2011].

When we wanted to take a bath, we had to report this to the boy, who immediately summoned the water-carriers. Humming rhythmically these coolies carried wooden containers of hot water up the three hundred and sixty steps to our house and poured it into a tub, into which 'Master' lowered himself.

'It happened quite often that Van Gulik and I had to attend the same cocktail party. He would greet the host (and hostess if there was one, a rare occurrence in Chungking) and then make his way to the person whom he either wanted to question or to tell something to, and then would disappear immediately. I, less experienced and perhaps more sensitive to this sort of cheerful socializing, would enjoy a glass or two, and later tiredly climb the hundreds of steps up to our house. Who had already been sitting quite a while at the table by the window at the front, under a bright lamp? Van Gulik who was carving seals with archaic characters or reading a Tang poem.

'His systematic method of working also helped spread his name and fame, something which he certainly did not discourage, but in fact discreetly encouraged. He once told me that he had just lunched with someone with whom he had taken the noon meal in another country a decade earlier. He had consulted his notes from this period and consequently was able to recall the former occasion casually, where and when it had taken place and which topics they had discussed. This naturally made a deep impression.

'Although he was a dutiful civil servant, Van Gulik was adept in evading work which did not interest him, especially when he thought it could be done just as well by somebody else. For instance, he was appointed member, and secretary, of the Committee on Facts and Evidence of the Allied War Crimes Commission. He handed all this work over to me and, although it was not always pleasant, I found it a not unwelcome change. The president of the committee was the Belgian ambassador, Baron Delvaux de Feuffe. We were given hundreds of dossiers about Japanese war crimes allegedly committed in China to study, and our task was to decide how they should be classified, in other words the *prima facie* probability of the alleged accusations.

'Our Ambassador, Mr Lovink, was a man of boundless energy, which was manifested among ways in long weekend hikes and climbing trips to the embassy bungalow in the mountains at Wang Shan, on which he was accompanied by most of his staff (whenever he went there, Van Gulik preferred to use a palanquin). Lovink was also at work in the mornings long before anybody else; although he was certainly not an intellectual type, he was well informed and charming. One day I was summoned to him, but when I entered his study he was talking to Van Gulik. I wanted to withdraw, but Lovink gestured to me to wait. I was extremely embarrassed because he was reprimanding my immediate superior in no uncertain terms. I can no longer recall his exact words but they made sufficient impression for me to repeat them fairly accurately:

'"For Heaven's sake Van Gulik, this has to stop now! Every day you don't turn up before eleven o'clock, when everybody else has long been at work, I personally a very long time. You have an obligation to be on time, because you are setting a very bad example. I haven't seen any political report by you for more than a year. I will no longer tolerate this. From this moment onwards, make sure that the reporting is back up to standard!"

'I can no longer recall why the ambassador had summoned me. I do remember very well that Van Gulik did not say anything in reaction to the accusations and that, when I returned to our shared office, he was sitting peacefully smoking and reading. Naturally, nothing was said about the unpleasant interview. I was curious to know what would happen the next morning. Van Gulik did not turn up at the office at 9 o'clock as the others did, and again not at 11, but as a sort of Chinese compromise at 10. He did not pick up his favourite tabloid newspaper, but placed a number of blank sheets of paper in front of himself, rolled up his sleeves and began to write, chain smoking as usual, dropping ash all over his clothes and scattering it over his desk, often coughing dreadfully. After the usual morning greetings, nothing more was said. He continued to write imperturbably with a steady hand, hour after hour, with no crossings-out, and he continued in this fashion for a while after lunch.

'All that I could see was that at the top of each page, the word SECRET was printed in capital letters. Our ambassador put great store by secret reports, because he had formerly been Head of the East Asian Affairs Service in Batavia. A confidential report was grudgingly accepted; a secret report was much better. When Van Gulik had finished, he gathered up the pile of papers, and showed me only the subject: 'The Life of Chinese Secret Societies (SECRET)', and with a wink said: "I am now going to the ambassador."

'After reading the report, Lovink appeared absolutely delighted. For the time being, Van Gulik did not need to do anything, and once again arrived at the office daily at 11 o'clock, or by way of special favour to the embassy, at 10.30. In one fell swoop, he had written an extraordinarily important, original report, which was to become the standard work about Chinese secret societies at the Foreign Office.

'In it he described the historical background of the most prominent of these societies and pointed out that, "They [were] in fact the logical consequence of the dearth of legal security in Chinese society, and the fragile protection the Chinese individual had enjoyed from his government throughout the centuries." In North and Central China above all it was the White Lotus Society which flourished; in West China the *ko-lao-hui* (Elder Brothers Society), in South China the *san-ho-hui* (known in the Dutch East Indies at that time as the *san-tien-hui*, the Three Finger Bond) and later along the Imperial Canal and the south-east coast the *hung-pang* (Red Bond) and the *ch'ing pang* (Blue Bond) thrived.

'Van Gulik's thesis was that the 1911 Revolution, which brought the Empire down, was principally the work of the secret societies, above all that of the *t'ung-mên-hui* (the United League), a precursor of the Kuomintang, the party then in power. In fact, this *t'ung-mên-hui* was a branch of the Blue Bond. In view of its historical importance, Van Gulik described this union in great detail. The report was not short of piquant details. Here I quote only the passage below taken from a summary of prominent Chinese who maintained close ties with a secret society or were indebted to them for their positions:

'"Chiang Kai-shek holds a high position in the mystical hierarchy of the Blue Bond, but Tu Yüeh-shêng, the richest merchant in Shanghai, holds a higher rank. I know from an absolutely trustworthy source that both Chiang and Tu must therefore be addressed as 'master' and on the rare opportunities on which Chiang, the President of China, is allowed an audience with the supreme leader, the mysterious Huang Chin-yung, he must enter as it were crawling as it were 'on his hands and knees.'

'General Fêng Yü-hsiang, usually referred to as the Christian general, also holds a fairly high rank in the *ko-lao-hui*. This combined with his military followers means that he must be treated with the greatest caution and that he remains a significant figure, independent of all the changes in the Chinese government."

'Van Gulik explored the position of this Tu Yüeh-shêng, whom Chiang-Kai-shek had to address as 'master', in greater depth and he illustrated it with a description of the way Madam Chiang Kai-shek was treated by Tu Yüeh-shêng:

'"One of the present leaders of the Blue Bond is Mr Tu Yüeh-shêng described in English in the Chinese *Who's Who* as 'financier and philanthropist in Shanghai'. Although he held no official position at all, he was the most powerful man in Shanghai and its surrounding area. He controlled some very large industrial enterprises, as well as being the leader of all the dock and transport workers' unions, not to mention of the associations of Chinese seamen, owners of opium dens and gambling casinos. The president of the Chinese Chambers of Commerce was one of his satellites […]. When Chiang Kai-shek launched his anti-opium campaign it was obvious that even the Generalissimo could not tackle Mr Tu. The campaign was organized nation-wide and opium was confiscated, opium-users were arrested and so on, but in Shanghai Chiang Kai-shek had to tread carefully; he simply could not afford to damage Tu's interests.

'The solution—in China—was very simple: the Generalissimo appointed Mr Tu president of the Opium Suppression Commission for Shanghai and Its Surrounding Area. Under his businesslike, extremely skilled leadership some opium-smoking tramps were publicly executed in a blaze of publicity, a scattering of small opium dens, with which Tu or one of his subordinates had an old score to settle, were officially closed with a great hullabaloo, and a few chests of inferior quality opium were publicly burned—and this having been accomplished the trade could peacefully resume its course.

'However, there was a time when Madame Chiang Kai-shek thought she could take on Old China. In the 1920s, after the Kuomintang leaders had won their great military victories and Chiang Kai-Shek had firmly established the central government in Nanking, Madame wanted to pay a visit to Shanghai to preach the gospel of the New Life Movement [its goal being to purge public life] there, and with a hankering for publicity set up a campaign to close gambling-dens and brothels. The Generalissimo strongly discouraged her plan; he would certainly not have trespassed on Tu Yüeh-shêng's territory. But Madame was still brimming over with her American ideals for a new China and wanted to push ahead with her plans. Tu let the Generalissimo know that naturally Madame would always be welcome in Shanghai, but just at that moment it was in the grip of a crime wave and the streets were not safe. Consequently, he suggested that Madame postpone her proposed trip indefinitely. Madame paid absolutely no heed to this unvarnished warning and travelled to Shanghai. Two days after her arrival, she was kidnapped in a closed car by 'unidentified criminals' and held prisoner for a week in a villa in the outer suburbs of Shanghai. She had a luxury suite and was treated with the greatest courtesy, but she was and remained imprisoned. After a week, she was 'rescued' by Tu's agents, who escorted her back to her hotel, showering many courtesies on her, larded with thousands of excuses about the 'dangers' of Shanghai. Shortly afterwards, Madame returned to Nanking."

'These are just a few quotes from Van Gulik's report. I myself experienced the fact that he personally maintained good relations with at least one secret society, namely the *ko-lao-hui,* which in Western China (especially Szechuan) was all-powerful,' Barkman went on to write.

'I had made a plan to travel overland to Kuanhsien via Chengtu and from there to hike upstream along the course of the Min River, not far from the Tibetan border, an area that was unquestionably under Chinese administration but was largely populated by Tibeto-Burmese tribes. It goes without saying that it was not a region in which one could travel safely, and Van Gulik advised me not to request the protection of the central Chinese authorities who were powerless, but to ask for that of the *ko-lao-hui* secret society. Therefore he introduced me to a venerable old gentleman who occupied a high position in it and, after a short conversation, thanks to Robert's intercession, he assured me that I would not encounter any great difficulties. He handed me a letter but said would also inform the representatives of the society concerned of my arrival. This intervention worked like magic. At no point did I encounter any obstructions. Quite the opposite in fact, when and where necessary I was discreetly given help and protection. A French vice-consul who had travelled through the region a few weeks before I did was relieved of all his possessions by robbers, even his clothes were taken and he was left in his undergarments.

'What was Van Gulik's relationship with this extremely secret society and how did it arise? Perhaps it happened through the intervention of General Fêng Yü-hsiang, a fellow-member of the lute club, who held high office in the *ko-lao-hui*? But Van Gulik had many channels in all strata of the population, and he might have made contact in a completely different way. He was acquainted with petty traders and keepers of small eating-houses and brothels who maintained covert relations. This was equally true of the embassy chauffeur, who sometimes supplied him with useful information. Van Gulik lived in different circles which neither impinged on nor indeed were acquainted with each other: one of the many puzzles surrounding his person which will probably never be solved.

'At the beginning of the time we spent together in Chungking I did wonder whether, in view of his completely 'idiosyncratic' training in Chinese, Van Gulik had actually been able to acquire a thorough grounding in Chinese political history. I did have the impression that this was not his strongest point but, over against this was the fact that we younger students of Chinese could not rid ourselves of the feeling that we saw China from "the outside", whereas Robert van Gulik was one of the rare figures who could see it and experience it "from the inside". An overall knowledge of the history of China and its relations with other countries was less important to him than a profound immersion in Chinese culture, Chinese people and their way of life.'

At the beginning of 1946, The Hague decided that Dr Van Gulik was to be transferred back to the Netherlands and would be replaced in Chungking by Dr Boon. However, Van Gulik found it very difficult to say good-bye to his beloved China and postponed his departure many times. Just as Carl Barkman had done, Dr H.N. (Han) Boon also wrote of his experiences in Chungking. After having spent a good five years, since 1940, in Washington and seemingly still with no prospect of a transfer, Han Boon had been hoping to take over the rather larger, better situated house from a departing colleague. This is not what happened:

'One fine day, at the end of January 1946, I was busy organizing a load of books, when I received a telephone call from the code room from my good friend Como Stuyt who said: "Forget it, because you've been transferred to Chungking." Of course, such a private message was completely impermissible, but in my ten-year career, I had been sufficiently schooled to display sincere amazement when later that day Ambassador Loudon officially informed me of it. As was usual, everything had to be done in a hurry, but the first priority was to find accommodation in America for my family—my wife and three children—because in Chungking, the wartime capital of China, there was no accommodation for women and children except—as I found out later—for Chancellor Stiphout who occupied a privileged position because of the presence of his wife and the charming Ray, his spaniel, as well as in other respects.

'However, this story is not about my own experiences but about Robert van Gulik, whom I was to relieve in the Chinese capital. As it was, it was an exceptional event to replace an experienced and very well-known Chinese scholar with a diplomat who had never set eyes on China, and possessed only the vaguest notions of the Chinese language and Chinese culture [hence another two Sinologists were posted to the embassy to replace Van Gulik]. I had already met Robert [...] in America, where he had been briefly seconded to the Council [Institute] of Pacific Relations [an NGO which made policy recommendations to the Pacific Council] after his departure from Japan. I had become acquainted with him at that time and sometimes accompanied him to the Bureau of Indian Affairs, where he astonished his American counterparts with his wide knowledge of various Indian languages. At the time he was involved in research into the relationship between Chinese and Indian languages, which might demonstrate that the Indian tribes originally entered the New World from Asia via the Bering Strait.

'The embassy in Chungking was accommodated in two houses, the main house, to which the chancellery was attached, served the ambassador and a few staff members as both office and residence. The other house was for the remaining sinologists and other staff, including the military attaché, Van den Brandeler, plus the Van Gulik family.

'In those first months after the war, travelling was not an easy undertaking and I spent a fairly long time, namely from 25 February to 5 April, in reaching there, partly because The Hague was under the impression that the transport from Calcutta to Chungking would be arranged by the local honorary consul, whereas when I arrived in Calcutta it had been presumed that The Hague had made the necessary arrangements. I was prepared for the fact that the airport [of Chungking] was situated in the middle of a river, but not for the fact that we would fly in between two high ridges of hills to land on a miniscule islet which was barely visible from the air: we pulled up about four metres from the end of the runway. Then all my troubles melted away as Van Gulik was waiting for me and had prepared the most cordial of welcomes. He drove me in one of the two cars the embassy possessed to the 'residence' where I was assigned a fairly spacious room, furnished with a desk, a bed and two chairs. The lavatory and bathing facilities were shared, which quickly led to a new discovery the next morning when I found that my toothbrush was damp, even though I had barely used it. I was told that, if the opportunity presented itself, the Chinese staff could never resist the temptation to brush their teeth. Luckily my baggage contained a second toothbrush, which I always carried with me thereafter like some precious gem and which was intended for my mouth alone.

'I already knew about Ambassador Lovink's restless energy from stories, but in this case the reality exceeded the bounds of the imagination. I arrived late in the afternoon of Saturday 6 April 1946 and therefore next morning at 8 o'clock was completely unprepared to have to participate in the obligatory Sunday hike, in which ten of us took part. As in so many shared activities, the Van Guliks were absent, but for everybody else was this "voluntary" exercise actually compulsory.

'In a letter to my wife, among other matters I wrote the following about this hike:

'"First by car down to the river, which we crossed on a rickety punt. On the opposite bank the hike began by climbing up flights of stairs and along small stone paths, barely wide enough for one person, which form the ubiquitous links between houses and villages. The landscape is fantastic: steep hills which have all been transformed into terraces by human ingenuity, nothing has been left to Nature, each tiny space has been cultivated with love and care; the Chinese in their slate blue clothes are a sharp contrast to brown water standing in all the rice-fields and the green of the plants. The whole scene is dotted with mud homesteads, even a few brick ones. Every so often, there is a hamlet, usually picturesquely situated against a slope. The tops of the hills are occupied by colourful small temples or memorials. The landscape is exactly like that in a Chinese drawing, except that in that case you think that it is a product of the painter's imagination, whereas the landscape is precisely as doll-like as it is represented there. There is no other landscape with which you can compare it."'

'After a four-hour walk', Dr Boon said, 'we came upon a country house which sometime earlier, when bombardment of Chungking as the wartime capital of China had been at its height, had been the embassy headquarters. Here we were a good five hundred metres above the city, and the fresh mountain air was bracing. We enjoyed a delicious lunch, served by boys who were stationed there, and afterwards stretched ourselves out comfortably for a few hours in the sun. We walked back, part of the way along the main road which passed the country house of the Generalissimo, guarded by a number of companies of soldiers. Close by was the palace of Tu [Tu Yüeh-sheng], the greatest proprietor of brothels and opium dens in Shanghai [...] After a while, [we] left the main road passing through innumerable villages teeming with hideous dogs which threatened to attack our own animals, but were driven off personally by the ambassador who threatened to beat them with his stick. Finally we reached the famous Burma Road, which ended on the other side of the river, opposite the punt. Then we climbed the flights of stairs again (I counted nine hundred steps) to the cars which brought us home again. These weekly hikes were a peculiarity of our representation, because the other missions were not headed by such energetic, sportsman-like chiefs as our *ta-shih* (ambassador).

'Thanks to Van Gulik, three days after I arrived, I was already being invited to a lunch at the *Wai Chiao Pu*, the Chinese Ministry of Foreign Affairs, where five Chinese and five foreigners devoured a typical Chinese meal which had to be eaten with the well-known chopsticks and was washed down with many small cups of rice wine.

'Van Gulik also did his best in other ways to introduce me to life in Chungking. He thought it of utmost importance that my first visit should be to the American doctor to lay in a stock of essential pills; even though these were prescribed for me personally, Van Gulik claimed a portion of most of the medicines because, as he was wont to say, it could never do any harm and might even do some good.

'A book—more than 500 pages thick—entitled *China Diseases* was a particular interest of his: in it the most frightful diseases which might assail to visitors to China were described in great detail. In fact, the inhabitants of Chungking were neither healthier nor more susceptible to disease than mortals anywhere else in the world, but it was advisable to observe certain precautions to ward off infection: drinking boiled water and refraining from eating eat raw vegetables, lettuce or unpeeled fruit. Occasionally something happened which gave one pause to think, like a swimming party in what appeared to be a small, clean lake, which later transpired to be a bathing-place for a large number of cattle whose hides already betrayed the fact that they were the breeding-ground of vermin and diseases.

'Nevertheless, Van Gulik's greatest concern was my complete ignorance of the Chinese language. He took it upon himself to teach me a few characters each day, using a small book I have since unfortunately mislaid. It was also necessary for me to take lessons from a woman teacher, because in Robert's opinion the various tones which were such an essential part of Chinese could be demonstrated better by a melodious female voice than by a male teacher.

'One remarkable peculiarity in this land was the difference in concepts of value. In China a human life was not worth much. Above all other animals, pigs were worth money, as we could observe during our hikes when these animals were transported over the steep mountain paths in baskets to prevent them losing valuable weight on the way to market. In one accident on the constantly overloaded ferry boats which crossed the broad, swiftly flowing Yangtze River, hundreds of coolies were drowned, but the thirty pigs on board were saved, because they would bring in money.

'In the long run these and other customs would often irritate specialists who tarried too long in China, so much so they answered sharply, especially on the telephone, where it was usual for the lower-ranking person to mention his name first. As one could not see on the telephone, this often led to the endless repetition of *"Wei, wei?"* (Hello, hello...) until our Jan van den Berg, undaunted in Chinese, replied with "With the undertaker", whereupon, with a grievous cry, the person spoken to slammed the receiver back on the hook, because something like this was a fatal portent. There was a famous story of an assistant military attaché of the United States who had been stationed more than twenty years in China who was in the habit of saying: "China is very simple; one half is shitting and the other half is carrying shit," a statement we could confirm during our hikes when we would meet endless rows of men who were transporting night soil on yokes, in the way milk cans used to be carried to the countryside, where it would be used as manure. Because, with the exception of pigs, no other animals were kept, human waste was essential.

'It did not take me long to realize that Robert enjoyed a great reputation among fellow scholars of Chinese at other embassies, including the Russian [his Russian colleague, Fedorenko, was an authority on the subject, a connoisseur of old Chinese poetry, and his Chinese pronunciation was better than Robert's]. At that time, Van Gulik's activities included carving Chinese seals; he had even made a new seal for the embassy. A special sort of character were used in carving these seals. When Carl Barkman had to go to the Land Registry to organize the cancellation of the tenure of our embassy on our departure to the new capital, Nanking, a crowd of curious Chinese gathered to praise the originality and artistic quality of our seal.

'Sometimes Van Gulik's exceptional relations with the most prominent Chinese and his rather eccentric attitude could cause difficulties in the embassy, especially with the ambassador, who believed that the work—even the unpleasant tasks—should be shared by everybody. Van Gulik was not happy when his turn came to look after consular matters in which he had no interest. When he was in America I had already heard from him that a tried and tested method to teach the chief not to assign you unpleasant or superfluous jobs was to say that you were sick, so that somebody else had to do the work for you. It was a strategy he had already employed in Japan on his chief, General Pabst. There came a time in Chungking when we were informed that Van Gulik had fallen ill, precisely when he should have been tackling a task which had failed to engage his interest. A few days later during a staff meeting doubts were raised about just how genuine this illness was. His personal servant kept "the patient" well informed about what was happening; therefore just at a critical moment Robert's servant knocked on the door and entered with the message that his master was feeling a little better and had done some work: a report about domestic developments in China, crammed with details which were completely unknown to the other Western missions [comparable to the famous report about the secret societies], was presented on a silver salver. Only Van Gulik could produce this sort of work, but later I did wonder what The Hague, which was so poorly informed about Chinese affairs and, in fact, was actually not interested in them, would do with such reports, except accept them simply as "for information".

'In the meantime, Van Gulik [who had long since been given orders to return to the Netherlands, but continually postponed this] was busy making preparations for his farewell. Initially I did not realize that this would require so much work: gifts arrived almost daily from Chinese friends, artistically written rolls of paper, scrolls containing good wishes in beautiful calligraphy, and the recipient had to give an appropriate reply. This led to my discovery that in China calligraphy was held in such high regard and that good wishes penned with the brush had just as much significance and value as a painting or drawing.

'While the farewell ceremonies were being carried out day after day, through his unique contacts Van Gulik was still able to perform another very beneficial service. Every day the ambassador was irritated by the fact that our guards, who had to be fed and clothed at the cost of the state, usually slept throughout their whole stint and could barely be bothered to stand up when the ambassador happened to be passing. In a staff meeting it was decided to sack these ne'er-do-wells, and this apparently went ahead without presenting any difficulties. On our next Sunday hike, we no longer found the Dutch flag flying on our country pavilion, and from which the furniture, plates and everything else which should have been inside it had disappeared. A cutting protest was made to the *Wai Chiao Pu* about this brazen theft, but as usual nothing more than a message of sympathy for this upset was received. A few weeks later, Van Gulik heard from our chauffeur, who played a prominent role in one of the secret brotherhoods in which China was so rich, that it was very important that the embassy re-employ the sacked guards. Good counsel comes at a price, but after a great deal of discussion it was decided to re-employ our guardians on probation. Who could have imagined our amazement when, on our next hike we once again saw the Dutch flag flying on our country house, and all the furniture stood back in its place undamaged and an excellent meal was waiting for us, of which the main course was 'peace fish'. Once again we learned that it was a mistake to allow the Chinese to lose face.

'Our chauffeur was to offer more proof of his excellent relations with the milieux so inaccessible to us. With much bowing and scraping he intimated to Van Gulik that he could recommend an insurance company to cover the transportation of our office furniture and similar items from Chungking to Nanking [the new post-war capital]. This business could give far more favourable prices than those offered by Lloyds, with which most of the embassies had insured their property for the rather perilous voyage along the Yangtze River to Nanking, more than a thousand kilometres away. Therefore we were insured by 'The Black Flag', a *kongsi* of robbers who had contacts with the bands which controlled the banks of the river. Our boat was allowed to fly the skull-and-cross-bones to show that the insurance payments had all been paid. When we arrived in Nanking, we discovered that some embassies, including the Indian, had scarcely a stick of furniture because the rest had been stolen on the journey and it would be months before the insurance would be paid out; all our stuff arrived without a scratch and was immediately set up ready for use. Long live the skull-and-cross-bones, we thought, but could not say this aloud, because they were bandits in the eyes of the Chinese government.

'In between all these happenings, Van Gulik's farewell gradually took shape. Despite its imminence, he was to take part in our departure to Nanking. This was a complicated exercise in itself: the secret embassy archive and the staff were to leave for Nanking by air but, before this could happen, the residence in which the chancellery was housed had to be transferred back to its owner, Mr Shui. The housing shortage in Chungking had swollen to such proportions that a dwelling such as ours could not be left unguarded even for an hour. When our landlord entered to attend the farewell dinner which was offered him, he brought with him an impressive entourage of nephews, cousins and other family members, whose task it was to occupy the embassy after our departure. While our landlord, who was suffering from stomach-ache, ate very moderately, his family members gorged themselves heartily. To make sure that all was secure, during the meal masons repaired the brick outer wall and built a gateway which could be closed off by large sturdy doors. Unfortunately, when the hour for departure came well after midnight, the heavily laden lorries could not pass through the door. However, there was no need to worry; after getting up a good turn of speed part of the wall where the mortar had not yet dried properly, and was also possibly of poorer quality, was pulled down, to the accompaniment of the loud lamentations of the owner, and we left for the airfield. Our plane was literally loaded up to the gunnels, so much so we could scarcely see the aisle. The pilot had even hidden his wife and child under his seat in order to transport them to the new capital. Notwithstanding, the take-off and the whole flight passed without incident and in Nanking we could begin a new, more spacious life. This farewell was tinged by an inevitable feeling of nostalgia, because we would never experience anything like it again. At the end of April 1946, I wrote a description of it to my wife:

'"In the meantime I do have a certain nostalgia for the picturesque hills, so very different to any landscape I have ever seen. The steep indentation of the contours of the land combined with the intense tillage and cultivation lend the landscape a striking, beautiful appearance, as if it had been engraved by an etcher with the utmost care and sense of proportion [...]. Chungking, in the centre of distant Szechuan, had represented virtually untouched China: a fertile province of 60 million inhabitants, almost completely free of famine. Rich in coal and minerals, it is a state in itself, one which throughout history has paid little heed to the central authority and even now is not unhappy about the latter's departure [...] Traffic moves on in an endless stream, and in the passes between the mountains, inns, even whole small villages, have been built along the road, inviting the weary traveller to rest. You also never see there the disturbed graves which are so much part and parcel of the Chinese landscape. The farmers plough their rice-fields using a very primitive implement, boys carry grass either to burn or to be fed the pigs [...]. Here and there walk pedlars lugging large boxes on their backs to sell their strange wares; women breast-feed their children; sick dogs lick away their vermin; everywhere children toddle in and out—a life of endless variations which never palls. The bright blue of the clothing forms a sharp relief to the brown or grey background of the villages. Above, the sun beats down mercilessly, peace and order seems to reign all round, whereas in reality every day brings a step closer towards financial and economic chaos."'

In the meantime, the moment for Van Gulik's actual farewell had dawned. Eventually he only left around the 15th of July, after an extended visit to Peking. The closer the date came, the less he wanted to leave, but Foreign Affairs would not budge. Actually, the embassy could not do without him. Indeed in Nanking he made even more impression than he had done in Chungking: both he and Jan van den Berg were tall, larger-than-life personalities to whom the Chinese, especially those from the south, formed a stark contrast. Externally Van Gulik seemed like a stolid Hollander, nothing like a wizened scholar; and he was actually no stranger to any human emotion.

Barkman remembered Robert's farewell at the station, for which he had ordered champagne. As he and Han Boon walked along the platform behind Robert and Jan, Han Boon said: 'Those two great figures between them possess almost all the knowledge about China it is possible for a human being to acquire.' Barkman had absolutely no quarrel with this.

Rather than exhibiting any great sympathy for the evolution of Asia, Van Gulik's ideas about Eastern people tended to be conservative and some people considered him a colonial. Although he was married to a Chinese wife, and in spite of his profound knowledge of China, he felt very European. Later he was never to resign his job as a civil servant: he continually rejected offers of chairs at the most famous universities in the United States and Europe because he felt strongly convinced that he wanted to remain a civil servant. Despite all its shortcomings in other areas, Foreign Affairs gave him the opportunity to carry out his work in the way which suited him best. He paid no attention to office hours: he played billiards in the afternoon and he preferred to devote himself to his books and studies after his family had gone to bed: 'It's quiet at night and I can work,' he used to say. This was the pattern he had already established in Chungking and he never really altered his character traits. 'No matter the circumstances in which he found himself, he was always able to display great originality, which drew attention to himself and made an impression,' said Dr Boon.

Since S.F. longed to see her father in Peking, she left Chungking with our son on April 13 1946, and I left for a tour of the newly-liberated areas, working my way gradually up North too. In Soochow I spent a most interesting week with the family of my wife's mother [from the photos a beauty, completely corresponding to the tradition that the most beautiful women come from Soochow; she died when Shih-fang was only four years old, but Shih-fang's grandmother, daughter of the former prime minister Sun Pao-chi, was still alive and living there], and reached Peking on May the 18th 1946. Thus I met for the first time my father-in-law Dr Shui [Chun-shao], and found him a fine old gentleman. He presented me with the dragon-robe he used to wear when he was a diplomat of the Chinese Empire. We stayed in Peking until July the 6th, living in the Netherlands Embassy in Legation Street.

Pl. 15. Shui Chün-shao, Shih-fang's father.

Pl. 16. Madame Shui, née K'uai, Shih-fang's mother.

Shih-fang remembered: 'Robert was very kind and attentive to my father, who just as the other family members developed an instant affection for him. He made an impression on account of his great knowledge of our culture and customs. He was one of us.'

Van Gulik himself wrote:

> During this stay in Peking I took part in a number of local music-associations, and we often visited the famous old Taoist monastery Po-yün-kuan (Hall of the White Clouds). The abbot, An Shih-lin, was a fine scholar and excellent lute-player. Unfortunately, he indulged—as I heard later—in all kinds of magical experiments with young women; this was discovered by the monks a few years later, and in the turbulent days when the Communist army was nearing Peking, the monks buried him alive. Later I used this material in my Judge Dee novel *The Haunted Monastery*.

In Peking too most of the time was devoted to cultural activities, but Robert was also interested in his wife's family and every individual member of it. Their family ancestral shrine, where the original family portraits were kept, no longer exists, and it seems as if Van Gulik saw every eventuality, because during the time he spent in Peking he had reproductions of the portraits made.

> 28-5-1946: 11-12 to Dr Shui, fetched the family portraits.

> 29-5-1946: After lunch with S.F. to grandmother [that is, the mother of her step-mother, a Manchu lady, who had cared for her and the other children better than their step-mother, who played mah-jong until 3 o'clock in the morning and lay in bed until noon; S.F. had not had a happy childhood: she and the other children from her father's first marriage did not live with him, but in another house, each with their own nurse], then to aunt, and to Dr Shui, where picked up photo and spoke to 12th sister.

> 30-5-1946: To the photographer Varjassof, reproductions made of family portraits.

> 8-6-1946: 2-5 An Shih-lin [the sexually overactive abbot mentioned earlier] and Kuan P'ing-hu came to play lute, 6 o'clock Dr Shui and wife, grandmother and 13th brother and Kuan P'ing-hu came to dinner. Kuan P'ing-hu played *Shui-hsien* and *Mo-tzu-pei-ssu*.[15]

---

[15]   'The Philosopher Mo-Tzû sorrowing over the silk'. (see page 138 *The Lore of the Chinese Lute*. Tokyo: Sophia University, 1940 [reprinted Bangkok: Orchid Press, 2011].

9-6-1946: 4th brother and wife, 7th brother [a younger brother of Shih-fang, she herself was eighth sister] and wife, and 12th sister came to dinner. [In the Chinese family system, the children of brothers were not considered cousins, but brothers and sisters, and all were numbered according to their birth order. This system also applied to the ancestors: the younger brother of someone's grandfather was called second grandfather and so forth.]

18-6-1946: 4 o'clock to Dr Shui to check the family register and dined there. [The fact that Van Gulik took so much trouble about the Shui family photos and the family register was greatly appreciated by Shih-fang's father and her other relatives.] I went to Wang Meng-shu on my own, looked at books and played the lute until 10 o'clock.

Pl. 17. Seated next to lute-playing abbot, Peking 1946.

After a brief holiday in India, mainly in Bombay, the Van Guliks embarked there (14-30 August) for the voyage to London, where they remained a fortnight. The former embassy secretary (A.F.) Calkoen remembered that (J.M.A.H.) Luns, also an embassy secretary in London, said to him: 'Will you pick up Van Gulik? He is a queer customer.'

Fredrik Calkoen discovered that this 'odd bird' was in fact an extraordinarily interesting man. From Calkoen's office, Van Gulik rang his contacts at the universities of Oxford and Cambridge to make appointments, and when he returned to London from his visits there, he carried with him invitations for chairs at both these prestigious institutions of higher education: 'Always useful to be able to show that you are not dependent on 'them' [the Ministry of Foreign Affairs in The Hague], when they want to send you to some unacceptable place,' he said to Calkoen. In London he met some old friends, including Frank Hawley, and he took Shih-fang to the great museums, devoting special attention to the Asian collections.

Chapter 8

FIRST PERIOD IN THE NETHERLANDS 1946-1947

After [our] arrival at Hoek of Holland, we went straight on by train to Nijmegen, to Villa 'Severen', my old home. Much had changed. Mother had died, and Father was living there now with Uncle Piet, now also a widower, and Aunt Riek, my mother's sister whose husband had died during the war.

13-9-1946: Arrived at Hoek van Holland at 6 o'clock [...] and in Nijmegen at 11.30. Father at the station, all [took] a taxi to 'Severen', where [we had] lunch, dinner and went to bed early.

14-9-1946: 9 o'clock I went alone to the Hunerberg Park and from there to the grammar school [one day after his arrival in the Netherlands!], where spoke to Headmaster Schwarz [of whom he was very fond and whom he admired] and Rutten [the caretaker].

16-9-1946: In the morning played in the garden with Shih-fang and Wimpie [we often come across this information in his pocket diary. Shih-fang enjoyed the family life there: 'We did enjoy ourselves at 'Severen', and I was very fond of my father-in-law.'] Lunched at home, at 3 o'clock went into town with Aunt Riek and Shih-fang, had afternoon tea with S.F. and we both visited Headmaster Schwarz, back in Beek at 6 o'clock. Dinner at 'Severen' and played billiards in the evening.

The F.O. appointed me Head of the Far Eastern desk, and we took a small flat in The Hague, half-destroyed by a bomb. I boarded up the windows with cardboard, painted walls and the floors and made the place more or less inhabitable—which was necessary as S.F. was then expecting our second child. Pieter Anton was born on December 10 1946, and S.F. sent a jubilant call to China: two *sons* born in quick succession made a profound impression on the Chinese family! Father—who had taken a great liking for my wife—was also delighted, and we passed many happy weekends at 'Severen', where my eldest brother Willem, who had worked on the Burma Road as a prisoner-of-war, joined us. His wife and child had survived a Japanese camp in Java, and now he was a major-general, in charge of military affairs in our Colonial Office. Ben, now a colonel, had also withstood the hardships in Siam and Burma, and was commander of Bandung, Java; soon afterwards he was appointed military attaché at our Embassy in Nanking.

Robert had quite a few domestic affairs to sort out in the relatively short period which the Van Guliks spent in the Netherlands. He not only did up the flat, he also had to pick up ration books, clear a mountain of baggage and household goods through Customs, and pick up a passport for their Chinese nanny at the Chinese embassy among other tasks. Until they came home on 20 December he paid regular visits to his wife and baby in Bronovo Hospital.

20-12-1946: walked to Bronovo at half-past 10, brought Shih-fang and Pietje home in a taxi. Lunch at home, 2 p.m. Wimpie fell over in the kitchen, failed to find Dr Gunst at home, fetched Dr Pel who stitched and bandaged the wound [and came to check on him the next day and took out the stitches six days later].

Besides all this Van Gulik also still found plenty of time to talk to friends and colleagues, he corrected an essay about Japanese *netsuke* (a decorative belt toggle) by Dr Volker, received diplomats and secretaries who were posted to China and wanted to hear about all sorts of things from them, played plenty of billiards, and also the Chinese lute occasionally, and visited libraries. Now he was working at home the whole day on 'Americana', without saying what this meant.

4-1-1947: 8.30 to Dr De Kat to have X-ray taken. Confirmed a duodenal ulcer. Went home to lunch via the ministry. Shopped in the afternoon, and had front and rear lights put on bicycle. Dinner at home, then tidied up and made chests into book case and stained it.

11-1-1947: Worked on Spanish in the evening.

His wife explained why he had suddenly begun to study Spanish and what he meant when he said he was studying 'Americana'. He was deeply interested in the ancient Maya culture and was hoping that at some time he might be posted to either Mexico or Guatemala. A number of data, including the objects given as grave goods, had led him to think that there must have been a connection between this civilization and that of China. He thought that some connections with the Far East also could be found in the field of astrology. It was a subject which fascinated him. But when he broached the topic with Van Roijen, the latter's reaction was: 'Mexico or Guatemala? That would be a great pity, you are our best specialist on China and Japan! Put the whole idea out of your head.'

As early as October 1945, shortly after his visit to America, Van Gulik had written Van Roijen, then minister without portfolio, a personal letter in which he expressed his desire to be posted to the Department of Foreign Affairs for a few months and, after that, in the following year to be posted somewhere outside the Far East, preferably Mexico:

> The reasons I am so keen on Mexico are as follows. First and foremost the climate there is ideal for my wife, who has been in more or less continuous poor health ever since the birth of our son and does not have sound lungs. Secondly, the country and its ancient culture are of exceptional interest to me. While I was in Washington, both the Carnegie Institution (Institute) and the Bureau of American Ethnology of the Smithsonian approached me to find out whether I could not find the time and opportunity to tackle the problem of the putative ancient relationship between the Central American and the Chinese culture. Loads of nonsense have been written about this, and there is interest in the opinion of someone who is familiar with both the Chinese and the American sides of the matter. This means that, besides my work at the mission, I would be living in a country in which I can dabble in my scientific hobbies. As you know, I am never happier than when, while I am simultaneously engaged in my practical work for my Country, I can indulge in purely scientific pursuits. In China and Japan this has proved to be a useful combination: the one reinforces the other. I believe that Mexico would offer another combination just as good. I can do the official work, which will free up a civil servant for another post, while my scientific work will provide me with good contacts with leading people in Mexico, and will not do the reputation of the legation any harm either. Finally a change of climate and surroundings will also do me a world of good, I feel stale, and I have not yet fully recovered from the effects of the bad case of food-poisoning I contracted here. At regular intervals my extremities swell, especially affecting my hands and feet, and a specialist at the Bethesda Hospital in Washington said that it could

well be a year before I fully recover, but that a change in climate might help to clear the toxin out of my body.

Years later he was to say to his friend Professor Boxer: 'If I could have spent a year or two in Guatemala, with almost no duties at the legation and plenty of holidays, I could have studied all of that. You [I] could have said to your [my] secretary: "You take care of the legation, I'm going into the jungle for a couple of weeks." I could have studied the Maya temples as well as their astrological system. I think I would have been able to discover whether or not there is a link to China.'

In The Hague, as *the* specialist in the Far East, his advice was asked on all sorts of matters; he was also consulted about the Middle East as well. In Leiden he browsed in the Chinese library and visited Professor Duyvendak. In The Hague he was reunited with many old friends, among them the Van Roijens, Theo de Josselin de Jong, Theo Rocqué and Arie de Visser. Here domestic matters consumed a great deal of his time—one reason he wanted to be posted abroad again and did his best to fix this up; he rejected an offer to become chief of the East Asia Directorate. Nevertheless, there was still time to play billiards, and he remained a loyal cinema goer and reader of English detectives. Occasionally there was a dance evening.

> 11-3-1947: at 2.30 spoke to Elink Schuurman [head of personnel department] about Washington [there was talk that Van Gulik would become a member of the Far Eastern Commission there], [...] 8 o'clock ate at Insulinde with Moesa's [an Indonesian in the Dutch Foreign Service] and S.F., danced at the Atlantic, went home at 10.

When he was a student, Robert had had a great deal of contact with the (Indonesian) Chinese community in the Netherlands. Now he helped to set up an exhibition of Chinese paintings and calligraphy in Amsterdam, for which he made a contribution out of his personal collection. He gave a lecture there in Chinese.

Chapter 9

WASHINGTON, D.C.
1947-1948

Then a message of his appointment to Washington as a member of the Far Eastern Commission arrived. He was given the personal title of counsellor (his appointment to this rank, the third highest class in the foreign service, followed on 1 January 1948).

> We left the Netherlands on 17 May 1947 on board the S.S. *Westerdam* and arrived in New York on 26 May, and from there we travelled to Washington the next day.

> 26-5-1947 (Whit Monday): Sailed into New York at 8 o'clock. Customs etc., 10 o'clock taxi to the consulate-general, lunch downstairs in the Holland Tavern, walked around the block with Shih-fang and Wimpie, 2 o'clock to Pennsylvania Station, arrived in Washington at 7 o'clock. S. (E.L.C. Schiff] came to fetch us, to the Roosevelt Hotel, suite 601. To station with S. where picked up 4 collies and on the way back dined in the Chinese restaurant *The Good Earth*, home at half-past nine where tidied up and early to bed.

Emile Schiff, then embassy secretary in Washington, made Van Gulik's acquaintance on a platform of Union Station, where he had been sent to welcome the new delegate to the Far Eastern Commission and escort him to his hotel. He had no idea what Van Gulik looked like, but the consulate-general in New York had passed on the number of the carriage and at least he knew where he should look for him. It turned out to be absolutely no problem, because the last passengers to alight from the carriage were a tall man with a cigarette in his mouth, the ash spilling onto his coat, a Chinese woman, two Chinese-looking toddlers and a Chinese amah; he confirmed that he was Robert van Gulik.

The whole family and its luggage could be fitted into Schiff's car and he drove them to the Roosevelt Hotel on 16th Street. When he arrived in the apartment, Robert rang room service, ordered meals for the family and, cool as a cucumber, left them to their fate and went to eat at a Chinese restaurant with Schiff.

According to what Emile had to say, what precisely Van Gulik did in the FEC was never really clearly defined. Whatever the case, Van Gulik often rang him around half-past three in the afternoon to invite him to play billiards at the University Club. He could not understand why Schiff always declined the offer.

Van Gulik had bought a car but still had to obtain his American driver's licence. In view of the fact that the examiner would be none too pleased were he to turn up at the place designated for the exam in his car without a licence, he asked Schiff to drive him there. After he had got out and the examiner had taken his place, Schiff looked for a spot to wait until they returned. He was never to find the spot because, after a few minutes the gentlemen had returned: after a few metres Robert had driven through a red light and was immediately failed. Not long after this the Schiffs left Washington and hence never knew whether or not Robert ever obtained his licence.

His pocket diary shows that Van Gulik had to attend quite a number of meetings of the Far Eastern Commission and, apart from this, informal contacts with the other delegates took up quite a bit of time, even though this was combined with a drink or dinner as often as possible. After all, Van Gulik had his own style, could accomplish a great deal in a short time and kept fixed office hours as little as possible. To go off to play billiards for hours on end in office time would of course have been unthinkable for the average civil servant.

Ambassador Van Kleffens was also troubled by the fact that Van Gulik did not keep to the designated office hours (9 o'clock in the morning to 6 in the evening). Van Gulik invariably arrived in the morning at 10 o'clock at the earliest and left in the afternoon at 4. He was summoned to give an account of himself, but in answer to the ambassador's question about why he never came on time, he answered cheerfully: 'Your Excellency, I am terribly sorry, but I have two small children and I have to take them to school and pick them up as well. This is why I always arrive late and leave early!' Mr Van Kleffens, who had no real answer to this, muttered something along the lines of 'discipline; everybody should be on time,' but this was the end of the matter and Van Gulik arrived late every morning and left early every afternoon.

First we rented there a large house in Georgetown, Q-street 2907, a re-modelled old residence, furnished in American Colonial style, near to Dumbarton Oaks and the beautiful Montrose Park; I arranged my library which was quickly expanding again, in a large room on the first floor.

My main work was to act as the Netherlands Political Representative to the Far Eastern Commission (FEC), the highest Allied organ that supervised and directed the Japanese Occupation (even though Van Gulik realized full well that this was altogether an American 'show' and that the Allies had at most a certain degree of say in the matter); our sessions were held in the former Japanese embassy in Washington. Soon I was elected chairman of the Economics Committee, and there I got my first actual experience of the American-Soviet quibbling. The Soviet representative was Mr Tsarapkin, who is now in Geneva. I had an office in the Netherlands Embassy too, and got a cubicle assigned to me in the Library of Congress, where I consulted literature on current Japanese affairs as well as on Sinology [the latter would certainly have taken priority].

The Georgetown house proved too expensive (rent 325 dollars p[er] m[onth], whereas my salary was 820 dollars p[er] m[onth]), so we moved to a less fashionable part of the town, 1100 E Street, in S.E. The advantage was its low rent (120 dollars) and its vicinity to the Library of Congress. Also we were there in a real American middle-class milieu, and rid of the over-sophisticated, snobbish quarter of high officials and diplomats. Moreover there was a nice park nearby where we could take our two sons. [They also frequently went to the cinema and saw such films as *The Unfaithful, Great Expectations, Possessed, Dishonored Lady* and *The Long Night*].

As to my scholarly work, next to reading up on Western sinological literature, and studying the rare old Chinese books in the Library of Congress, I now made an English translation of the anonymous Judge Dee novel [*Dee Goong An*], just as an exercise. I had never read modern detective-stories—my knowledge of the subject being limited to Poe and Sir [Arthur] Conan Doyle—but being confronted daily with the array of pockets in our "drugstore on the corner", I used to pick up a few; I found them much inferior to the Judge Dee story I was translating.

S.F. and I found life in Washington an interesting experience, but all in all we did not particularly like it. We were most happy, however, with our weekends in a small log cabin we had rented in the mountains of Maryland, and we enjoyed long car trips

(I first drove a Chevrolet, thereafter a Studebaker), particularly on long car trips in the South. The southern towns like St. Augustin presented a quaint mixture of Dutch, and Netherl[ands] East Indies colonial atmosphere; it struck me that we treated the Indonesians much better than the Southern Americans the negro[e]s, and both of us were shocked at the social discrimination, which was quite new to us. We loathed Miami and the other fashionable resorts, but had a very good time in Tampa, on the w. coast of Florida. There I could again indulge in my favourite sports: swimming and boating.

We made a trip across the Mid-west, but were struck everywhere by the deadly uniformity of American life. We were not sorry when in the autumn of 1948 I learned that the FO had appointed me Political Adviser to our Military Mission [in fact the embassy] at Tokyo. S.F., however, had misgivings about having to live among the Japanese, whom she knew only from experiences during the Japanese occupation of Peking; she doubted whether our children would be safe! I tried to explain she had only seen the worst Japanese in the worst of circumstances, but she was convinced only after I had taken her to a few Japanese restaurants in New York, and then she saw how polite and kind Japanese waiters were.

Commenting on this Shih-fang said that she had not really been convinced, and went to Japan filled with apprehension. There a great shock awaited her: to her absolute amazement she saw how Robert, who was a prominent scholar of the centuries-old culture of her own country and felt completely at home in it, suddenly without the slightest difficulty immersed himself in the culture of Japan, a land towards which her own feelings were hostile, and seemed to feel completely at home there discussing their books and art with his friends among Japanese scholars in their own language. She never really completely recovered from this shock. She found the Japanese alien and closed; she was afraid of them and could not get used to the country, not even when Robert was later posted there again, this time as ambassador, and she tried to learn the language. Shih-fang did realize that Robert was held in high esteem in Japan because of his great knowledge of the language and customs.

We left Washington on Sept. 30 1948, and when we arrived in San Francisco heard that a large shipping strike was on, and that we had to wait. So we took a flat in a hotel, for the FO had decided that I might as well profit from the delay by having a long holiday. This proved a very nice holiday indeed, for we visited Berkeley University where I had many sinological friends and where I gave a few lectures, and we thoroughly explored the Frisco Chinatown. When the strike went on and on, I had to leave by plane, alone. I left Frisco on Nov. 14, and flew via Anchorage to Tokyo, where I arrived on November the 18th 1948.

17-11-1948: Lost day because of route via the Pole Circle.

Chapter 10

SECOND PERIOD IN JAPAN
1948-1951

Van Gulik arrived at Haneda, the airport of Tokyo, at 5 o'clock in the morning of 18 November 1948. He was met by Baron Lewe van Aduard, the acting *chargé d'affaires*, and Captain Van Kispal, who took him to the embassy. They arrived just at the moment the flag was being raised and stood to attention while the bugler, Sergeant Boerboom, played a few notes of the national anthem. Afterwards Van Gulik said: 'That's not how it should be played. Give me your bugle for a moment', and he blew a beautiful solo, which the rather glum-looking Boerboom could not match; later the two were able to get on very well together.

After breakfast Robert went straightaway with the gardener, who again greeted him with an extra deep bow remembering the beautiful characters he had once written on his smock, to look for the place where his former house had stood. Only the concrete foundations remained. It was a nostalgic moment. How many happy hours had he not spent there among his beloved books and paintings, nearly all of them now also gone forever, and with Kachan, his devoted Japanese girlfriend. During the war the embassy had been hit by incendiary bombs and only the main building—the ambassador's residence—was still standing.

> No, nothing will remain... The poet says it all: our hopes, our dreams, everything will disappear at the moment inimical fate decrees that this will be so. All that remains is the summer grass, which will sprout afresh each spring.[16]

After lunching at the embassy with his colleagues, he and Lewe went to inspect the house assigned to him by the military government, and naturally that very first day he also went to the

---

[16]   Citation from Robert van Gulik: *The Hot Springs of Odawara*, <judge-dee.info>, 2013 [*Beside the Hot Springs of Odawara*, unpublished, 1936].

Kanda quarter to visit the bookshops. His house had once been the dwelling of a Japanese general, a beautiful building completely constructed in Japanese style, situated in the Meguro quarter. His great friend Frank Hawley, now correspondent for the London *Times*, lived close by; Frank had divorced his Japanese wife and had married a Canadian, Gwynneth.

While awaiting the arrival of his family, Van Gulik devoted a great deal of his time and attention to putting the house and garden in order. Even though he employed a gardener, he also liked to work in the garden himself. He bought a wooden board from an antique dealer, which he embellished with finely carved characters and placed in the garden. He also designed a plaque for the entrance-hall of the embassy.

On 18 December, Robert picked up his wife and children and the nanny, Mrs Ritchie, in Yokohama.

Both S.F. and I were happy here. The general leading the Chinese Military Mission was an old friend of S.F.'s father, and his sister came to Japan to teach Chinese in a Girls' High School. Thus S.F. had a large circle of Chinese lady friends. We made a corner-room overlooking the beautiful Japanese landscape-garden into a Chinese dining room, and there regularly organized gatherings with Chinese and Japanese friends—foremost among the latter old Hosono Endai who had taken Japan's defeat philosophically and said it all belonged to the country's destiny and in the long run would produce good results. The largest room I used for my study, and there laid the foundations for a second Chinese library. At that time Chinese books and antiques were ridiculously cheap in Japan (the Japanese concentrating on things western), so my collection grew rapidly. Practically every Sunday I went with Frank to the booksellers' quarters in Kanda and Hongo, having dinner together afterwards in some small Japanese restaurant, just as during the pre-war days.

For my scholarly work these three years in Japan were a period of production, as appears from the list of my publications [the translation of the Chinese detective novel *Dee Goong An;* an erotic story dating from the Ming period; the erotic colour prints from the Ming period; an article about the small Chinese zither; an essay on Taoist magic; and two of his own Chinese detective stories from the Judge Dee series, *The Chinese Bell Murders,* and *The Chinese Maze Murders*]. I also re-wrote entirely the manuscript of my work on *Chinese Pictorial Art*, embodying the data gathered in Chungking, and new material found in Japan, so that it became twice its former size.

[…] Noticing that the book market was flooded by third-rate crime-novels about Chicago and New York by younger Japanese writers, I decided to publish my English translation of *Dee Goong An*, just to show them how much excellent material there was in ancient Chinese crime-literature. I financed that edition myself, and it sold so well that within six months I had my outlay back, plus a tidy profit. Chinese and Japanese authors liked to read it, but felt no urge to write such novels themselves since, as they frankly said, the subject was not sufficiently "exotic" to them. Therefore I decided to do it myself, as an experiment, and wrote *The Chinese Bell Murders*.

18-1-1950: 2 o'clock with S.F. to Meijiya [a supermarket]. Flat tyre on the way back. Picked Wimpie up from school, dinner at home 6-7 attended a council meeting of the Asiatic Society at the British Embassy on my own. Began on a new detective novel in the evening.

15-2-1950: Worked on a detective novel in the evening (typed it out up to Chapter 18).

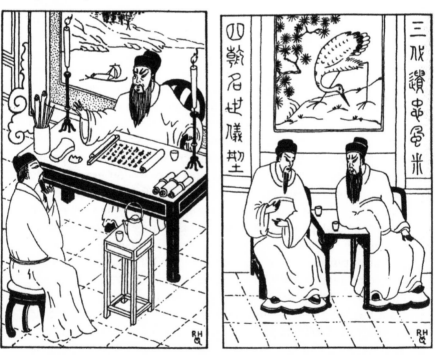

Fig. 3A: (left image): Judge Dee discusses a case with Sergeant Hoong. From *The Chinese Bell Murders*.
Fig. 3B: (right image): Judge Dee drinks tea with Lin Fan, a wealthy merchant from Canton. From *The Chinese Bell Murders*.

28-2-1950: Operated on at 8 o'clock. Gall-bladder and appendix removed. [During his time in hospital he borrowed a book of cartoons, a genre of which he was very fond, from Major Gout; later he produced comic books himself].

10-3-1950: 12.30 discharged from hospital. At home sat in the library until 4 o'clock, 4-6 in bed. Dinner and worked on a detective novel in library until 10 o'clock.

16-3-1950: Finished new detective novel after lunch.

I wrote part of the *Chinese Bell Murders* in the Military Hospital after a major operation (removal of gall-bladder and appendix), and I got some vicarious satisfaction from describing the torture-scenes, for the post-operative period was very painful! When I showed the ms to a Japanese publisher he said he liked the genre, but could not publish this particular novel because the Buddhists were shown in an unfavourable light and Buddhism was then quite popular in broader Japanese circles. So I wrote a second one, *The Chinese Maze Murders*. That was accepted, but the publisher insisted on having a colourful cover with a nude woman on it— else, he said, he could not sell the book; the cult of the nude was then rising in Japan, and there came into being even a splendid class of "carnal literature"—*nikutai bungaku*.

I protested that the Chinese did not have an erotic art, and I wanted to keep the illustrations of the book completely authentic. But my publisher who—like many of his colleagues!—was a man with few illusions left, remarked that if I searched for it, the ancient Chinese would certainly prove to have had an erotic art. Then I wrote postcards to a few dozen booksellers and curio-dealers, and indeed received two positive replies: one from a Chinese bookseller in Shanghai who wrote he knew a Chinese collector who had a few erotic Ming-albums, and a curio-dealer in Kyoto answered that he had the actual printing-blocks of such an album. Then I discovered there had indeed existed in China in the 15th and 16th century a cult of the nude and the "body beautiful", and I could design a book-cover with an undressed female in Ming style.

This discovery led me to a study of Chinese erotic art, and then of sexual life, and so I wrote my large work *Erotic Colour Prints of the Ming Period,* later followed by *Sexual Life in Ancient China.*

The Chinese Maze Murders was translated from my English original [that Agatha Christie had read and of which she wrote: "I have thoroughly enjoyed the book; the entire book has a rare charm and freshness, and I hope that it will be a huge success]

into Japanese by my friend the
Japanese Sinologue Professor
Ogaeri Yoshio, an expert in the
old Chinese novel. I myself began
on the Chinese version, which I
would complete later in India;
in Japan I was kept too busy
with other studies. And my aim
in publishing *Dee Gong An* and
The Chinese Maze Murders had
been reached. I had brought this
field to the attention of modern
Chinese and Japanese novelists.

Van Gulik's *Erotic Colour Prints
of the Ming Period* is a pioneering
study of a field which Western
scholars of Chinese had never
ventured into. And it is a splendid
work. In addition to the Chinese
text of the erotic albums, to which

Fig. 4: Cover of the Japanese edition
of *The Chinese Maze Murders*.
Black Orchid surprised in the
bath.

he applies his own translation, he also wrote detailed descriptions
and annotations on this topic in his own hand. The fine prints and
the wood-blocks which he purchased for his collection, because of
their outstanding artistic merit, together formed an album entitled
Hua-ying chin-chen (Various Orders of Battle in the Flowery Camp).
The frank eroticism of these prints is allayed, Van Gulik later writes
(*De Boek Illustratie van het Ming Tijdperk/Book Illustrations of the Ming
Period*, 's-Gravenhage, 1955), by the sensitive lines and the delicate
colours. This art breathes a combination of sensuality and mysticism,
which absolves the subject of any vulgarity. This spirit is expressed in
the last two lines of the final poem in the album, namely:

> The supreme ecstasy lasts but a single moment
> The ocean of suffering is boundless.

Especially during the second half of the Ming period in China, a
refined culture devoted to a life of pleasure, of which Nanking was a
centre, had emerged. This was the time at which the most beautiful
erotic prints were produced, but under its successor, the prudish
Manchu dynasty, this art was considered immoral and disgusting.
Consequently, hardly any trace of it can still be found in China.

The author opens his book, *Erotic Colour Prints of the Ming Period*, with a quotation in Sanskrit, followed by the English translation:
The Lord said:

> He who can behold Me in all things and
> All things in Me, he shall never lose
> Me nor shall I ever lose him.
> (*Bhagavad Gitā*, Ch. VI, 30).

Not everybody is free to make a closer acquaintance with these prints and his detailed views about Chinese sexual life expressed in the exceptional book because, to keep sensation-seekers and voyeurs at bay, the author required a stipulation from the very few libraries which were able to obtain a copy of the work from him, insisting that these books could only be consulted for academic purposes by a limited number of serious scholars in the field. He even went so far as to have the original printing-blocks which he had bought planed smooth. This does arouse the serious suspicion that, by removing the possibility of any further editions, he wanted to ensure that his work would accrue in both rarity and value.

Van Gulik displays a phenomenal fund of knowledge, not just of the philosophical Taoist and Tantric Buddhist terminology which this study demands, but also of both the everyday and the literary terminology employed in the sport of 'clouds and rain'. His knowledge also extended to the devices used in love-making: the ring or silken band wound around the base of the penis to maintain an erection, the *olisbos* or dildo (usually referred to in Chinese as a 'Burmese bell)' which women use to masturbate (either an artificial penis made of ivory or in the form of a small silk bag, filled with mercury, flour or the dried stems of plants which swell when they come into contact with moisture) and the double *olisbos* which can be used by both lesbian partners. Van Gulik remarked that there was a very tolerant attitude towards lesbianism in a country in which so many women were forced to cohabit.

The strict conditions he placed on the publication of his coloured prints was well suited to the period in which it was first published. However, in the current era, in which people are so much more open to such matters than at the time he was writing, it is fortunate that this important work has again been made available in reprint for the scholarly community (Brill: Leiden 2004). Following are a few examples of the prints from this work, with the accompanying text.

Fig. 5: From *Erotic Colour Prints of the Ming Period*, 1951. Volume III, Plate 4.
'The Way In the Manner of the Academicians'.[17]

Description:
A shadowy courtyard corner. On the table covered with a mat, a
book and a rolled up scroll. The man, wearing an official's cap, has
lowered his trousers; those of the girl are lying on the table. One of
the girl's boots has slipped off.

From the poem:
She is a little bashful and gently pushes him away, because this is
quite a departure from the ordinary! Looking over her shoulder she
gently cries out: 'Hurry up a bit! And please don't say anything to
the others!'
     Signed: The Candidate from the South.

---

[17]   Members of the Imperial Academy (*Han-lin*) apparently frequently practised
       pederasty and were thought to prefer anal coitus, even when copulating with a
       woman.

Fig. 6: From *Erotic Colour Prints of the Ming Period*, 1951, Vol. III, Plate 18.
    'Supporting the Homeward-Bound Tippler'.

Description:
Somewhere in the open, in a secluded spot behind a rock and a
blossoming tree. On the right one sees the edge of a cliff with an
agaric growing among a tuft of grass. Two swallows are in flight
in the sky. The man is fully dressed and wears an official cap; the
woman is also dressed for the outdoors. The maid holds up the
robe of her mistress.

Poem:
A pair of young swallows sporting together during the long spring
day has excited the passion of the lovers. She has lowered her red-
embroidered trousers, and now they imitate together the way of
the birds while mating.
    The gauze robe flutters in the wind. It is not easy to keep it
properly raised, but the maid servant lends a helping hand. Working
diligently to help the pair, her own lust will certainly be roused.'
    Signed: 'The Bold Immortal'

Fig. 7: From *Erotic Colour Prints of the Ming Period*, 1951, Vol. 1, Plate 13. From the album 'Secret Handbook for Devoted Lovers'.

Description:

This print depicts a bedroom scene. An elderly man wearing a silk belt with a ring to keep his member in an erection, is about to deflorate a young girl. The bed is drawn in detail, including the golden curtain hooks. The couch is covered with a padded quilt, its inside is decorated with a motif of swallows and plum blossoms.

On the left a young woman is standing ready with a tea tray. Attention is drawn to the large clothes rack on the left and the pair of tabourets on the right. These motifs together with the large bronze candlestick are very common in such pictures.

To these and other plates Van Gulik added a few others entitled *Chiang-nan hsiao-hsia*, Beguiling Time in a Summer South of the River (that is to say, south of the Yangtze River). Since time immemorial this region, the author noted later, had been home to many centres producing the wood most suitable for making woodblocks, the finest quality paper, the purest ink and the best brushes; it was the home of great artists, famous writers and a host of art-loving, high-ranking civil servants who had retired to fine country estates, "I have had enough of governing and I am tired of serving"—as Goethe so compellingly expressed it. Finally, Chiang-nan was also a place in which a large number of rich merchants, who were only too happy to patronize the arts and learning, had made their homes. Van Gulik was to add yet another, more subtle element to this mixture: the prevailing *fin-de-siècle* atmosphere, a mood of pensive resignation in the transience of all earthly things, but yet accompanied by a feverish striving to make all these same worldly things as perfect as possible; the mood of hypersensitive nostalgia, which has also frequently characterized the apogees of a culture in other places. In Van Gulik's eyes—and the whole of his work bears witness to this—the Ming period was the absolute pinnacle of Chinese culture; everything which came out of China after it counted for almost next to nothing as far as he was concerned.

These prints of *South of the River* have no text appended and Van Gulik thought that they were probably not meant to be included in any erotic album, but had been intended to be used to decorate the inside of a bedstead. They were the last known examples of the famous erotic coloured print. Van Gulik observed that, although they were imbued with a great skill and originality, in some of them he also detected the onset of decadence and obscenity—'the wilted flowers of the summer, which would presently fade into the chilly autumn of the Manchu dynasty'.

Fig. 8: From *Erotic Colour Prints of the Ming Period*, 1951, Vol. I, Plate 20. From the album 'Whiling Away the Summer South of the River'.

Description:
Shows the corner of a garden terrace. The man is reading in a chair. He holds the book in his right hand; his left is hanging down holding a fan. A naked women is squatted between his spread legs and practises [fellatio]; she holds his member in her left hand and with her right supports herself on the arm rest of the chair. The man tickles her vulva with the toes of

his left foot. Another woman is standing on the left; she fans the man with a feather fan, and holds a towel in her right hand.

In his academic work, *Sexual Life in Ancient China*, which appeared later, Robert van Gulik draws the edition of this rich material to lyrical, almost utopian conclusions:

> The Chiang-nan material again stresses the fundamental concerning the ancient Chinese attitude to sex, namely an unreserved joyful acceptation of all the varied aspects of human procreation, ranging from the smallest biological details of carnal congress to the most elevated spiritual love of which that congress is the seal and confirmation. Viewed as the human counterpart of the cosmic creative process, sexual intercourse was looked upon with reverence and never associated with moral guilt, or sin. The cosmic prototype hallowed the flesh, never considered as an abomination. No difference was felt between, for instance, the rain sprinkling the fields, and the semen fecundating the womb; or between the rich wet soil, ready for the seed, and the moist vagina of the woman prepared from sexual congress. Further, in the polar ideology of the *yin* and the *yang*, woman had her appointed place: second to man, but only in so far as Earth is second to Heaven, Moon to Sun. No sin attaches to her biological function, on the contrary, it makes her the Gates of Life.

However, when looking at the erotic prints, it is difficult to speak of 'unreserved, joyful acceptation' when a rather elderly man, who has to rely on the use of artificial appliances, deflowers a young maid. This is just one of the examples which can be cited which show that it is necessary to make some adjustments to the idealized picture Van Gulik sketched of sexual life in ancient China. Perhaps the author should have paid more attention to the prudishness revealed across the centuries in Confucian China (before the Manchu dynasty), although this does not detract from his general thesis, because this prudishness had more to do with form and external appearance than with the substance.

More interesting is his tentative conclusion, however contestable it might be, that the attention paid to sexual relations in China was and is an important factor in the survival of the Chinese people and their culture down through the centuries:

While other great civilizations perished, theirs remained; and while other races disappeared, dispersed or lost their political identity, the Chinese survive in ever increasing numbers, and retain their identity, both racial and political.

The historian must try to analyze such phenomena, he must study the underlying political, economical, social and moral factors. In doing so, however, it must always be realized it is not given to us to penetrate till the ultimate reason of the growth and decay of civilizations, just as we shall never know the ultimate reason of life and death of individuals.

Yet, in the case of China, a historical survey of Chinese sexual relations, the mainspring of life, makes one inclined to the belief that it was primarily the careful balancing of the male and female elements, studied in China as far back as the beginning of our era, that caused the permanence of Chinese race and culture. For it would seem that it was this balance that engendered the intense vital power that, from remote antiquity to the very present, has ever sustained and renewed the Chinese race. (*Sexual Life in Ancient China*, p. 336; this book is still the standard work in this field).

In this book and in the *Erotic Colour Prints*, Van Gulik quotes at length from old Chinese sexual manuals which give information about the many different positions and postures, the rhythm, and the number of movements and many other informative matters relating to the sexual act.

An active sex life was recommended as extremely healthy, but warnings were also given about indulging to excess. The latter reminded Van Gulik of an inscription in a Peking brothel he had once read about somewhere:

The Gate through which we entered life can also prove a Gate to Death,
But how many men have awakened to this truth?
At night the "Iron Fellow" must be used with careful consideration,
Longevity and the conservation of youth depend on a man's own actions.

In the world of the Orientalists, Van Gulik was recognized as one of the very greatest, despite the fact that a few professional Chinese scholars dismissed him as an 'amateur scholar'. Later, in his obituary of Van Gulik (*T'oung Pao*, 54, p. 116 *et seq.*), the Leiden Professor of

Chinese Language and Literature, A.F.O. Hulswé, had this to say: 'A brilliant amateur? To a certain extent this is correct. He eschewed the "central tradition", the major issues in Chinese history and society, the philosophers. He went in search of untrodden byways which offered him matters just as interesting to him, especially on account of their relative obscurity. However, as soon as his interest was aroused, no amount of trouble was too much for him to get to the bottom of it. Almost all his studies bear witness.' Via the byways and the things he discovered along them, Van Gulik penetrated more deeply into Chinese life, especially that of the scholar-official, than did by far the large majority of his contemporary Orientalists. It would not be going too far to claim that, in a certain sense, he was an adherent before its time of the *Annales* School and its approach to historical scholarship. Above all, through both his academic work and through the Judge Dee novels he brought ancient China to life in a way which was both fascinating and intelligible to the modern student.

Later, in the Netherlands, Van Gulik the collector possessed a very disparate group of artefacts from China and Japan. In *De Koorddansers en Andere Herininneringen* (The Tightrope Walkers and Other Memories; Nijgh & Van Ditmar, 1985), Rico Bulthuis describes an evening spent with the Van Guliks in The Hague in 1964. They had invited him and his wife to dine with their artistic friends Don and Ly Vermeire and Antal Sivirsky:

> The dinner with Robert and his wife followed the usual pattern; as the people in The Hague say, in the Indies fashion. Robert frequently retreated into the kitchen, returned with *saté*, poured beer, loaded the table with small dishes and said when the meal was finished: "Now then, the ladies can spend some time here chatting together, and the gentlemen will accompany me upstairs, where I want to show them something extraordinary".
>
> My second wife, who had only recently been introduced into these circles and was the youngest member of the company, could not believe her ears! The ladies could chat. They had to remain behind and gossip! In English or in the laboured Dutch of Mrs Van Gulik who poured coffee.
>
> When they arrived upstairs, Robert ushered his 'gentlemen' into his study, locked the door, took a row of books out of a rack and produced a black lacquer box from behind these books. He put it down on a small table. He pressed on the two copper, or perhaps they were gold, springs which closed the box and laid the lid on his writing table.

We saw lying there a number of objects in red silk fittings. Ivory rings, strangely notched sheaths with bulges, rods with protuberances on them and many more such artistically decorated objects whose significance or use we were at a loss to guess. Early Chinese free expressionism?

"Rich elderly mandarins used these things", said Robert, "around their 'young gentleman' to be able to serve their concubines more ardently. In fact, these are rare examples. A complete set. Very special."

Don and I roared with laughter, which made Robert smile somewhat bemusedly. Antal was the only one of us who did not seem to find it interesting. Downstairs the ladies chatted haltingly about the cold weather in the Netherlands and about the whims of nurses.'

In this Japanese period when he first began to take a serious interest in Chinese erotic literature, Van Gulik discovered that books and manuscripts which were no longer procurable in China could still be found in Japan. At his own expense he published a Chinese story of the Ming era, *Ch'un-mêng so-yen* (An Inconsequential Story of a Spring Dream), which he had furnished with an introduction and annotations. The plot was a simple one, frequently found in this genre. A brilliant young scholar is roaming through the mountains on his own, delighting in nature. Unexpectedly he meets two incredibly beautiful young girls, whose family names are *Li* and *T'ang*. They live in a sumptuous country house and are surrounded by an army of servants. They invite him to partake of the evening meal, during which they pass the time constantly exchanging poems and songs. He spends the night and the three of them make love. This is described in detail. As the day breaks, the call of the cuckoo is heard and the young man wakes up. He realizes that he has slept in the open air, lying between a plum and an apple tree, both in full bloom. The girls and their magnificent house have vanished. Hence, it had all been nothing but a dream, and the girls had been fairies, the spirits of the plum tree (*li*) and the wild apple tree (*t'ang*). The morning breeze scatters their red and white petals over him as he continues his journey, contemplating the transience of all earthly pleasures. This was a theme with which Van Gulik was very much at home: 'No, nothing shall remain...our hopes, our dreams, all shall disappear...'

In Tokyo, as he has already said himself, Robert van Gulik occupied himself with his various studies. He did very little at the embassy. It was an open secret that he did barely a tap of work but, if something important did crop up, he could always produce a good contact, give the right advice or had prepared a clever, incisive report in next-to-no-time. No one, not even his top man, would ever have dreamed of telling him that he should turn out more work. After all, he was *the* expert on China and Japan, and he stood above the law.

Ambassador Lovink, who had once dared to reprimand him during the time he was in Chungking, later wrote: 'Van Gulik was a potent figure. I have always had great admiration for him. We worked together in Chungking for three years. Unforgettable years, because they were remarkable. What he did not know about the language, history, culture, life, thought and way of doing things of the Chinese was not worth knowing. Intuitively he saw and could visualize what was really happening. There are not, nor have there ever been, many masters who were his equal. He *lived three lives:* his own, [and that of] the Chinese and the Japanese. Indubitably a remarkable achievement because he genuinely could cope with all three, and even had the gift of being able to immerse himself in them. On many, many occasions, what his own "I" was, was an enigma. I sometimes had the feeling that a second person was living alongside him.'

In these words, Lovink aptly captures the experiences of many of the other people who knew Van Gulik.

Visits to the city of Nagasaki were very important to the Dutch embassy in Tokyo, certainly to a Japanese expert like Robert van Gulik, who happened to have been posted there. The compelling reason was that for several centuries the Dutch had maintained a trading-post there, one which indirectly played a significant cultural role. It goes without saying that trade was the top priority of the Dutch but among those people posted were men with a wide breadth of interests (among them Kaempfer, Titsingh and Von Siebold) and in no small way they contributed the West's ability to form a clearer picture of this faraway, unfamiliar country and the Japanese had also been offered their first introduction to Western sciences.

As early as January 1949, Van Gulik paid a visit to Nagasaki on embassy business. He was accompanied by the Japanese scholar Krieger and two officers posted to the embassy, Major Gout and Captain Van Kispal. His chief goal was to foster Dutch (and his own) cultural interests.

Here too he lived his 'three lives'. On the day of his arrival, as official representative of the Dutch embassy he held talks at military headquarters and the chamber of commerce about the reconstruction of Deshima, the small, artificial island in Nagasaki harbour which had been home to the Dutch trading post for three centuries, at a time when all other foreigners, with the exception of the Chinese, were banned. This business concluded, he seized the first opportunity he could to visit a pair of *Chinese* temples in this Japanese city. In an antique shop he purchased a *gekkin* (moon guitar); he walked to the (*Japanese*) Suwa Shrine, where the patron god of the city resided, and looked out over Nagasaki, covered with a mantle of snow, seemingly more romantic than ever. His next visit was to the museum, where he wrote scrolls (in finely calligraphed Chinese characters) for a Japanese friend and scholar, Hirayama, with whom he then proceeded to the grave of Zūfu Jōkichi, which is located in the Kotaiji, a Zen temple. In the evening Van Gulik read a detective story.

The next day, accompanied by Watanabe Kurasuke, whose library he had admired earlier, he visited an elderly geisha and afterwards he enjoyed a drink with Dutch officers. The day after, three former geishas accompanied Watanabe to demonstrate how to play the *gekkin*, the moon guitar. After the demonstration, they all lunched together. In the afternoon Hirayama went with him to pay another visit to the Kotaiji where a Buddhist memorial service was read for Zūfu Jōkichi and they walked to his grave to make offerings. This accomplished, their first stops were the museum and a bookshop, then on to the officer's mess.

Jōkichi was the young son of Hendrik Doeff (Zūfu), who as "chief" on Deshima was in charge of the Dutch trading-post at the beginning of the nineteenth century, and of Uryuno, one of his regular Japanese girlfriends. The Dutch were forbidden to take their wives to Deshima; only prostitutes from Maruyama, the pleasure quarter, were permitted on it. Initially these *Oranda-yuki* were only allowed to spend one night at a time there, later this was raised to three days and, towards the end of the eighteenth century, the 'five-day system' came into effect.

The doyen of Dutch Japanese scholars, Professor Vos, gives a vivid, particularly readable description of the situation on Deshima:

> [...] The *Oranda-yuki* were sophisticated girls, who clearly dis-
> tinguished themselves from their modest sisters by their behav-

iour. They interspersed their conversation with Dutch and Malay, shook hands and gave kisses (*umakuchi*, 'delightful mouthing'). They wore bracelets and rings set with precious stones, drank coffee and ate chocolate [...].

The names of the girlfriends (confidantes) of many chiefs and doctors on Deshima are known. Children were born out of various relationships and their fate in a society as closed as that of the Japanese must have generally been far from enviable [...].

Maruyama ni	In Maruyama
sangoju wo umu	are women who give birth
onna ari	to [beads of] coral.

The coral beads mentioned in this *senryu* [a form of short satirical poem] refer to the exotic eyes of the half-Japanese children. Hendrik Doeff, who was appointed chief in 1805, six years after he arrived in Japan, was famous as a scholar and as a lover. Doeff's special girlfriends were Sono'o, Iroha and Kotaki [...] and Uryuno [...]. He had a daughter with Sono'o [...]. Uryuno gave him a son, Jōkichi. To his bitter disappointment, the Japanese authorities refused him permission to take Jōkichi with him to the Netherlands. However, before his departure he took pains to see that Uryuno and her son were properly provided for. The latter had died at the early age of seventeen in 1824.

Maruyama no	A farewell in Maruyama
wakare ichiman	means [a distance of]
sanzenri	13,000 miles.

[...] In view of this and other love affairs, it is no wonder that the stereotypes which so often crop up when speaking of other peoples and races also took root in Japan. It was assumed that Dutchmen were possessed of phenomenal sexual prowess, which they could drive to even greater heights by the use of secret elixirs.

Oranda no	How efficacious is
yakuryoku mekake wo	the Dutch love potion
notautase	my sweetheart convulses ...[...]'

[From Professor Dr F. Vos, *Het dagelijks leven der Nederlanders op Deshima* (Daily life of the Dutch on Deshima), in: *Vier Eeuwen Nederland-Japan*, published by De Tijdstroom Pty Ltd, Lochem 1983, p. 24-25.]

In the period in which The Netherlands was under French rule (1795-1806) and during the subsequent Napoleonic Wars, contact between Asia and continental Europe was severed almost completely. The upshot was that, after 1808, Dutch ships were not able to make the voyage from Batavia to Deshima. Hendrik Doeff and his staff were stranded there, cut off from supplies, money and goods to trade, and having to throw themselves upon the mercy of the Japanese. He made good use of his unexpectedly free time to compile a dictionary and, as a true patriot, he thwarted any English ships which might venture to sail in and try to usurp the Dutch role. It was a typical Van Gulik gesture to take the time to pay his respects at the grave of Doeff's son.

On their return to the hotel several high-ranking Japanese liaison officers happened to be sitting in the lounge. When Captain Van Kisool entered, they neither stood up nor offered any greeting. This Dutchman, who had spent some time in a Japanese prisoner-of-war camp where he had picked up some Japanese military expletives, swore at them in their own language, whereupon they sprang up and saluted. When Van Kispal told this to Van Gulik, who had not been present during this incident, although Van Gulik did show some understanding for his action he was nonetheless disapproving: 'As foreigners here, we should not abuse the people of this country.'

The visit came to an end for Van Gulik and his travelling companions when a telegram arrived from the embassy in Tokyo asking in a rather peremptory tone when the gentlemen might at last consider coming back. They travelled back to Tokyo via Kyoto, where Van Gulik and Krieger spent a leisurely couple of days visiting countless temples, *objets d'art* and libraries.

> 26-1-1949: With the Gouts to Golf Drive Washington Heights, Shih-fang first golf lesson. Returned home, played with the children.

The Van Guliks did not play golf, but he was interested in *everything* and omnivorously wanted to find out about and hence gain knowledge of whatever he could. It seems he also wanted to discover if his wife was drawn to things. When he had learned about something, this did not mean that he always wanted to devote more time to it; his motto was often: 'Now I know about it and it's not really my thing.'

Gout was engaged in intelligence and his work in this field brought him into fairly frequent contact with Van Gulik. He recalled that Van Gulik had compiled a simple code book for the American Navy which was based on... Blackfoot Indian!

The official work was of absorbing interest. I could follow closely Japanese reactions to the various policies of the Military Occupation, and after the war in Korea had started, I also went there regularly.

Besides the Netherlands interests, I also tried in an unofficial way to bring about a better understanding between Japan and Korea, but without much success. The intelligentsia on both sides were prepared for it, but President Syngman Rhee [of Korea] was violently opposed to it and SCAP (Supreme Command Allied Forces Pacific, in short General MacArthur) was wavering.

As stated above, I had purposefully ignored precisely Japanese literature of former times, because I thought such a study would lead me too far afield. That I now changed my attitude is thanks to a young Japanese girl-writer. She was a graduate in classical Japanese literature, wrote in beautiful calligraphy and she had a very fine understanding of the niceties of general Japanese culture. During two years met regularly in old-style Japanese restaurants and tea-houses, went together to Japanese exhibitions and tea ceremonies, and I thus became interested in classical Japanese literature, especially *haiku* [and *waka*] poetry.

He had made the acquaintance of this young woman, who would play an important role in his life, through his friend Frank Hawley, for whom she worked. Ikeda Etsuko is mentioned in the pocket diaries by her given name, Etsuko, or often simply as E.

14-2-1949: [...] dinner at home, 7 o'clock fetched Etsuko from Shibuya Station; went with her, S.F. and [the governess] Mrs Ritchie to the Imperial Hotel, where [there was] a lecture on Japanese woodblock printing. Went home with both Hawleys, Redman and E., where whiskey was drunk and songs sung until 12 a.m.

30-3-1949: embassy in the morning, 12 p.m. returned home for lunch, 4 o'clock to the embassy where wrote letters until 5. In jeep to Shimbashi Eki [the station at which he usually made his appointments with Etsuko], where met E, together to the Esquire for dinner.

S.F. and Mrs R. to Japanese opera.

Most foreigners had a summer cottage at the seaside or in the mountains; the Van Guliks were among them:

I had rented a small house in the mountain region of Karuizawa and there went in the summer with Shih-fang, our three children and servants. Frank and his Canadian wife had also a villa there, and together we explored the historic sites. Shih-fang, though keeping to her Chinese standards, became friendly with Frank's wife, who held modern Western ideas on marriage and the position of women. Our marriage was and is founded essentially on Chinese principles: S.F. is concerned with the "within". She cares little about the "without". This implies that we never speak about my office-work, neither about my scholarly activities. When I go out alone, she does not ask me where I go, and when I come does she does not ask me what I did.

Thus my home has always been a real haven of rest and relaxation for me: on crossing our threshold, I leave all my "outside worries". People often wonder how I could be active in so many different fields without becoming a schizophrenic patient; the answer is the happy organization of our home life.

We speak Chinese when we are alone, Dutch and English with the children, and although we have had the usual differences in meaning in the course of the more than twenty years of our married life, these never concerned matters of vital importance.

In this piece, Van Gulik, who was always on a quest to find the ideal woman, is tending to over-idealize his (Chinese) marriage. Is he doing this to convince himself? Or for posterity? He must have known that a Chinese woman, the daughter of a mandarin no less, was also unquestionably a *woman* who could be just as inquisitive and jealous as her Western sisters.

When Shih-Fang was asked whether it had mattered to her where Robert went and what he did when he was away from home, and whether this, as he writes, was based on Chinese principles, she responded: 'Of course that is not Chinese! But he hardly ever talked to me, nor did he speak much with the children; he told me nothing about his work and other activities, and therefore I never asked about them. Robert was *always* busy with something. When he did come home, he usually disappeared straight into his study. When we had guests he usually also took his food in there. Sometimes we did attend an exhibition or go to the cinema together, or perhaps did some shopping. Occasionally we took an evening stroll in a quiet area close to our house.'

Van Gulik writes further:

Since Shih-fang has the innate tact of a mandarin's daughter, she has been doing very well as a diplomat's wife, being not really interested in politics she makes an excellent listener, a quality especially appreciated by male diplomats and politicians! I vividly remember a remark which was made by a prime minister when he had been seated beside Shih-fang during a banquet. He said I was lucky indeed to have a wife with *such* a fine understanding of European politics. The fact is S.F. had been two hours listening to his views on Europe, nodding politely from time to time, and saying how extremely right he was.

Her sense of duty made her acquire a sound knowledge of Dutch, and she occasionally reads Dutch novels, especially those describing family life in the nineteenth century, because it resembles Chinese life. Of my books she has read only my Chinese work on the loyal Ming period. My Judge Dee novels she has looked at but she doesn't like them [and she likes the erotic Ming prints even less] because they tell too much about the bad sides of Chinese society; brothels and illicit love-affairs belong to the 'outside world' and are subjects not mentioned among old-fashioned Chinese 'young daughters'. After spending twenty years in the international milieus, it still shocks to hear Western women mention them—what with the films she sees has given her a rather dim view of Western civilization, and made her cling all the more firmly to Chinese traditions.

Van Gulik gives a lecture in English about Chinese detective novels at the Imperial Hotel, and he delivers a talk about the classical lute to a Japanese musical society. He remains a connoisseur of good food—preferably Chinese or Japanese—and plays billiards with Dutch friends and acquaintances. In this period—spring 1949—he is also complaining more often about stomach aches and has X-rays taken, but he still continues to eat often and well. And, despite a host of throat and nose ailments, many visits to various doctors, swallowing all sorts of medicines, he remains a chain smoker. He will not or cannot change his cherished way of life.

In the summer the family are often to be found in Karuizawa where it is cooler and Van Gulik spends the weekends with them. Then suddenly, just for a moment, his former Japanese girlfriend Kachan re-appears in his life; he gives her a lift in the car to a village near Karuizawa:

3-6-1949: Telephone call from Karuizawa about Pietje [whose arm had been dislocated], 9.30 to the embassy where collected petrol. Okaya Katsuyo [Kachan] was there, accompanied her and Tsuyuko to Karuiszawa. Dropped Katsuyo at Takasaki Station, arrived at Karuizawa at 2 o'clock.

He had lived with her for seven happy years, but she was not a very well-educated girl and they had probably grown apart.

1-6-1949: in the morning with S.F. and the children to the Dispensary, then to Meijiya. Took everyone [home], I went to the office on my own, 12 o'clock to Tokyo Station where met E., together to Yaomatsu, went home 5 o'clock, with S.F. and Wimpie to Mrs Ch'ien [her Chinese lady friend] and chatted until 6 o'clock. Dinner at home, Hawley came for a drink, 9-10.30 strolled with S.F. in the moonlight.

Kachan did try to make contact with him on another couple of occasions:

21-6-1949: embassy in the morning. Katsuyo comes, ate *unagi* (eel) together in Hanabiki.

23-8-1949: To the office where Katsuyo comes to talk and was handed 10,000 yen [then roughly $2,500 or €3,000].

Just as many other Japanese directly after the war, she was plagued with financial difficulties. On 1 October she came again and was handed another 5,000 yen at the office.

A few years after the war, Tokyo presented a pretty sorry sight. The Allied bombardment had wrought enormous destruction. Office blocks and houses were not the only victims, carcases of cars lay scattered around everywhere, too many to be tidied up. How harrowing the housing shortage was only properly dawned on Van Gulik one evening as he was strolling past one such ruined car, very close to the embassy, and caught sight of a small light burning inside it; people were living inside it.

Apart from a few exceptions like Van Gulik, the foreigners lived almost entirely outside of Japanese society, in a sort of mini-United States. To find one's way in the city, one had to depend on American traffic signs and names. One made one's purchases in 'Washington Heights' (*Omotesando*), in shops for foreigners in which one paid in dollars.

It goes without saying that Japanese society was not completely unaffected by the occupation, and it has to be said that its more beneficial aspects predominated. By and large, the occupying force (Allied in name, but actually American), usually opted for a humane and constructive approach. Over-eagerly—sometimes naively or without full cognizance of the situation—it set about introducing a large number of reforms. Its point of departure was that Japanese aggression had been spawned by its feudal social structure, its militaristic ideals and the presence of large capitalist concerns, called *zaibatsu*. These last had to be radically eliminated.

A new constitution was introduced, one which guaranteed parliamentary democracy and fundamentally altered the status of the emperor, who became 'the symbol of the state and of the unity of the people, in whom his sovereignty is vested'. The aristocracy and aristocratic titles were abolished. Far-reaching reforms democratized the 'feudal' agricultural system. The former family hierarchy was replaced by a system of family law based on the equal rights of all members of the family. Education was reformed and the chauvinistically nationalist textbooks were replaced. The formation of free trade unions was regulated by law and anti-trust laws were designed to break the power of the *zaibatsu*.

Did all this mean a complete break with the past? Under no circumstances, and if anybody was sceptical about the real significance of these reforms, that person was both a conservative and a Japan expert like Van Gulik. No society—certainly not the Japanese— allowed itself to be fundamentally changed within a short period of time by a number of measures, some existing only on paper, imposed from above and from outside. In the 1920s, before the rise of the militarist period in the 1930s, Japan had already had experience of a more democratic system. In some instances the reforms the occupier imposed created a situation which could be compared to that of the 1920s. The power of the political parties was restored, and certainly strengthened by the undermining of the class composed of the large landowners, the military and the court clique. Undeniably it could correctly be described as a break with the recent past.

Once the occupying force was satisfied they had extirpated the greatest 'evils' in Japan, root and branch, and that, indisputably, there was a solid basis for a parliamentary democracy, it turned its attention to regulations which would bolster the Japanese economy. Initially these attempts were received rather apathetically by the people. These were the precursors of preparations for drawing up a peace treaty which would herald the end of the occupation, then surplus to requirements. The peace treaty was ready in 1951 and was signed by forty-eight countries, among them the Netherlands. The Soviet Union, China and India were not among the signatories. The United States and Japan also seized this opportunity to conclude a security treaty, a logical response to the international situation as it was seen at the time.

As early as 1948, when the writing was on the wall that the Communists would prevail in China—and it should be remembered that this was viewed by Washington as an extension of Soviet communism—it was important to the United States to set Japan firmly on its feet economically and to offer it military protection. The economy recovered quickly in the 1950s (partly because of the demand for supplies required by the Korean War) which meant that Japan was able to enter into agreements with various countries in Southeast Asia about the payment of reparations, which was combined with the extension of credit loans.

Van Gulik followed all these developments closely. His greatest interest was in the reactions of the Japanese who generally remained extremely self-contained, but now, after their crushing defeat and standing in complete awe of the American occupation force, more than ever before they were increasingly beginning to express their cautious criticism of the United States. As Van Gulik's over-riding interest was in cultural matters, he enjoyed the advantage of being constantly updated on Japanese public opinion and the political climate on the ground by his contacts in that field. Of all the branches, it had always been intelligence ('secret service') work which had fascinated him the most, all the rest was boring beyond belief.

On one occasion, when Ambassador Mouw happened to be absent for a few days and Van Gulik was acting head of mission, an official entered his room with an urgent, top-secret coded telegram, which commenced with the words 'To be deciphered by the ambassador personally'. The room was full of Japanese with whom Van Gulik was scrutinizing and discussing scroll paintings. The official informed him that he and he alone should decipher the telegram immediately, but Van Gulik waved it aside dismissively saying: 'Impossible, I do not have the time to do it', and stuck the telegram in his pocket. When the ambassador returned a few days later, the telegram had still not been deciphered! Eventually it proved too late to comply with the instruction, which turned out to be of little importance (the official concerned could no longer recall what it was about: it just happened to be one of those problems which solves itself). This was not the only occasion on which Robert treated his diplomatic work cavalierly, but every time he did so, he was spared any disasters. Nor was this the only occasion on which he happened to be engaged in something other than office work at the chancellery. Sometimes he could be found sitting on the floor of his room there clad in a kimono writing characters on large sheets of paper.

Despite everything, Van Gulik remained an exception on account of his great simplicity, unruffled demeanour and innate modesty; he did not thrust himself into the limelight. He did not need to do so. If one asked him a question, one was always given a sound and well-considered answer; the range of his knowledge of many subjects was incredible—as a colleague at the time noted, 'he picked up everything immediately' and never needed long to study anything.

In August 1949 a request arrived from the embassy in Washington asking if Van Gulik could comment on a report about *Communism in China* submitted by Sub-committee 5 of the House Foreign Affairs Committee. His commentary (dated 28-8-1949), in which he also gives his opinion of the American *White Paper on China* which had appeared not long before, is remarkable. It betrays a rather narrow-minded vision, one to which we were not accustomed, even from the arch-conservative Van Gulik. The gist of his argument is that:

> ...in the final phase of the war the national armies [Chiang Kai-chek] could certainly have broken the power of the Chinese communists, but American interference obstructed this. The pro-Russian policy of the American government had led to such excesses as the dispatch to China of Mr [John S.] Service [...] who later had to be dismissed on account of his political views [actually, Service was one of the few American diplomats who understood what was happening in China, but he fell victim to Senator McCarthy's witch hunt for 'suspected' communists]. The United States forced the national government to negotiate with the communists and forbade it to take military action.

Another remarkable argument Van Gulik puts forward is to suggest that, had such a military action been mounted against Yenan, it would not have weakened the anti-Japanese front:

> After all, because of the blockade of Yenan the armies under General Hu Tsung-nan were being kept out of the battle against Japan.

He pursues his thesis further:

Through its support [?]America gave [the Chinese] communists face [prestige], by and large considerably strengthening their position in the eyes of the Chinese people, and hence laid the foundation for their present success. This is not to say that, had America given him a free hand, Chiang Kai-chek could have broken the power of the communists [which contradicts what has been argued above], but the Russians would have had to strengthen their commitment to assisting the Chinese communists in Manchuria into the saddle and the communists would have needed to expend more time and energy on expanding their power.

It could be McCarthy himself or perhaps Senator Judd of the Taiwan lobby holding forth. One may think whatever one wants about the actions of the United States in China and ponder the grievous errors which were made, but Van Gulik's remarks betray such a lack of judgement not only of the capability of the Kuomintang but also of the strength of the communist armies, that one simply cannot avoid wondering how he could ever have permitted himself to write it. Moreover, everything he says contradicts the tenor of the contemporary despatches from the embassy in Chungking, on which he himself had worked. It seems as if, somewhere along the line, he had had a change of heart. In Tokyo he had intensive contact with the Taiwan- Chinese military mission/embassy and might perhaps have been influenced by it.

He did take the trouble to stress that his criticism of American policy did not imply that Chiang Kai-chek was an 'affronted innocent'. Corruption had reached stupendous proportions and the contact between the Kuomintang and the broader strata of the people and the intellectuals was no more than a distant memory. Chiang had lost his grip on the real situation. He was so under the influence of his immediate circles—an impenetrable barrier of petty politicians and sycophants—and his beliefs in his own party ideology had become so inflexible that he could or would not see where the greatest communist threat lay. The ultra-nationalism which Chiang had cultivated so assiduously was in fact easily adaptable by his enemies and communism, decked out with a few ultra-nationalist slogans, was the logical extension of the theories that Dr Sun Yat-sen had set out in his *Three Principles of the People*.

Van Gulik concluded that the controversy between the Kuomintang and the communists,

...is not one of ideological differences, it is actually the struggle for supremacy between two power groups, both shaped in the same totalitarian mold and both relying on the nationalist sentiments of the Chinese people. Communism in China is not a foreign doctrine to be imposed on the people by force, it links up with how the Chinese people have lived for centuries.

Here Van Gulik is again at his best. Few then could have foreseen that the communist ideology, or what passed for it, would evolve into such an efficient, ubiquitous instrument of power in China, nor could they have predicted Mao Tse-tung's struggle for supreme power, which visited so much disaster on China, ultimately culminating in the infamous 'cultural revolution'. Van Gulik's views on both China and Japan should certainly never be shrugged off, but his view of the world often strikes one as unrealistic and naive; he was and remained a 'specialist', but indubitably a very exceptional one. This leads neatly to the question of whether Van Gulik was a good diplomat. Naturally he was most at home in Far Eastern countries with whose cultures he was thoroughly conversant. Despite this penchant, in other countries he always held the name of the Netherlands high and he was able to win respect, trust and friendship. He was proud to serve his country and attached great importance to his official status. Certainly he utilized all the practical, personal opportunities and facilities it threw in his path. His position, even later as ambassador, never saw him lapse into arrogance; he remained himself: 'an ordinary person', but none the less one with a natural authority, unruffled and unassuming. It was his political horizon which was limited. In the diplomatic field he was always a specialist and would always have been passed over for the highest posts in the foreign service (at that time Tokyo was not one of them). Nor was that ever his ambition. His first priority was invariably his work as scholar and author and to this he devoted most time. The fact that, despite his poor health, his unbounded energy enabled him to achieve such an incredible amount as a scholar and writer and to acquit himself of his duties as diplomat in so honourable a fashion, is an achievement which can only be admired.

Van Gulik commenced his career before the war, in an era in which there were no massive flight links or networks providing means of swift communications. Then the Netherlands was still neutral and there was much less work in foreign posts than there would be later. Importantly, he began in the interpreting service, a corps of specialists who were allowed a high degree of latitude in their own field, albeit this was because most knew not one word of the Japanese, Chinese of Arabic in which these gentlemen immersed themselves. After the war, the character of the Dutch foreign service changed fundamentally but by then Van Gulik had established his reputation as an expert and a scholar and he was permitted the freedom to which he was accustomed. As the years went by, this latitude allowed him to continue to follow a steady path of studying and writing, every so often devoting a burst of time to his real work. His great intellect meant that he required less time to deal with his diplomatic duties than most others. However, for that little bit extra, that effort above and beyond the normal call of duty which a diplomat, competing with colleagues from so many other countries, has to expend if he is to be really successful, Van Gulik had neither the time nor above all the inclination.

He was an eccentric and unconventional diplomat, but one gifted with high intelligence and oriental subtlety. A high-ranking official in the department had this to say about his work as ambassador: 'Naturally one could never rely on him to carry out his instructions to the letter, but he would never do anything stupid.'

What did begin to annoy Van Gulik—and he was far from alone in his irritation, which worsened in later years when he was the man-in-charge—was the mounting cavilling and diminishing support from the department. Perhaps this provides the answer as to why, when one of his sons showed some interest in his father's profession, Van Gulik advised that the diplomatic service no longer had much to offer and he wondered why none of his sons had shown any interest in studying medicine. Thomas did become a doctor and he has the impression that, had his father been able to live his life over again, he would have also wanted to become a doctor. Throughout his life he showed a great interest in the subject and a host of diseases and medicines exerted a strong fascination on him: he always had the *Codex Medicus* close at hand.

While Robert was busy in Tokyo supervising the publication of his fine *Erotic Colour Prints of the Ming Period*, the Korean War broke out:

> Sunday 25-6-1950: Lunch at home. Hawley rang up to say that war had broken out in Korea.

Throughout the entire year 1950, Van Gulik worked on his various books and articles in the field of Sinology, and he had no time for, or perhaps no interest in, Japanese literature.

The evidence of his pocket diaries shows that he had almost given up his once almost daily meetings with his literary friend Etsuko. At the end of 1950, Christmas celebrations brought them all together again, if only momentarily:

> 25-12-1950: 7 o'clock picked up Etsuko with S.F. [who was pregnant], and went together to Hawley where [ate] Christmas dinner with both Jordans.

At the beginning of 1951 he purchased a *p'i-p'a*, a short-necked Chinese lute, which he would play occasionally in the evenings. Once again his contacts with scholars, painters and wood-carvers relating to his books and their layouts intensified. An old Chinese friend from his first Japanese period, Sun, picked up the thread of working with him on Chinese texts and calligraphy. And then:

> 17-2-1951: Half-past one in the morning drove S.F. to Seibo Hospital.

> 28-2-1951: Pauline born in Seibo Hospital, 8¾ pounds. Visited the hospital with Wimpie at 8 o'clock, saw S.F. and baby. Lunch at home with Pieter.
> When I sped in my car to the hospital through the dark streets, the headlamps caught the glitter of a gold-lacquered Chinese Buddha in the shop-window of a curio-shop. I stopped and had a look at it, and found it a very beautiful statue. S.F. considered this a good omen, so next day I bought it and it still adorns my library.

Robert was again suffering from serious stomach complaints, and walking had become painful, so bad that he even had radiation therapy for his foot. But the single-minded scholar spared neither himself nor his family and continued to devote himself entirely to his work. Hence, despite everything, he somehow managed to summon up the energy to plunge into a round of increasingly boundless cultural activity.

In July 1951, he received a telegram advising of his imminent transfer to New Delhi as Counsellor. As the first stage of the relocation, after the household had been packed up and all the farewell dinners attended, the family embarked on the *Sangola* in Yokohama on 12 December. Even though Etsuko had scarcely rated a mention in the pocket diaries in 1951, she came on board to say good-bye:

> 2-12-1951: [...] Hosono, Versteegh, Wiersum and Paddy O'Neil came aboard. The Ambassador and Lewe came to say good-bye.

Dinner on board. At 9 o'clock Jongejansen and Etsuko came to say their farewells.

The Van Guliks disembarked in Hong Kong. They moved into the Miramar Hotel in Kowloon, 'where the Barkmans have also just arrived on the *Tjiluwah*'. Of this period Carl Barkman recalls:

'We had just been transferred here from Moscow, and there was a joyful reunion with our former Chungking friends. Robert often drove with me to the consulate-general for long discussions; he also typed large sections of his new Chinese detective novel there. A few times I drove the family around all sorts of places of interest in Hong Kong and the New Territories, some of which we were discovering ourselves for the first time. When we moved into our flat, they came there for afternoon tea; besides this, we also visited antique shops and Chinese scholars. My post in Hong Kong was consul for political affairs. The consul-general was Dr K.E. (Kai) van der Mandele, who gave a dinner at which, among the other guests, the Van Guliks and we met the Chinese communist dissident, the famous general Chang Kuo-t'ao. He had been one of the founders of the Chinese Communist party but in 1935 had lost out to Mao Tse-tung in the struggle for the leadership and three years later had transferred his loyalty to the nationalists. Chang spoke at length on these matters from his own personal experience. He confirmed that Stalin had never trusted Mao and that the Russians thought Chou En-lai a much more trustworthy, more stable leader.

One unforgettable excursion which included the entire Van Gulik family, all the Van der Mandeles, ourselves and our children and a colleague, Hagenaar and his son Robert, took place on a Sunday in January 1952. We went to the *Ch'ing-shan-sze* Monastery on Castle Peak in the New Territories, where we viewed the temple and enjoyed a delicious vegetarian lunch. The scenery was splendid, the temple impressive and Robert the most erudite and wittiest guide anybody could ever want.'

[In Hong Kong] we passed three delightful weeks (said Van Gulik himself), meeting many old Chinese friends from Chungking, and making new ones, and also ransacking book-shops and curio-dealers. Memorable were gatherings with lute-players and protracted Chinese dinners with writers, painters and calligraphers. I also delivered a few lectures there.

A curious occurrence was that S.F. and I, while trying to locate a friend's house in the back streets of Kowloon, came upon a very small shrine dedicated to the famous ancient master-detective of the Sung period, Pao Kung; on a side-altar stood a small statue of Judge Dee! We burned some incense there, and my wife claims that then there was established a *yüan* [緣], a "mystic bond" between the old judge and me; subsequent events would seem to prove that she was right!

On 16 January 1952 the Van Guliks embarked on a cargo ship, the *Sirdhana*, for the voyage to Calcutta via Singapore, Penang and Rangoon. The entries in his pocket diaries reveal that in each of these places Robert looked up his Dutch diplomatic colleagues but especially sought out a large number of Chinese scholars, art connoisseurs and antique dealers.

The Van Guliks particularly enjoyed the few days they spent on Penang, '...a beautiful island, a paradisal corner, where China and S.E. Asia have blended in harmony'. Robert writes that one very hot day they made a trip to the famous Buddhist Temple of the Supreme Joy, *Chi-lo-sze* (*Air Hitam* in Malay). They clambered up the many steps to the top, Shih-fang with her young sons Willem and Pieter, while he carried Pauline on his shoulders.

Arrived in the main temple, we burned incense, and S.F. maintains that thus there was established a *yüan* between this island and us. We did indeed come back there ten years later!

Of course, when they were in Rangoon they simply had to visit the Buddhist holy site, the *Shwe Dagon* Pagoda, where they had an interesting conversation with the monks.

Shih-fang's family was Buddhist, but 'in the Chinese fashion', that is to say it had become intermingled with all sorts of other elements. It has been said that Robert believed 'a little' in Buddhism. He personally tended to give somewhat evasive answers to this question. If one had to stick a label on him, one would have to put 'Zen' on it, he once remarked. Apparently he was attracted to the mysticism and intellectual exercises in Zen. He was not one for interminable meditation sessions or for prayers. Later he was to refer to himself as, '...pre-Council of Nicaea Christian'.

But he was also fascinated by Tantric Buddhism and Taoism, as well as in the hexagrams of the *Book of Changes*, the *I-ching*. In fact, he wanted to know everything, understand everything, in as far as it lay within his power to do so.

Chapter 11

INDIA
1952-1953

After a brief ten-day stop in Calcutta, where they visited antiquarian bookshops—Robert will also undoubtedly have taken a few Urdu lessons and worked on a detective novel at night—the Van Guliks arrived in New Delhi by train on 17 February.

> I had visited India in 1942, 1943 and 1946, so this was the fourth time; it was a great disappointment. Independent India was groping for the proper attitude, and not necessarily succeeding too well. Among the government officials in N. Delhi, especially among those of External Affairs, one met many solid and cultured misfits; when one tried to talk to them about Indian culture, they would look superior and ask 'How is your golf nowadays?', and when one spoke about golf, they would look even more superior and say, 'You Westerners think only of sports'.
>
> All the best Indian scholars and artists shunned New Delhi. One had to go to Bernares, Madras, Calcutta etc. to meet them. I was especially irritated by their patronizing criticism of the Netherlands policies in Indonesia, and our 'colonial' attitude—subjects about which they possessed very little real knowledge.

Worst of all Van Gulik found the work at legation uncongenial because he and his chief, Ambassador Winkelman, did not see eye to eye. The gulf between the way they lived their lives and their ideas was so wide as to be unbridgeable. Winkelman was the scion of a Roman Catholic merchant family and was first and foremost a businessman. He had not been educated beyond a commercial college but, as the representative of a Dutch tobacco firm, he had fulfilled the role of honorary consul for many years. This experience had made him not unfamiliar with a number of aspects of the work of the foreign service. In the eyes of this ambassador, who advocated fairly strict ethical norms, Van Gulik was a cuckoo in the nest, imbued with divergent ideas about what was *comme il faut*, which was a closed book to him. Furthermore, Winkelman was in the habit of personally penning extensive political and economic reports about India (the texts, in bad Dutch, interlarded with English, were corrected by his secretary), an occupation which did little to encourage Counsellor Van Gulik to do much in this field himself.

'Winkelman was utterly devoid of culture, and adored the Indians, so therefore we had many heated quarrels about policy', Robert noted. A story which did the rounds was that on one occasion he had said to the ambassador that there could not be two captains on one ship.

Whatever the situation, Van Gulik did manage to organize an official trip to the Netherlands, allowing him to escape Delhi for almost a month. On 21 September 1952, he flew to the Netherlands where he succeeded in cramming an unimaginable number of activities into a few weeks. In The Hague he held consultations about appointments to the consular posts in India, finances (including his own) and matters of policy. No doubt, he will also have taken the opportunity to vent his spleen about Ambassador Winkelman in the right places. A short time thereafter the latter was replaced—coincidence?

In The Hague, Leiden and Amsterdam he met up with a large number of old friends and frequently played billiards with his brothers Wim and Ben. He played yet more billiards with his father and uncle in *Severen*, the old family house. In Nijmegen he dropped in to both the old and the new grammar school. He visited libraries, institutes, scholars and publishers, with whom he discussed his books. In the evening, he often dined on Chinese or Indonesian food with friends and then went on to a nightclub to take in a show and to dance. One such club was *Charlotte Chérie* in the Lange Houtstraat in The Hague. Occasionally he went to *Pension Meyer*, now 'with Lenie', now with 'Loekie' or 'Hilly'.

The jottings in his pocket diary show that even before his left for the Netherlands, Van Gulik had been suffering 'severe bouts of abdominal pain'; later they were to recur. Apparently these attacks gave him no trouble at all in the Netherlands, although he did suffer from back ache, as well as having trouble with a knee and a foot, alongside some other minor ailments which he did not allow to curb his irrepressible energy.

> 9-10-1952: The ministry in the morning, dropped in on Wim and talked about a doctor in connection with my back ache, 12.30 to the Witte [gentlemen's club], lunch in Harrison, 4-5 [Publisher] Nijhoff showed book, 6.30 Terwisscha and [Arthur] Jansen came [civil

servants in Ministry of Foreign Affairs], dined together in Royal, afterwards *'t Jagertje, Charlotte Chérie, Plaza* and *Savoy*.

On 21 October he was back in India where he energetically resumed his busy routine, more of which was spent on cultural activities and socializing than on office work. Naturally the Lenies and Hillys were, almost, a thing of the past. He devoted himself to his hobbies and his family; he undertook numerous excursions with his wife and children.

Nevertheless, his work at the embassy, working under an ambassador with whom he could not see eye to eye often made him irritable. By and large he was a man with a good external command of himself, but every so often he could erupt in a burst of pretty bad temper. His chauffeur, Abdul, had a small accident with the Chevrolet and Van Gulik dismissed him on the spot. However, no later than the next day, he noted in his diary: 'Abdul re-employed'.

He found Professor Chang Li-chai willing to help him with the translation of his *Chinese Maze Murders* into Chinese. Robert had once again gone about this in his usual fashion: he visited several professors at the university, on a few occasions had invited those with whom he thought might be able to improve his work to dine with him in a restaurant, built up a friendship with them and then, and only then, asked them to help him with this work. There were two Indians to assist him with his book, *Siddham*, about Sanskrit studies in China and Japan and the way the writing of Sanskrit evolved there (a topic which they had actually suggested to him) and Chang Li-chai, who frequently ate a Chinese meal at the Van Guliks with his wife and three daughters, for the translation of his Judge Dee novel.

The situation [at the embassy in Delhi] improved when [in February 1953] we got a new ambassador, Baron Floris van Pallandt, a career-diplomat, expert on French literature and modern art.

Our private life was rather pleasant. We occupied the large councillor residence in part of the Chancery, Ratendone Road 4, and there I housed my library which, during the three years in Japan, had waxed to over three thousand items. My best friend became Hilary Waddington, the only Briton retained in the Indian Archaeological Service; he was also in charge of finances, and even the Indian government realized that for that job one needed a completely honest man! Later they got rid of him in a disgraceful manner. Together with Hilary I visited many archaeological sites, and he taught me a great deal about the technique of "digging up the past". He was a voracious reader of detective-stories, and liked the manuscripts of my Bell and Maze Murders. When I had written the third, *The Chinese Lake Murders*, in Delhi, Hilary read it chapter by chapter, and drew the picture to the flower-boat for the end-papers.

Pl. 18. In his library in New Delhi.

To people who were unacquainted with him, Robert's great friend Hilary Waddington gave the impression of being a rather eccentric intellectual. He was a bachelor in his forties, who could both behave and express himself in an extremely unconventional manner. Once during a dinner with Ambassador Van Pallandt, who was a man of imperturbable savoir-faire, he recounted such indelicate stories that the former reprimanded him: 'Mr Waddington, I forbid you to say any more on this subject.'

I also had very pleasant and instructive association with Indian Sanskrit scholars [among them Professor Raghu Vira and Dr Lokesh Chandra], and on their request wrote my book *Siddham,* on the history of Sanskrit studies in China and Japan. I made also Tibetan friends and enlarged my knowledge of Lamaism.

The greatest attraction the *Siddham* script held for Van Gulik was the calligraphic possibilities it offered. Although this aspect had been neglected in India, Buddhist monks in China and Japan developed it to a high degree. Its popularity in these countries had grown with the rise of Tantric Buddhism: *Mantrayāna*, the esoteric 'School of the True Word' (*mantra*: magical formula, *yāna*: the spiritual struggle to achieve the eternal and indestructible). The central tenet of this doctrine is that the highest ecstasy of unification with the deity by the combined realization of *karunā* (all-pervasive mercy) and *sunyatā* (comprehension of emptiness) can be achieved by the believer. Two fundamentally different methods could be employed to attain this unification: by meditation, or, physically, by mystic sexual union with a female partner.

Tantrism reached its zenith in China during the Tang dynasty (618-907 CE). The colourful tantric pantheon, the complicated amulets and magical spells, written in the intriguing Siddham script, the splendid ceremonies performed by priests in magnificent robes, heightened by the chanting of magical Sanskrit texts—all of these elements, Van Gulik wrote, had won Tantrism its own place in the opulent life of the Tang court. Its popularity had extended to ordinary people because its introduction of elaborate burial rituals, the reading of masses for the dead and séances for the exorcism of evil spirits.

Fig. 9: 'Seed letters', calligraphy with a wooden pen written by the Japanese monk Cho-zen (17th century), illustrating the essence of a deity or sutra, in this case the Heart Sutra, one of the most beautiful and best-known sutras in Buddhism. From, *Siddham*, 1953.

Long before the advent of Buddhism, the Chinese had become accustomed to Taoist magical formulas. They were so steeped in them that they believed such a formula could only be efficacious if it were written correctly. Consequently, after approximately 600 CE, the Siddham script was often employed for the writing of Tantric magical formulas and amulets. In this study, Van Gulik devotes a great deal of attention to its calligraphic aspects.

However, he does not restrict his study to this aspect but ventures into a wider field. For instance, he poses the question of how it was possible that at a certain time in China, which considered itself the centre of the world and the only civilized culture, a foreign religion like Buddhism, whose doctrines diverged so widely from the Chinese way of thinking, was able to exert an influence on almost all the facets of Chinese culture. One important factor was that perhaps the Indian monks who came to China distanced themselves from the land of their birth and did not introduce any alien political ideas. Buddhism underwent a process of sinification and was quickly accepted by the Chinese as part of their tradition and civilization. This explains why, with the exception of a few famous Chinese pilgrims such as Fa-hsien, Hsüan-tsang and I-ching, the Chinese exhibited very little interest in India, not even in the language of the holy books. Knowledge of the Sanskrit script was considered enough in itself; they identified it with the language. Nevertheless, the study of that script and knowledge of Sanskrit phonetics were important not only to Chinese Buddhism but also to Chinese philology. It laid the foundations for to the development of a system for the compilation of Chinese dictionaries on the basis of phonetic principles. One of its enduring consequences has been that right up to the present day the reconstruction of the pronunciation of classical Chinese is facilitated by it.

In his study, Van Gulik points out that the work carried out down the centuries in the field of the Siddham script by Chinese and Japanese monks should be measured by more than simply historical and epigraphical yardsticks. He goes on:

> Anyone who has had the opportunity to assist at Shin-gon [Doctrine of the True Word] ceremonies which to this day are still being conducted regularly in Japanese temples and monasteries, and who has seen the magic flames of the Homa-fire [offering to the gods of pure butter cast into the sacred flames] rise higher from the altar as the *mantra* and *dhāraṇī* [mystic syllables such as *om*] are being recited with ever-increasing intensity—he will probably share my view that here we approach a borderland, as yet only dimly perceived, and the horizon of which lies beyond this apperception of the logical mind.

The Mantra-śāstra [treatise about mantras] is still fully alive in Japan. But, as was pointed out above, it would be rash to assume that this esoteric knowledge is really completely extinct in

China. There the Sect of the True Word has long ceased to exist. But does not its essence hover still in the Buddhist temples and monasteries that are scattered over China's vast territory, both in the mountainous country-side and in the crowded cities—an essence that manifests itself every time and in every place where the powerful Mahā-mantra is intoned by the monks? Its echo will linger on forever, for once enounced its sound will mingle with the seating crowds in their perplexity, as it merges also with the mists drifting in the eternal serenity of distant mountain vales. Thus the Mantra stands for all-pervading Compassion—without which everything is Emptiness.[18]

Taoist magic also continued to exert its fascination on him. In China he had become acquainted with the 'mango trick'. Subsequently he devoted an article to it which was published in 1954 (*Transactions of the Asiatic Society of Japan*, Third Series, vol. III). A mango stone is planted in the ground by a magician who then covers the spot with a cloth and mutters some spells. When he finally takes away the cloth, his audience sees a shoot appearing. Then the magicians re-covers it and mumbles some more incantations. When he removes the cloth again, a mango sapling is revealed. He repeats the operation several times, and finally a small mango tree bearing ripe mangos appears before the eyes of amazed spectators.

The year 1952 ended for the Van Guliks with an important event in their private life:

On December 5, 1952, our fourth child was born whom we called Thomas Mathijs, two old names of the family. He was a sturdy boy of 8½ pounds, but in his first year much given to crying in the night. I carried him around in the house but he would only stop crying when I took him to my library; there he would pat the books with his hands, and laugh happily. S.F. took this as an auspicious omen: Thomas would in due course become a scholar (he is twelve now, and indeed seems to be the only one of our children whose intelligence is definitely above average) [he became a surgeon]. I may add that in China a baby is shown a tray on which is a writing brush, a small sword, and a piece of silver; the child's future is derived from the object he touches first, a scholar-official, a military official, or a merchant.

---

18   R.H. van Gulik: *Siddham: An Essay on the History of Sanskrit Studies in China and Japan*. Delhi, The Jayyed Press, 1980, pp. 138-139.

Pl. 19. Family photo in New Delhi, 1952/1953.

In fact, Robert was just as superstitious as his wife. His thought processes were a curious mixture of the mystical and level-headed logic, a product of both East and West. In both worlds he moved in the most heterogeneous circles. Perhaps the reason was that he was such an elusive figure himself. He always seemed enveloped in an air of mystery. He did nothing to dispel this; in fact it seems that he went out of his way to encourage it. Occasionally the Van Guliks would consult a clairvoyant, and now it appears likely that the omen relating to Thomas' future perhaps prompted such a visit:

> 1-1-1953: 5-6 Srivastava [an Indian scholar who was often in Robert's company] and the soothsayer came to talk.

In all the countries that the Van Gulik's visited, they had intensive contact with the local Chinese community. In India it was not large but it was cultured.

> There were two or three refugee Chinese scholars in Delhi, so Chinese contacts were not lacking all together. At one of our Chinese gatherings I put on my Chinese dress I often used to wear in Chungking (for western clothes were absolutely unobtainable there, and those one had one had to save for formal occasions), as shown in the picture here. [Robert delighted in wearing Chinese clothes

and his 'excuse' for doing so is not only unnecessary, but unfounded. From Chungking you could order everything in Calcutta].

Van Gulik spent the whole of the month of June 1953 on furlough in the Netherlands. This time it was to have his eyes examined by a good specialist in Amsterdam, after cataracts had been diagnosed in Delhi. His foot was also X-rayed and he was prescribed an arch support. Apart from these medical interludes, his furlough passed just as pleasurably as the previous one, crammed with meetings and discussions, books, billiards, drinks and dinners, although he went to

Pl. 20. The Van Guliks in Chinese attire, New Delhi, 1952/1953.

bed earlier more frequently. On 3 July he was back in Delhi and he travelled on to the cooler climes of Mussoorie, where his family spent the summer and his two elder sons attended the Sacred Heart boarding school. It was nearly a day's journey, first by car and then into the mountains in a palanquin with bearers.

> All in all S.F and I were glad when our term in India came to an early close, although it was for a rather unexpected reason: I got trouble with my eyesight, and it was found that I was suffering from a premature cataract. One has to wait a couple of years until a cataract has ripened, then it is cured by the removal of the lens. Pending the operation, however, one has to be under medical supervision, but complications occur. Since medical facilities in India were not of the best, the F.O. appointed me Director of African and Middle-Eastern Affairs, in the Ministry in The Hague. The post was not chosen at random: they remembered my work in Africa, and thought that this gave me the necessary background. Since the Directorships are scheduled to last three years, that would give me ample time for having both my eyes fixed.
> We left Bombay on the S.S. *Asia* on September 9th 1953, landed in Genoa, and went by train to Holland.

Chapter 12

SECOND PERIOD IN THE NETHERLANDS 1953-1956

[Initially] we had to rent a furnished house in The Hague, for empty houses were not to be had, and anyway we would have needed an extremely large one for housing my library and art-collection; all that remained in storage.

It was quite nice to be in Holland now for a longer period, and I liked my work in the F.O. very much; I had *i.a.* one good expert in Arabic and Islamic affairs on my staff [Dr Graf] and from him I learned a tremendous lot. I also had private lessons in Arabic colloquial, and did much reading up on Arabic literature, *i.a.* the Koran and the Arabian Nights in Burton's unexpurgated translation. My experiences in Africa and Egypt, brief though they had been, now came in very useful. It was also an advantage to become familiar with the F.O. routine, and to learn how they viewed the work in the Embassies abroad.

In due course the cataract was successfully removed from my left eye, and one year later that of the right. S.F. liked our stay in Holland, for now she had real opportunities for improving her Dutch, and becoming acquainted with life in Holland and all its problems—foremost among those that of servants!

In the Netherlands Van Gulik also remained true to himself. He often visited his club (the Witte), the *Haagse Kunstkring* (The Hague Art Circle), the Pulchri Studio (an organization of artists) and the *Tong Tong*, the club for old Indies hands. Friends were many and there was conviviality a-plenty.

He also had more time for his family in this period.

30-9-1953: In the morning with S.F. and 2 sons to V&D [a department store], bought a bicycle for Wimpie and a monkey for Pietje, lunch with S.F. in a hotel, birthday cake for Wimpie with 9 candles.

10-10-1953: In the morning Thomas had pus in his ear, doctor not at home. Did shopping, lunch at home, 3 o'clock Dr O. arrived and diagnosed a middle ear infection for which prescribed sulpha drops. Dinner at home, read detective novels in the evening.

On 12 October as he was selecting scrolls to be shown in an exhibition in Amsterdam, busy helping to set up the house and purchasing a car (Thomas was sick and Pauline had to remain in bed with a high temperature), news came that Robert's father had been admitted to the hospital in Nijmegen, and half an hour later that he had died. Robert was very attached to his father, whom he greatly admired and for whom he had enormous respect, therefore his passing was a grievous loss. The family home *Severen* in Beek near Nijmegen, where Robert and later Shih-fang had spent so many happy hours, was no longer the house it had been, even though Uncle Piet still continued to live there. Robert's mother, who had been even more an ally than his father, had died at the beginning of the war while Robert was posted in the Far East.

Willem and Pieter went to the Frederik Hendrik School, where they needed extra coaching because, like most children of diplomats, they had attended a number of schools, each with its own curriculum; none of them a Dutch one. The capacity to adapt that is expected of such children is tremendous; often they feel that they are strangers in their own country and have difficulty in making friends. Willem's teacher, Miss Hazelnoot, seated him the front row and, as he spoke no Dutch, she repeated everything for him in English. However, he learned Dutch pretty quickly and after a few months was able to express himself in the language. Prior to this English had been the language spoken at home, or Chinese whenever his parents needed to discuss something that they did not want him to know, without realizing that in the meantime he had managed to understand Chinese reasonably well.

Father Robert was once again assailed by bouts of stomach pain. He consulted a doctor about the problem and, once again, was advised to rest and prescribed a diet. Consequently, he began to take things more quietly.

> 19-11-1953: Lunch at home, 3 o'clock went into town with S.F., visited the Maurits House [an art museum]. Took tea in the Ho-p'ing Restaurant, back home via the shops.

> 20-11-1953: Worked at home in the morning. Lunch at home, 3 o'clock with S.F. to [brother] Ben, on my own to Aunt Em for her birthday afternoon tea. After that with Ben and S.F. to Garuda

[Indonesian restaurant]. I went on alone to [Institute of] Social Studies, spoke to George Dèb [who gave him Arabic lessons]. Dinner at home. Worked on carving [woodblocks] in the evening.

4-12-1953: In the morning bought Saint Nicholas presents with Pauline. Lunch at home. Attended Saint Nicholas party at school with Willem and Pieter.

In the company of Shih-fang he visited Leiden in preparation for an exhibition of Chinese art (including his collection of scroll paintings) at the National Museum of Ethnology, and attended the viewing days of art auctions. They also went to the zoo in Wassenaar with the children or to Meyendel, a recreation area in the Wassenaar dunes, and the beaches at Scheveningen or Kijkduin. They might visit the Panorama Mesdag (a panoramic painting of Scheveningen in the late nineteenth century) or eat *poffertjes* (a Dutch treat, like a light pancake) on the Malieveld.

24-12-1953: 1 o'clock picked up Ben for lunch, decorated the Christmas tree with him and the children. Dinner at home, afterwards turned on the Christmas tree lights. Worked in the evening.

28-12-1953: 9 o'clock to the bank, withdrew money, 10 o'clock to Amsterdam with Wimpie. Visited the Rijksmuseum and lunched there.

Besides these cultural excursions, in the Netherlands he again also worked on Judge Dee and Chinese crime fiction:

In searching for plots for my three Judge Dee-novels (*Bell*, *Maze*, and *Lake* Murders) I had been consulting old Chinese crime-literature and thus found the *T'ang-yin pi-shih* [Parallel Cases from under the Pear Tree], a 13th century handbook of jurisprudence and crime-detection. Since my library was in storage, I could not engage upon complicated sinological research; as this text could be handled without consulting other sources, I chose it as main subject for my studies; the book was published in 1956.

In the meantime foreign friends had read the typescripts of my three novels, and told me they thought there could be interest in these new type detective stories also among broader circles of Western readers. I showed *The Chinese Maze Murders* to a few Dutch publishers and W. van Hoeve Ltd. accepted it for publication, in English. Favourable press reviews attracted the attention of the

London publisher Michael Joseph Ltd., and they decided to publish
The Chinese Bell Murders as an experiment.

While Van Gulik continued to keep up a constant stream of
cultural and social activities alongside his work at the ministry, his
stomach began to play up again. He spent the period from 20 January
to 9 February 1954 in the Prinsengracht Hospital in Amsterdam
where he underwent abdominal surgery. It was typical of him that
on the day he was discharged he did not go straight home: 'taken to
The Hague in a hire car via the antiquarian bookseller Huizenga'.

He could work quickly and hence could deal expeditiously with
his daily round of tasks (policy and practical matters). Meetings at
and about the various institutions with which he was connected
consumed much more of his time, but whenever he had to visit
either the Africa Institute or the Oriental Institute in Leiden, he
always made sure to link this up with talks with Chinese scholars
at the Sinological Institute, or when he called in on the Islam Room
in the Institute for the Tropics in Amsterdam, he would drop in on
Jaap Kunst for a chat about gamelan music and to cast his eye over
the collection of *wayang* puppets. He was trustee of a study centre
and a member of the Africa Commission chaired by Professor Jan
Donner. As a member of the Arabic and African Divisions for this
broadcasting station, he had regular contact with Hendrik van den
Broek of the *Wereldomroep* (Radio World Service). As well as these
activities, he gave Chinese language lectures to one group of Leiden
students and taught another group calligraphy. Also in Leiden, he
gave a lecture about *Taal en Techniek van het Chinees Penseel* (Language
and Technique of the Chinese Brush) and organized an exhibition of
Chinese woodcuts. Besides all this, he delivered a lecture about the
Middle East to the Naval Staff.

In March 1955, he spent a fascinating, culture-packed fortnight
in Rome visiting his friend and colleague Dr H.N. Boon who
was ambassador there. The purpose of this visit was to mount
an exhibition and give a talk about the art of Chinese painting, in
Italian, at the invitation of the famous Tibetan scholar Professor
Guiseppe Tucci, whom he had met in Delhi. Interspersing a whole
host of activities—visiting private art collections, discussions with
Orientalists, sightseeing—were the customary dinners, meals in
Chinese restaurants and many cups of coffee at the El Greco.

Van Gulik had prepared his lecture meticulously. On one occasion
he had been surprised in his office at Foreign Affairs attempting

to fix a roll of white shelf-paper to the door with drawing pins. He explained that in roughly four weeks' time he was to present a lecture about the art of Chinese painting and calligraphy in Rome and hence wanted to practise, among other subjects, a Buddha in a circle in one single brush-stroke. Because he was to hold the lecture in Italian, he was also assiduously learning the language and he had rung the Italian ambassador to send him someone—preferably a charming lady—to help him perfect it. He will have spoke the Italian with a Dutch accent, because even his English, which he wrote perfectly, was coloured by an unmistakable Dutch accent. His wife also confirmed that, although he read and wrote Chinese (not to mention the archaic forms of Chinese) far better than she herself did, every so often he had difficulty with the tonality of spoken Chinese, even though he refused to admit this.

Under Van Gulik's leadership, the Africa and Middle Eastern Section was less turbulent than it was to become in later years. With the exception of the budget negotiations, it seldom had to field parliamentary questions, and when it did these were principally to do with either the relationship between Israel and the Arab states or apartheid. The chief function of the section was to supply the departmental leadership with information about this region. Nevertheless, this period was not without its moments: when Prime Minister Muhammad Mossaddegh nationalized Iranian oil, the Algerian War, the Suez Crisis and the first steps in the decolonization of Africa. The last generated a string of regular proposals to do with the recognition of new African countries. These proposals were invariably authorized by the Council of Ministers with the note that the Minister of Finance had remarked that this recognition must not cost any money.

As Van Gulik, who was blessed with an above an average in-telligence and memory, required no more than a few hours per day to handle his work, he was free to spend the rest of his time doing research and writing his publications or checking galley proofs. He worked according to a strict timetable, which commenced at 7 o'clock in the morning with chopping the kindling to set the fire, followed by breakfast and taking the children to school, after which he went to the office, and later worked on his Judge Dee books until 11 o'clock in the evening. Thereafter, between 11 and 1 in the morning he could relax by reading a detective story.

His favourite member of staff was Bob (A.H.) Croin, LLB., who enjoyed himself tremendously during the two years in which he worked for Van Gulik. He had the greatest admiration for this 'fascinating personality', who could be pretty extreme in his personal relationships with others. If he liked somebody, that person could do no wrong; on the other hand when he disliked somebody, he had no hesitation in crucifying them. For reasons he found difficult to explain, as the only things they had in common were a youth spent in the Netherlands Indies and a partiality for English-language detective novels, spiced up perhaps by a taste for political analysis, Croin apparently fell into the first category. He could always drop in on him for whatever reason, and they enjoyed endless conversations about books, graphology, hieroglyphics, Chinese painting, calligraphy and so on.

During the midday break they used to take a short stroll through the town, munching a bread-roll or some other snack, looking at books, both new publications and antiquarian volumes. After the debates on the budget in the States-General, which usually went on until deep into the night, they were in the habit of drinking a beer or two in one of the night clubs in the Lange Houtstraat. On one of these occasions Van Gulik was shocked when two attractive young ladies presented an act which turned out to have a lesbian theme.

His humour could be malicious. Once during the lunch-break, they happened to meet an impeccably dressed civil servant from their department (Homburg hat, glacé kid gloves) on the front steps of the ministry. 'Ha', said Van Gulik, 'Croin and I are going to have a bite to eat, would you like to join us?' 'How delightful', said the person concerned, who probably had visions of an expensive restaurant. However, to his dismay, Van Gulik shot to an adjacent automatic food dispenser and asked whether he would prefer a ball of fried rice or a small rissole: 'You had better take your gloves off.'

On another occasion they happened to be walking along Spui Street where a cinema was advertising *Casablanca*. 'This falls within our field of expertise,' said Van Gulik, 'so we should see it'. They only arrived back at the Ministry around half-past four.

He was such a forceful character that everyone in the department, from the highest to the lowest, listened to him. Sometimes he could be very rude. Once Croin had thought up a fairly complex proposal but had not yet committed it to paper. When Van Gulik asked him what he was doing, it took him more than a quarter of an hour to explain. He added that he was about to write it down. 'Don't bother', said Van Gulik and was immediately on the phone to the secretary-general: 'Croin and I have cooked up a little plan.

May we come along?' Permission granted, Van Gulik proceeded to give a summary of the plan in three minutes, so succinctly and persuasively that the secretary-general had to give his consent. Hence his staff member could have only 'enormous admiration for this man'.

At the time everybody knew that Van Gulik always left a coat and a hat hanging on his hat-stand in order to give the impression that he was in the building. He also did this when he was playing billiards in his club, the Witte, situated diagonally opposite across Plein from the Ministry. If anybody enquired for him, his secretary were instructed to say he was with the minister. Should the minister be looking for him, the usher had orders to apprise him of this in 'the Witte'. The upshot was that in the department he acquired the reputation of being lazy, unconventional, witty and exceptionally casual, apparently refusing to take matters seriously.

Despite his frequent absences, he made sure that he always attended the policy meetings with the secretary-general. He was also given to unleashing a burst of his malicious humour and his love of teasing during these meetings. When one of the directors, whose nickname was 'The Rabbit' on account of his protruding upper front teeth, failed to arrive and kept everyone waiting for him, Van Gulik sat reading the paper. After a while, he lowered it and said mournfully with a very serious face: 'Myxomatosis...'.

On yet another occasion, a colleague happened to be delivering an exceptionally exhaustive, long-winded, tedious exposition. As he paused in the middle of his argument, Van Gulik suddenly loudly addressed the chairman saying: 'I say, are you sporting a moustache at the moment?' This completely discomposed his serious fellow director-general.

Nevertheless, people also recall his extremely lucid, brilliant lectures on the subjects which caught his imagination, including one about the cultural differences between Chinese, Japanese and Indian civilizations, which he delivered in the main auditorium of the Ministry.

During this Dutch period he began to spend more time at home, went less frequently on his own and included his wife in everything.

31-12-1954: stayed up with S.F and let off fireworks.

29-8-1955: 9-10 to Ministry, then picked up S.F. at home, together went to Poelgeest Castle in Leiden, where [there was] a Sinological Congress. Heard the lecture by Cheng Te-kun and lunch. [Went to] the Beukenhof [Restaurant] with S.F and Mrs Franke [wife of the German sinologist Herbert Franke], afterwards visited the Burcht [reconstructed ruin of a motte and bailey castle] in Leiden and attended reception in the auditorium [of the university], spoke to Hofstee.

Robert encouraged Shih-fang to take dancing lessons and study English and the artist, Jan Willem Maronier, painted her portrait on 18 March 1956. He took French lessons from the crammer Gerritsen, who had coached many students for their attaché examination. His interest will certainly not have been in the spoken language, but he will have wanted to polish his 'diplomatic' French (texts of treaties and memoranda and the like) about which Gerritsen was extremely well versed.

> 30-4-1956: 10.30 into town with S.F., Pauline and Thomas, tried on uniform [he knew that he would shortly need an ambassador's costume in Beirut; had formerly been the uniform of Ambassador [Van] Troostenburg de Bruyn which he had been able to purchase second-hand]. Went to the fun fair and afterwards to Meer en Bos [Lake and Wood], where ate pancakes for lunch, 3 o'clock home, 4 o'clock I [went] to throat specialist Buysse, dinner at home.

> 4-5-1956: 8 o'clock to Leentje [de Vries-] van der Hoeven, for farewell evening [being held] for Chinese calligraphy students [Wil] de Vries, [Roland] Van den Berg, [Jan] de Jong, [Michele] Ondei, Gan [Tjian-tek], [Erik] Zürcher and Miss [Kitty] Granpré-Molière.

In May 1956 Robert and Shih-fang spent a week in Paris. Once again it is remarkable how thoroughly he prepared for such a trip and how meticulously everything slotted together. They paid a visit to both the Dutch and Chinese ambassadors, almost every day took a *Paris-Tourisme* organized bus tour around Paris and its environs and went to museums to ensure that Shih-fang saw all the important landmarks, as well as finding the time to meet the whole top echelons of French sinology.

'He could be difficult about his posting', recalled the incumbent secretary-general Van Tuyll, 'and he was highly displeased with his appointment to Lebanon, a post which he considered beneath his dignity.'

In May the Van Guliks paid a round of farewell visits in The Hague, Leiden and Nijmegen, and endured the customary round of dinners, lunches and cocktail parties given on the eve of leaving for a posting. On 31 May Van Gulik went to Soestdijk Palace, where he was sworn in as ambassador by Her Majesty Queen Juliana.

They left for Marseilles via Paris on 6 June. In Marseilles they embarked on the *Marseillaise*, which arrived in Beirut on 12 June.

Chapter 13

MINISTER IN THE MIDDLE EAST
1956-1959

We had a fine voyage across the Mediterranean, and when I stood at the railing with S.F., Pauline and Thomas (Willem and Pieter we had put in the Quaker Boarding School in Holland), we got a most favourable impression of St. George's Bay and the city of Beirut, basking in the sun. This Mediterranean sunshine stayed with us the greater part of the three years we were in Lebanon, and we retain the most happy memories of this country of sun, sea and flowers.

Initially they took temporary lodgings in the comfortable Hotel St George close to the bay. It offered delightful opportunities for swimming (and rowing) and in the evenings they liked to sit on the terrace.

23-6-1956: Legation in the morning, paid courtesy visits to the Dean and the Japanese envoy, lunch at hotel. Rested in the afternoon, S.F. did shopping with Miss B. And the children, 5-7 took tea with S.F. on the hotel terrace, dinner in room. In the evening sat with S.F. on the terrace.

The Legation was a rather small building in an unfashionable quarter, so I had received orders to find a better place. By a stroke of good fortune I could rent the palace of the former Turkish governor of Lebanon, a beautiful building in old Turkish style, in the centre of the city, behind the palace of the President. The two wings had been separated; the British ambassador had the right and now I took the left wing. Since the building is surrounded on all sides by other houses, it is difficult to take a good picture of it. ...The place was built like a fortress (for in the old days there was occasionally trouble between the Turkish governor and the population), with walls several feet thick and many vaults underneath—the old prison; these vaults I had converted into a garage and wine cellar. [In front of this small palace were Turkish looking guards in fine military uniforms].

Pl. 21. Minister with kavass (doorman), Beirut 1956/1959.

I furnished the hall and the rooms on the right in conventional style, utilizing old Dutch paintings on loan from our Service of Monuments. The spacious left hall I made into an old style Chinese library. [Besides his desk, he installed a Chinese table and two imposingly large chairs—a sort of throne for a mandarin—made of ebony inlaid with mother-of-pearl. On one occasion the wife of a colleague with whom he was friends caught him sitting on one of the thrones, clad in his beautiful Chinese robe: 'I think I was a Chinese in a former existence', he said].

Especially during the first year, however, I had little time to study in this now so splendid *Tsun-ming-ko* (study in which 'clarity is venerated'). Besides organizing the Legation in Beirut, I had to go regularly to Damascus in Syria, to look after the Legation there [Van Gulik was accredited as envoy to both countries; in Damascus A.C Vroon was acting *chargé d'affaires*]. In the summer it was a beautiful 3 hour drive through the mountains, but in winter it took much longer.

[…] It was the first time I was fully responsible for extensive Netherlands interests, and I was determined to make a good job of it.

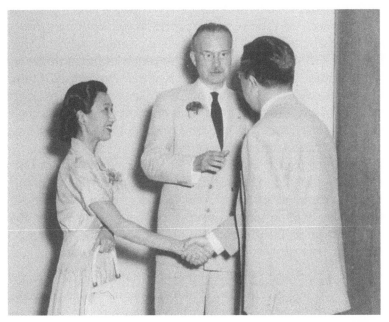

Pl. 22. The Van Guliks being welcomed at a reception in Beirut 1958.

Representatives of Dutch commercial life remembered him as an exceptionally pleasant and interesting man, highly learned and remarkably informal; not to put too fine a point on it, untidy, more the professor than the diplomat, a man who did not seem to overexert himself but was on good terms with the Dutch community; someone who devoted himself entirely to your interests when you needed him professionally.

> I traveled widely in both countries, and made also trips to neighbouring Jordan. The F.O. charged me with a special mission to the King of Saudi-Arabia, and I visited Djeddah, Ryadh, thereafter Baghdad. Other trips took me to Iskenderun in S. Turkey, and Istanbul in the north (where I had been appointed one of the Curators of the Netherlands Archeological Institute).

The only reference to the Suez Crisis, which threw the whole of the Arab—and also the Western world—into tumult, we find in Van Gulik's notes is:

3-11-1956: To a cocktail party [...]; to the chancellery picked up telegrams, deciphered them at home the whole evening.

On 29 October 1956 Israel had opened the attack on Egypt, its goal being the seizure of the Suez Canal which the Egyptian president, Nasser, had nationalized. This action was immediately followed by what was in fact a supporting British-French military intervention. However, under heavy pressure exerted by the United States, all troops were forced to withdraw. In the Arab countries, this incident, which temporarily caused a profound crisis in NATO, was seen as a huge victory for Nasser. For the next decade, the Arab world would continue to be fascinated by Nasserism.

During the Suez Crisis, Van Gulik discovered that the public took his red-white-and-blue Dutch flag for the French tricolour, and this generated an inimical attitude. Consequently he personally designed an orange flag with a silver lion rampant and arrows for his car; apparently these aroused memories of that of (Tsarist) Russia, and as a rule the car was allowed to pass freely.

From Beirut S.F. and I passed a delightful holiday in Greece, and I spent two longer holidays in Rome, staying in the Embassy there headed by an old friend, Dr H.N. Boon, who was an expert on Etruscan art. On one of these visits to Rome, the Oriental Institute [*Instituto Italiano per il Medio ed Estremo Oriente*] of the famous Tibetologist Professor Guiseppe Tucci, the contract for the publication of my large work on Chinese Art (*Chinese Pictorial Art as Viewed by the Connoisseur*) was drawn up; it was published [in Rome] in 1958, in a limited edition of 900 copies with the specimens of paper and silk. These I had made in the bombshelters of Chungking during the air raids.

What Van Gulik himself called his 'large work' was certainly no sinecure. He invested enormous amounts of time, energy and love on it. Among the topics Van Gulik explores in this 'large work' are the reasons Chinese painting only became known in the West so much later than ceramic art. He attributes this principally to the reluctance of Chinese collectors and antiques dealers to show or sell outstandingly superior scroll paintings to foreigners. Moreover, there is an immense Chinese literature about painting and calligraphy which is difficult to encompass, even for experienced scholars of Chinese, whereas that about Chinese porcelain is more limited in size and written in simpler language. Even in the 1920s, Western books about Chinese painting were still only being written by art lovers and connoisseurs with no training in Chinese studies. Only later did change begin to creep in.

In Van Gulik's opinion, this was tantamount to the neglect of an important and difficult topic of study: the experience and knowledge of traditional experts in Chinese art accumulated over the centuries. He did his best to make a contribution towards filling this gap, although he was extremely conscious of just how very much work still had to be done in this field. In his book he says little, as he remarks, about the beauty of Chinese scroll paintings and about their profound philosophical background. So much had already been written about this that he thought it would 'not be out of place to examine the art of the brush from a more technical and practical point of view'. This corresponds completely with his own thoughts on the subject which were always directed towards the 'technical, craftsman-like' aspects of art. Whenever he purchased a scroll or an antique vase, a mark or a crack did not bother him, as long as the piece was an interesting object to study, which is why his interest ran deeper than just the beauty of an *objet d'art*. It is also an explanation of why the interior of his house was less tastefully furnished than might have been expected.

Finally, in his foreword to this book, Van Gulik admits that he would not for all the world have missed both the joy and the sorrow which he had experienced in twenty years of collecting. The happy hours spent with connoisseurs and collectors of art in China, Korea and Japan and in studying favourite paintings and calligraphy, brought to mind the words of the poet Li T'ai-po, that 'besides this world there is another, not of people'. Nor indeed would it have been good had he not felt the pain which is aroused by having to relinquish beauty. 'Because', he says here, 'it is perhaps this pain which eventually will teach us resignation—a valuable lesson in this transient life.'

Commenting on this volume, Van Gulik's friend, the ambassador and scholar Chen Chih-mai, says that 'the work as usual is based entirely on Chinese and Japanese sources', a valuable work because, among other reasons, in the second part there is 'a very important chapter about the way in which forgers are able to fool even the most astute connoisseur'. But in one respect, regarding the crucial matter of determining authenticity, he does not think the book comes up to expectations. The reason for this judgment is that the book does not go into the extremely important matter of the various techniques used by different painters—the diverse sorts of linear treatment (*miao*) of the painters of life studies and the divergent sorts of brush strokes of the landscape artists to indicate (*ts'un*) the contours of rocks and hills, which are considered by Chinese and Japanese experts to be the most prominent criteria to determine the genuineness of a work. Dr Chen Chih-mai attributes this oversight to Dr Van Gulik's 'lifelong inclination to concentrate on less well known (obscure) sources, often at the expense of standard works.'

Talking of his life in Lebanon, Van Gulik continues:

> Our spacious residence was eminently suited for entertaining guests, we could seat 24 at our [large, round] table, for which S.F. had, in Damascus, a fine table-cloth woven. Besides diplomats and officials we also had there many gatherings, with Arab and Chinese scholars, and professors of the two universities in Beirut, The American University and the Catholic St Joseph University. From all these experts I learned much about Classical and Arab history, [Moreover, Van Gulik also took regular Arabic lessons] and we visited almost all the important historical sites: Baalbek, Byblos and Tyre in Lebanon; Palmyra and Aleppo in Syria, Jerusalem and Jerash in Jordan; Antalya in Turkey, and Delphi, Epidaurus etc. in Greece. I became specially interested in the Crusader castles, and visited all the important ones.
>
> Looking back upon my three years in the Middle East, I think that for my personal education this confrontation with the foundations of my own western culture, and of the Christian religion, was of decisive importance. I realized that though I had become partly "Chinese" in my thoughts and emotional life, the larger and most essential part of me was still thoroughly western. I also realized that this was as it should be, for one must remain true to oneself in order to be able to understand others. I read much on the history of the Christian creed, and decided I was neither a Protestant nor a Catholic: I preferred to consider myself a Christian from before the Council of Nicaea: for then the Christian creed became mixed with politics. Ever since I have remained a strong supporter of ecumenical ideals (aiming at greater unity of all the various Christian churches).

This ideal which occurred to Van Gulik in Beirut is all the more comprehensible when one remembers that the Christian half of the population (the other half was almost without exception Muslim) was divided up into a great many denominations: Maronites, Greek Orthodox, Greek Catholic, Armenian Orthodox, Armenian Catholic,

Protestant, Syrian Catholic, Roman Catholic, Syrian Orthodox and Chaldean Christians.

When the Van Guliks arrived in Lebanon it was a charming place, not just because of the mild climate, the natural beauty and peace which still prevailed there, but not least because Beirut was an important Arab and cosmopolitan cultural centre. As heir to a large number of successive Mediterranean civilizations, Lebanon possessed a rich heritage and its own personality. Art in all its forms flourished there. It was a land of Greek and Phoenician temples and theatres, of cedar forests and snow-topped mountains. Moreover, at the time it was the country which could boast of the highest standard of living of all the Arab countries and, with the exception of the oil sheikdoms, the highest per capita income. It was said to be a nation of journalists and bankers: apart from the many imported foreign papers, hundreds of papers and magazines were published in Beirut, in Arabic as well as in Western languages. Copious amounts of money from the Arab oil states flowed into the banks, casinos, hotels, restaurants and nightclubs of Beirut. There was an excellent selection of films (which the Van Guliks very much appreciated!) and the statistics for cinema visits were among the highest in the world.

Van Gulik's son Willem has never seen so many films in his life as he did in Beirut. His father told him that watching films was a source of inspiration for thinking up plots for the Judge Dee novels and was also useful for writing the dialogues. But: 'If my father thought that the films were poor quality, he rose resolutely to his feet and left the cinema, while we—often against our wishes—had to follow.'

The Lebanon was a republic with a parliament chosen at general elections held by secret ballot (active and passive women's suffrage since 1953). However, as in many southern countries, there was a strong linkage between the political parties and their regional or local interests, between members of parliament and their 'clients' or sponsors, and corruption was also rife. The political system was set up to maintain a delicate balance between the Christians and the Muslims. The parliamentary seats were divided up in a proportion of 6:5 between the two religions. The president of the republic was chosen in parliament by a two-thirds majority, and custom decreed that he must be a Maronite; the minster-president was Sunni Muslim, and the president of the parliament a Shiite.

Because Beirut was one of the centres of political and cultural life in the Middle East, there were frequent official visits by heads of state from neighbouring countries. Hence I met a number of interesting personages.

But most important to me and to S.F. was the beach in Beirut; we went there almost daily to swim and sunbathe. When our eldest son Willem had finished his boarding school in the Netherlands, he came to us in Beirut, where he was placed in the British Quaker School in Broumana, in the mountains. Pauline and Thomas attended the British primary school in Beirut. Now the family was practically reunited; only Pieter still remained at boarding school in the Netherlands, but he spent his holidays with us.

Van Gulik's daily diaries of the period reveal that he spent a great deal of time with his family. He also continued to be enormously active, but now often took a rest in the afternoon or went to bed earlier in the evening. Occasionally his stomach complaint played up on him in Beirut and he also had some trouble with his heart. Therefore the doctor ordered Robert to have a cardiogram and he took a break for a little while.

As did his father before him, Robert van Gulik allowed his children a large latitude of freedom; he would never make any attempt to influence their three greatest choices in life: religion, work and partner. He also respected their opinions in lesser matters. When on medical advice Pauline had to spend a year in the Netherlands, where she was sent to the Quaker School in Vilsteren near Ommen, she was very unhappy there. Worst of all were the holidays in a 'children's boarding house'. When she spent the next summer holiday in Beirut, her father asked: 'Do you want to go back to Ommen?' When she replied in the negative, he said no more nor was it ever discussed at any time afterwards. It was assumed as a matter of course that Pauline would remain with her parents in Beirut, where she attended the British school. This incident made a deep impression on her. What she also remembers as very special in her recollections is that throughout his whole life her father undertook so incredibly many activities, but was never in a hurry, took plenty of time for everything and gave no one the idea that they had to hurry up.

From these years Willem retains some of the best memories of his youth. After the boarding school in Vilsteren, his parents' decision to allow him to come to Lebanon and spend the first years of his secondary schooling there was a very welcome change.

In fact, for me personally this period meant the first conscious experience of family life, something which really took some getting used to at first. After various sojourns in boarding schools (twice in India and once in the Netherlands) and in guest families or children's boarding houses, where we spent the school holidays, initially I addressed my parents as 'Mr' and 'Mrs'! Despite all this and the fact that I was going through puberty, I never felt any rebellious tendencies towards my parents. On the contrary in fact, it was in this particular time that a special bond developed between my father and myself. I learned to know him well from close daily interaction. I stood in awe of him, sometimes with admiration, sometimes also in fear, because of the booming violence which was poured out over one's head as if from a terrifying deity when he was annoyed about something.

We did a great deal together, shared experiences and were in a manner of speaking mates with each other. Lebanon was a glorious country, prosperous, rich in natural beauty, good climate offering all the pleasures of the Mediterranean region. Not without reason was it often dubbed the Switzerland of the Middle East. For me as a youth poised on the threshold of manhood, Lebanon was a real paradise. Where in the world can you go deep-sea diving in the sea in the morning and still that same afternoon, after driving for a couple of hours, go skiing in the snow-clad mountains peaks in the middle of the cedars?

Father and I regularly visited the Sporting Club on the bay, not far from Hôtel St. Georges. We swam and rowed (actually it was canoeing on flat-bottomed, surfboard-like closed canoes with long paddles) a lot. With his height of almost two metres and his sturdily built figure, he made a great impression when clad in a bathing-costume, naturally of course among the female members of the club who tried to catch my father's attention via me.

Of course, I can recall the residence very well. The immensely large entrance hall, which had a large open fireplace and from which the drawing rooms branched off to the left and right, was completely clad with marble. Thomas had no difficulty riding around it very fast on his racing-bicycle without bumping into any piece of furniture. [It was] ideal for large receptions (it could hold 500 guests without any difficulty). I see my father standing in front of the fireplace, under the portrait of Her Majesty the Queen, as he gave a speech on the occasion of national days or, for instance, at the Saint Nicholas gathering for the children of the Dutch community in Lebanon. His speeches were always full of humour and pleased his listeners. This was also the case when the hall was used as a

Pl. 23. At the Sporting Club, Beirut 1958.

chamber of weddings held according to Dutch law. As I remember,
Father acted a number of times as marriage registrar.

For me, the Chinese library, on the left after entering this space
was the 'sacred hall'. Encircled by towering book-cases, twice a
week I would sit down on an ebony Chinese stool opposite my
father seated at his desk for Latin lessons and to be tested. No Latin
or Greek was taught at the British School in Brumana (a Quaker
school founded by the famous Kees Boeke), and as the idea was
that I should eventually attend a Dutch grammar school, in which
Latin was taught from the first year, my father took this task
upon himself. Later I profited greatly from the lessons when after
returning from Lebanon I was placed in the third class of the Jac.
P. Thijsse Lyceum in Overveen. He was remarkably patient during
the Latin lessons. It was wonderful that he usually harked back to
anecdotes from his own years in the grammar school in Nijmegen
and actually used the same teaching methods as Sormani, his Latin
teacher, a famous Latinist for whom he had enormous respect and
who had been Dr Schwarz's predecessor as headmaster.

When I accompanied my father on the many visits paid to
well-known tourist sites dating to the Roman era (Baalbek, for

instance, where I once saw a production of *Hamlet* in the middle
of the columns and the ruins of the greatest Roman temple there
under a starry sky—immensely impressive), I would feel rather
nervous. These were precisely the moments for me to be tested by
Father to see just how much I had learned about Latin and Roman
culture. Inscriptions carved into the marble had to be translated, so
I was also being taught on the spot. But the baptism by fire came
in Rome, when I was allowed to accompany Father to Italy on my
own and we stayed with the ambassador, Dr H.N. Boon. There I
was struck by the deep bonds of friendship between the two and
I enjoyed listening to the many stories, recounted with a certain
understated humour, with which they regaled each other.

Also memorable were the official trips to Damascus, Amman,
Palmyra, Jerash, Jerusalem and other places, on which once again
I alone might accompany him. These journeys through the desert
by car could be adventurous and fascinating. On one of our trips
through the Bekaa Valley, the chauffeur Edouard suddenly made
an unannounced and unexplained stop, stepped out and took
a carbine out of the boot and used it to shoot a couple of large
birds out of the sky. It seems that they were a special delicacy of
the region. The hunting trophy disappeared into the boot and we
continued our journey. To my great astonishment Father merely
shrugged his shoulders and did not say another word about it.
These were also educative excursions because I heard a great deal
about the history of the Christian faith. I remember vividly how
much an impression a visit to Bethlehem and a walk along the
route of the Via Dolorosa made on my father.

Our Lebanese chauffeur Edouard, with whom I got on very
well, was a Christian, as were most of the household staff. Once
I felt very sorry for him after he had plucked up the courage to
knock at the door of the Chinese library to ask Father for a rise in
salary. Apparently it was not the right moment because his request
elicited a veritable tumult of wrath, accompanied by a torrent
of abuse in French, English and Arabic, which was audible sixty
metres away in the kitchen quarters. I was witness as Edouard,
who was as white as a ghost, fled from the library and told me at
the entrance that he had been dismissed.

However, next morning, looking out of my bedroom window
into the side street beside the house, I spied the black Ford Fairlane
parked outside the side entrance, while Edouard, his official khaki
cap perched nonchalantly on his head, was busy placing the Dutch
tricolour next to the bonnet as he did every morning. It seemed

he had been reinstated [in precisely the same way as Abdul the chauffeur in India, who had been dismissed but had been reinstated in his function the next day]. That was how Father was, he could fly into an ungovernable rage, and then the best option was to run for cover, because his punches could land hard. Nevertheless such an outburst of temper and rage, during which he could barely utter his words (he began to stutter), was soon over and forgotten.

One evening, sitting opposite my father at his desk in the study-library for my usual Latin lesson, I noticed that he seemed rather unsure of himself, as if he wanted to say something but could not immediately find the words to say it. Suddenly he shoved a book to me across the top of the desk, saying: "Here, you should read this attentively—you are now at an age for it." I think the title of the book was, *The Sexual Life of Man*. In itself it was a good book, and father had clearly been at some pains to find it. Aware of the fact that at the age of thirteen most of my friends were Arab boys of my own age, who matured early, he must have intended the provision of this book to be more of a reference work. Whatever the case, all the sexual instruction which I ever received from Father was confined to this one gesture; we never had a proper discussion about its contents. [What is remarkable is this shyness shown towards his own son by the author of *Sexual Life in Ancient China*, which is not in the least bit prudish, who in his own youth at the same age had created a rather mature impression and thought that the school children in the Netherlands, in contrast to their counterparts in Java, were very puerile about sex].

To this I must add that Father never missed the opportunity, solicited or unsolicited, to give a commentary on the appearance of the beauteous sex, both those he happened to come across in his environs as well as the girls of my age.

The Van Guliks spent the 14th July to 22nd August 1957 in the Netherlands on furlough and to hold official talks. All the appropriate civil servants, friends and family were visited. He also had a session with Minister Luns and finally an audience with the Queen.

9-8-1957: 9.30 in the ministerial car to Soestdijk, 11-12 talk with H.M., afterwards with Prince Aschwin [Prince Bernhard's brother, who was a Sinologist and a connoisseur of Chinese art], returned at 2.

15-8-1957: S.F. to Soestdijk [where the Queen said to her: "I have read your husband's Judge Dee novels. They are very exciting!"]

On 22 August 1957, Van Gulik and his son Willem flew to Beirut via Rome, where they spent a few days with Ambassador Boon. He and Willem visited Professor Tucci as well as a number of tourist attractions such as Castle Sant'Angelo, the Colosseum, the Villa d'Este, Odescalci Castle and an Etruscan Museum. Shih-fang had to have an operation in the Netherlands and remained there until 28 November 1957.

Van Gulik continues the story of his life:

A routine of life having been established [as envoy Van Gulik was now his own boss and he had even more freedom than before], I now had more time for my own work. I translated a treatise of a Chinese collector [*Scrapbook for Chinese Collectors*, the English translation with the Chinese text was published in Beirut in 1958; he sent a friend and colleague—the envoy in Israel—a copy with the dedication: "For Han Bas Backer, as evidence that we in Beyrouth do not sit still! Robert"].

[I] also did more reading in ancient Chinese crime-literature and old novels. My Judge Dee novels, the *Maze, Bell* and *Lake Murders*, were so favourably received by the Western press that I decided to write more of them.

I found this a very pleasant relaxation after official and also after scholarly work; in doing scholarly work one has to be a kind of slave to the facts, and a very diligent and conscientious slave at that! But when writing a novel, however, one is *master*: one creates personalities and circumstances, according to one's own sweet will. [Later Van Gulik goes a step further and writes:] In the course of the last fifteen years, the writing of novels has become an integral part of my existence, as necessary to me as my academic research. Without academic research it would not have been able to continue my diplomatic career, in which one is occupied only with affairs of momentary importance. The academic research offers a welcome escape, because everything one does in it is of enduring value, even the mistakes which one makes, from which others can learn.

After the remark that when writing a novel it is possible to allow one's imagination free range, which is not the case with academic work, he continues:

Hence writing novels became an essential third facet of my work, a relaxation which kept alive my interest in diplomatic and academic work.

Also since I found, even in the most unexpected places, [an] astonishing lack of understanding of the Chinese and their way of life, I thought my Judge Dee novels might also serve the purpose of making this subject better known in wider circles; hence I went on to do my utmost to keep my novels authentic till the smallest details.

Van Gulik succeeded exceedingly well in this. There was a period during which the U.S. State Department made these Judge Dee novels compulsory reading for American diplomats who were posted to China because they were the best possible introduction to the background to Chinese life.

In the personality of the scholar-civil servant Judge Dee, Van Gulik drew a picture of what he wanted to be himself; he also found something of his father in it. This upright, intelligent judge became a familiar figure to millions of readers throughout the whole world. And the same can be said of his assistants: the faithful old Sergeant Hoong and the three highway robbers converted by Dee: the hedonistic, rough and ready, gutsy Ma Joong; the somewhat mysterious fighter Chiao Tai; and the thrifty, handy, realistic Tao Gan. They serve and respect him with doughty fists and touching loyalty. In the last series Judge Dee acts alone. When the author killed off Sergeant Hoong, he received protests from faithful readers who did not want to be parted from Hoong.

As was the custom of his time. Judge Dee had three wives. However, they remained vague personalities for the reader, as indeed did most of the other female characters, the majority of whom were prostitutes. Judge Dee lived, as did Van Gulik himself, in a man's world, and hence the men took centre stage.

His assistants took care (as Ab Visser has remarked in a radio portrait of Van Gulik) 'of all the colourful business, the fights and the "common" element, while the aristocratic Judge Dee provides the deductive, analytic brain. It is not just their historical, oriental and slightly occult sphere and characters which make the novels and short stories so extremely readable, they are all also enhanced by their ingenious plots, in which Van Gulik followed the traditions of the English school of deduction. Nevertheless, what stands out in these stories is the dominant influence of Judge Dee himself, who without budging an inch from his legal principles, primarily hands down judgements which are humane and wise and who is of an exemplary, in no way at all weak-kneed, integrity.'

Fig. 10: Judge Dee and his three wives. From *The Haunted Monastery.*

Van Gulik acknowledged that Judge Dee and his four assistants had now began to be part of himself.

In the judge, traditional Chinese ideals of the just and learned scholar-official merged with my own picture of the ideal western official, of which my Father had been such an excellent example [and it is also clear that to a high degree Robert also identified himself with Judge Dee]. Sergeant Hoong is the faithful Watson. I adopted him because such a type occurs in every Chinese crime story, rather than because of deep personal sympathy. Ma Joong represents the less desirable side of myself in whom an interest in women and a bohemian-style of life predominates. Chiao Tai represents the latent militarist virus in the family (for which our ancestor Thomas Gullicke may be responsible!) and Tao Gan gives the opportunity for venting the cynical views all diplomats come to hold during various phases of their chequered careers.

I decided to keep in my novels to a—largely imaginary—chronology. In this history left me great freedom, for in the official biography of Judge Dee in the T'ang Dynasty it says only: "In the first half of his career he solved hundreds of difficult criminal cases"—nothing more. The first thing to do was to give the series a beginning and an end. Therefore I wrote in Beirut *The Chinese Gold Murders*, describing the beginning of Judge Dee's career, and *The Chinese Nail Murders* describing the end of his career as district magistrate.

Elsewhere Van Gulik noted that while writing *The Chinese Gold Murders*, for the first time he had found a formula which he felt was satisfactory and which would probably be acceptable to both Western and Asian readers. He felt that now Judge Dee's assistants had become real people and that other characters, like the abbot and Miss Tsao were also real personalities. Only Dr Tsao did he find rather exaggerated and insufficiently convincing. He now introduced fewer characters, but there were twenty-two nevertheless. Van Gulik thought that *The Chinese Nail Murders* would be his last Judge Dee novel.

In his postscript to this last novel, Van Gulik explains that the preliminary work for these books had cost him the most time, but it had afforded him the greatest pleasure, not least because it could be done in snatches, in between other activities. The first step was to discover three usable plots in the Chinese sources – in itself a sort of detective work. When three suitable plots for a novel had been found, the second step was to create a background of people and geographical surroundings.

> The most fascinating part is every time to be able to see, as the people and their surroundings began to take shape, that everything gradually came alive and as it did it created new possibilities to expand on the plot. [...] The last phase in the preliminary work was to set out the times and the places substantially. The first thing to do was to draw a plan of the town, an animated task which often suggested new developments. Every old Chinese town had approximately the same landmarks—in the first place of course the tribunal, then the temple of Confucius, the Temple of the War God, etc. The rest of the city one can design according to one's fancy, incorporating special features of towns actually visited or lived in. [...] The last phase of the preliminary work was to draw up a timetable, divided in as many days as the action occupies, and

subdivided into morning, afternoon and evening. In the novels there is little mention of dates or hours, because the ancient Chinese did not live by the clock as modern life compels us to do. But I needed a time-table for my own reference, so as to know where all my people were at a given moment, and what mischief they were up to.

All this preliminary work having been completed, I could at last start writing. With plots, persons and places ready, the actual writing proceeded comparatively smoothly, all kinds of odds and ends coming to mind and finding their appropriate place. Although the plot remained unchanged, as I wrote the centre of gravity often changed radically. People who were intended to remain in the background, pushed themselves into the footlights, others who had been given a leading role, crumpled up into bit-players. One enduring difficulty was to prevent my characters from getting out of hand, as the persons quickly came so much to life and I was tempted to let him or her engage in all kinds of activities that had no direct or indirect bearing on the plot—and such as are out of place in a detective novel. These two novels [the *Gold* and *Nail Murders*] I wrote in a comparatively short time (if I remember correctly, the drafts took me only six weeks or so) and in a period when the political situation had become tense. As is well known a civil war developed in Lebanon between the Christians and the [Muslim] Arabs.

By this time, even in peaceful Lebanon, fanatical Nasserism began to stir. The first note about this in Van Gulik's pocket diary was:

30-5-1957: ...Attempt to oust the government of Gaffi and Saeb Salam. Soldiers occupied the city. A. van Sprang [Dutch journalist] arrested.

The civil war about which Van Gulik wrote broke out in 1958:

10-5-1958: Bombings and political crisis begin during the weekend.

11-5-1958: Barricades and shooting near chancellery.

15-5-1958: Day off from office [Ascension Day], 23 to office for telegram in cipher. Compiled political report and sent it. Curfew introduced.

18-5-1958: [Sunday] Morning worked on article for Italian Encyclopaedia [he wrote a trilogy of articles for the *Enciclopedia*

Universale dell'Arte on Chinese art], 3 o'clock walked to Capitol with Willem and Thomas, occupied by soldiers. Afterwards to Amir, where saw French film *Miss Striptease*. Dinner at home, read in the evening.

19-5-1958: 19 hours Nahas [the Lebanese councillor, a courageous man who later saved the archive and was decorated for his action] rang about bomb near chancellery.

20-5-1958: Morning chancellery temporarily removed to house.

14-6-1958: 10 o'clock with S.F., Willem and Thomas to Brumana [the mountain village where they had rented a summer house]. Fixed up the house. That morning fighting in Beirut near residence.

15-6-1958: Brumana. Brodhaags [agricultural attaché and wife] came for coffee at 11, because of the worsening situation I returned to Beirut with him.

19-6-1958: Drafted telegram about evacuation.

27-6-1958: Randall the British consul came to talk about evacuation timetable.

8-7-1958: I returned alone [from Brumana] to Beirut, 1-3 lunch with Chinese ambassador, Wang Kiding, for Chinese Muslim mission. Worked at home, dinner alone, 10-11 heavy exchanges of fire, slept in Thomas' bed and barricaded the window with cushions. Attack on ABC. Revolt has lasted 60 days. [Wang Kiding was the Taiwanese ambassador; despite the fact that the Netherlands did not have diplomatic ties with Taiwan and these contacts were unauthorized, Van Gulik continued to maintain them, albeit as unofficially as possible].

The UN had to interfere, first an observers team, then an American armed force. Our legation being right behind the President's palace, which was besieged by the rebels, we were in the firing line. I sent my wife and children to the Christian mountain village of Brumana, and more or less barricaded the Legation—an easy matter, for it was exactly for such eventualities that the old Turkish governors had built it! I calculated the angles bullets could take through the windows, and indicated safe space by washing lines hung in the rooms. Our walls were so thick that even machine gunning only dented them. I must add that the rebels had officially and solemnly stated that they would not shoot at the diplomatic missions, but, as my neighbour the British ambassador remarked wryly: "They are such lousy marksmen!"

The larger part of my two novels was written when I was sitting all alone in the large palace at night, the shooting outside going on and on and the smell of the cordite drifting in through the windows. [He slept in his study on his large Chinese bench inlaid with mother-of-pearl, with a loaded pistol beside him, a Colt .45 which he had been given by the American Navy; he had asked The Hague in vain for machine guns]. Part of that eery atmosphere is reflected in these two books.

When the rebels started to explode small sticks of dynamite in our gardens, my British colleague and I decided we would evacuate our residences, and move temporarily to the St. Georges Hotel, on the beach. And there we stayed till the truce was signed.

11-7-1958: Chancellery transferred to hotel [St Georges].

15-7-1958: First reports of American landing in Lebanon at 2 o'clock, dinner at home, in the evening put the finishing touches to *Lake Murders*.

Van Gulik had written the first draft of *The Chinese Lake Murders* in New Delhi, with a view to eventually publishing it in Chinese. However, all manner of things intervened and he only took another look at the manuscript in 1957, in Beirut. When his publishers demanded another Judge Dee novel, he completely rewrote the novel; he gave the book a new beginning and, instead of the obvious state councillor, made the silk merchant the guilty party. Even though Van Gulik thought it was a better novel than the *Bell* and *Maze Murders*, the books was still too complicated and too long for his taste.

It had been a tense and confused period which I found of absorbing interest. I fear that my years in the Far East and war-time experiences had made me a bit callous as regards the human suffering brought about by the civil war, for I positively enjoyed the tense and irregular life, including the rather boisterous late nights in my improvised office in the hotel, with a crowd of war correspondents, including Alfred van Sprang.

Each morning he convened a meeting in the hotel with the remaining representatives of Dutch businesses; experiences were exchanged and, where possible, solutions found to problems. The

Hague had ordered that Dutch women and children be moved out of the danger zone to safer destinations.

Willem van Gulik, who had not yet become a boarder at the school in Brumana during the initial period and had remained with his father in Beirut, was taken there and brought home each day in the car. He experienced some tense moments, including dangerous roadblocks. Once the edge of the road close to a ravine had been smeared with car oil, but Edouard spotted this in time and just managed to jam on the brakes before they plunged into the abyss. Apparently the diplomatic car which drove back and forth each day had aroused the suspicions of the Muslim fanatics, but the situation improved when, at Edouard's suggestion, they offered a lift to a regular group of country girls who had to walk along the road from their village to the next to go to school each day.

Willem says:

> The daily journey (about an hour each way) was considered dangerous, too great a risk, and I became a boarder at the school. My roommates were all Muslim: from Pakistan, Iran, Iraq, Syria and Kuwait. Consequently I was immersed in Muslim culture, participated in the Ramadan fast, and heard their side of the story about the problems in the Middle East. At that stage I little realized how long the aftermath of the civil war would drag on and its dramatic consequences, not least for Lebanon.

However, before he became a boarder at Brumana, Willem had all sorts of interesting experiences in Beirut.

> For me, the outbreak of the civil war in Lebanon ushered in an adventurous time. Our house, which had actually been built as a fort, lay precisely in the line of fire on the border between the Muslim and Christian quarters. Situated with two sides along the public thoroughfare, from the kitchen balcony especially, it offered a good view of what was happening in the street. Barricades and checkpoints were set up around the house and, and whenever I had the chance, I mixed with the soldiers and the guerrillas. Imbued with a sense of the theatrical, the Lebanese citizens also walked around heavily armed—pistols which they nonchalantly displayed under their coat flaps in their trouser belts, showing that they were not to be trifled with.
>
> Actually the whole affair struck me as a vaudeville performance. Surreptitiously joining the soldiers on the barricades,

I was treated to firing a round from a machine pistol into the air. Initially the Lebanese soldiers emptied most of their magazines into the air—their aim being to make a noise—rather than actually aiming them at persons. Matters turned more serious when the bombing raids came. The road ambush on the kitchen (northern side) of the house was a sort of checkpoint, and it was there I saw a woman, who had hidden a large number of hand grenades under wide black skirts, being hauled out of a taxi. Tanks carrying marines from the American Seventh Fleet regularly rolled down the street, and I and my Arab friends were sometimes given a ride in them. What made a really big impression on us was that they had built-in refrigerators in the vehicles, from which ice-cold bottles of Coca Cola were handed out. My Muslim mates spoke of their horror at the fact that, on account of the swingeing heat of the Lebanese summer, the American marines walked around with bare torsos, something which was regarded as exceptionally undignified in Arab culture. I told this to Father, who understood immediately, and also reported it to the American commanders.

As the situation worsened and the Dutch were advised to evacuate, Mother, Pauline and Thomas found a safe haven in a mountain villa close to my school in Brumana. For a little while I remained with Father in the house in Beirut. We slept in the same room, the barred windows partially reinforced with sandbags on the window sills. In order to make an impression on the militia around the house, I appeared on the barricades with Father's service revolver in its holster on my hip.

Our neighbour, the British ambassador, was assigned an extensive guard by the Lebanese police. In order not to be left behind, Father employed a gigantic Turkish (or Druze) mercenary, who posted himself on the steps up to the house every day, dressed up to the nines in his traditional costume, bandoliers over the shoulder, an enormous sword with its sheath inlaid with semi-precious stones, and a war-like moustache. I still remember how the guards of the adjoining British premises, who had to continually pass in front of our entrance, greeted this martial apparition at our main entrance with great respect.

In fact the civil war did not last long: the Nasserite groups accepted what they had first rejected, namely the formation of a mixed Christian-Muslim government on condition that it would adopt a middle course between the pro-Western and the pro-Arab directions. This civil struggle did not incur a fraction of the suffering and destruction which later civil wars in the Lebanon were to cause.

31-7-1958: Morning General Chehab [Sihab] elected president in parliament.

8-8-1958: Returned to Beirut from Brumana with Willem and Pieter. W. and P. to the Sporting Club. We left the Hotel St George and moved back into my residence. Lunch at home with the boys, rest in the afternoon, 5-6 did shopping with boys in the neighbourhood, dinner at home from tins, worked in the evening.

9-8-1958: 8.30 S.F., Pauline and Thomas came from Brumana with small presents for my birthday. Office for the first time at home. Mulder and Van Ginkel from UNOFil came to have a beer, later Borgerhoff Mulder [KLM representative] and Mrs Brodhaag. Lunch at home. In the afternoon looked at weapons check by the soldiers outside. Extensive Indonesian dinner [*rijsttafel*]. Worked in the evening.

3-9-1958: Lot of shooting in the evening.

Robert van Gulik continues in his notes:

In Beirut I wrote in rapid succession two more Judge Dee novels, viz. *The Haunted Monastery* and *The Red Pavilion*, and made a draft for a third one, *The Lacquer Screen* [elsewhere Van Gulik named this the last Judge Dee book, the plot of which he thought up during delightful bus trips in Greece in the autumn of 1958. It was in fact the first novel in the new, altered series of Judge Dee novels].

Studying the reviews of my preceding novels, and letters about them, also from Chinese and Japanese friends, I noticed that many readers thought that the large number of *dramatis personae* a strain on the memory, and the chapter headings in Chinese style (two parallel lines) a bit contrived. Therefore I decided to write the second series of 5 Judge Dee novels in a different manner, letting Judge Dee be accompanied by only one of his lieutenants, and keeping the figure for the *dramatis personae* as low as possible. I also discarded the chapter headings and modified the introductory passages, giving them a direct bearing on the story itself. I found that in this manner I could devote more space to the character description.

Fig. 11: A chain fighter defeats the assassins. From *The Red Pavilion*.

The writing of *The Haunted Monastery* gave him so much pleasure that within six weeks he had begun work on his next book in the new series: *The Red Pavilion*, which he wrote in exactly one single month. This novel developed around two characters, 'the Crab' and 'the Shrimp', who some way or another emerged from his imagination; Van Gulik always considered the pair to be one of his best creations.

> Finally, I tried to improve my illustrations, and made a careful study of the Ming illustrated block prints in my collection. Copying and recopying these made me discover a number of interesting prints so that I began to collect notes for a comprehensive work, *The History of the Chinese Book Illustration*; these notes keep accumulating and someday I hope to be able to publish that book. So here again

my Judge Dee hobby, and my scholarly work mutually benefited each other. [*De Boekillustratie van het Ming tijdperk* appeared in The Hague in 1955, published by *De Nederlandse Vereniging voor Druk- en Boekkunst.*]

That I wrote four novels in three years must, I think, be explained by the fact that although outwardly my life was extremely busy, my inner life was very satisfied and quiet. Both S.F. [and I] liked our existence, our children were happy, and I had neither the time nor the inclination for emotional adventures; my 'lowly instincts' found an outlet in my novels.

[Only very rarely indeed in his notes did Van Gulik betray anything personal. What he writes here confirms the impression that prior to Beirut—and later every so often—he was compelled by a huge inner turmoil. His boundless activities in all sorts of fields, including the sexual, and his smoking of one cigarette after the other all hint at this.]

My book *Erotic Colour Prints of the Ming Period* which I had published in Tokyo in a limited edition of only 50 copies, had aroused the interest of anthropologists and sexologists everywhere, it was quoted widely in medical literature, and many specialists in the field, including Prof. Kinsey, urged me to publish a second edition, in a form accessible to a wider circle of students. In Beirut I re-wrote the book on a broader sociological and anthropological basis, and it was published by the famous Orientalist house E.J. Brill in Leiden. [*Sexual Life in Ancient China*, Leiden, 1961]

Here Robert forgot to mention that in the same period he had also written three Judge Dee short stories, *New Year's Eve in Lan-fang*, of which he had 200 copies printed in Beirut at his own expense and sent them to friends as a New year greeting; *The Murder on the Lotus Pond* and *The Coffins of the Emperor*. These were later published in an anthology of short stories entitled *Judge Dee at Work*.

In the meantime, Van Gulik had found a better location for the chancellery in Rue Najib:

19-11-1958: 11 o'clock inaugurated the new chancellery with champagne.

In the summer of 1959 the F.O. informed me that they planned to appoint me Netherlands Minister to the Federation of Malaya. Kuala Lumpur was [then] a much smaller post than Beirut, and the local Netherlands interests were limited. However, since Indonesia had severed relations with Holland, Kuala Lumpur rapidly assumed great importance for us, for it became the observation-post for Indonesia. Moreover it was known that the Federation would try to mediate between The Hague and Djakarta, to solve the New Guinea impasse. The F.O. added that, in view of these facts, it planned to raise our legation there to an Embassy. If, however, I preferred to have a second 3-year term in Beirut, they would raise no objections.

16-6-1959: to office for cipher telegram about transfer.

I consulted S.F., and she was in favour of the proposal. She liked Beirut but said she would like Malaya even better, because of the large Chinese community there. I myself had made up my mind at once: for me the East was calling again, and my childhood memories of Java came back in full force! I would live again in the surroundings where I had passed such a happy childhood. So S.F. and I were in perfect agreement: we liked the Middle East, but were convinced we would like Malaya even better.

13-7-1958: 1 o'clock to Minister [of Foreign Affairs], asked for *agrément* for Philipse and informed [them] that I was leaving.

Then came the familiar hectic weeks of packing and leave-taking. S.F. went to Holland first to rent a house and make arrangements for the schools for Willem and Pieter. I followed three weeks later, travelling via Istanbul, to inspect the Netherlands Institute there, and see the famous Chinese porcelain collection in the Tokapi Museum. After a brief stay in Holland, where we put Willem and Pieter in a good boarding-school in Haarlem—our old family-home—S.F., Pauline and Thomas boarded a ship for Singapore. I flew ahead by K.L.M.

Before Van Gulik left Beirut, he had handed over leadership of the Legation to the Secretary to the Ambassador, Iwan Verkade, who had been specially posted there briefly for that very purpose and had arrived there on 9 August, Van Gulik's birthday. Despite all the hectic activities at this time Van Gulik still found the time to have lengthy discussions with Verkade, in which an incredible series of topics were passed in review. Van Gulik used to say that he considered himself a civil servant first and an academic second; 'I'm not really an artist'.

Iwan Verkade said:

His interest in the theatre extended to his trying to write a Judge Dee stage play. I read the manuscript in Beirut. This revealed that he had not yet explored stagecraft. When I remarked on this, he looked at me grumpily and said: "What do you mean?" The piece commenced with a long scene, a dialogue in which two minor characters talked about the events which had happened. Knowledge of this was essential to understanding the rest of the play. I said that this technique, which Ibsen might have been able to essay, was old fashioned because the present-day member of the audience is in a *hurry*: only the action which takes place on the stage interests a modern audience. This is the reason that, for instance, Vondel's *Gijsbreght*, in which heralds described battle scenes which the audience does not see in long verses, is a play which is now only performed above all out of reverence; it will not bring in any money. Van Gulik never completely forgave me my criticism. However, he did write to me later from Kuala Lumpur:

'Looking at it in hindsight, my play which you so kindly read for me, does not please me at all; it can be *read* with pleasure, but would completely collapse on the boards. I now regularly go to various Chinese theatrical performances with my wife and, by doing so, attempt to educate myself—if at least I am not too old to do so.'

[Verkade added] The original theatre script has become a very successful novel; if I remember rightly it is *The Willow Pattern*.

Chapter 14

AMBASSADOR IN MALAYSIA
1959-1962

Malaya [Malaysia] proved to answer all our expectations: contrary to India, this was a young independent Asiatic country that had assumed its new status with dignity, and few complexes. The credit for this achievement must go partly to excellent British statesmanship, partly to the Malayans themselves, a friendly, relaxed kind of people, with an innate sense of decency. The Premier, Tungku Abdul Rachman, became a personal friend, and we still maintain contact.

Van Gulik arrived in Kuala Lumpur on 6 October, 1959. He presented his credentials as envoy on 16 October and later, as ambassador, on 26 July, 1960. With his sensitivity to ceremonial and correct procedure, he obviously enjoyed the decorum and traditional customs still adhered to at the Malay court. These filled him with nostalgia for the erstwhile Netherlands Indies.

Pl. 24. On the way to present his credentials to the king of Malaysia, Kuala Lumpur, 1959.

Nevertheless, the ceremonial could prove extremely taxing. A rabid smoker (at least sixty a day), he was overcome by frequent bouts of coughing, which attacked him especially whenever he had to exert himself. This is what happened when the king died and the entire diplomatic corps had to follow the cortège through the city on foot, a distance of three miles. The solemn procession wound on its way to the accompaniment of the soft beating of muffled drums and the loud coughing and spluttering of the Dutch ambassador. Van Gulik was not very happy about this fatiguing walk in the tropical heat, but consoled himself with the idea that it was a very rare occasion which would not be repeated in a hurry. Five months later, the new king also passed away...

> Everyday life was an exact replica of my childhood in Java: the large house and garden with the singing birds and the gibbons, the cosy informal meals in the Malayan market-stalls, the Malayan dances and the shadow-play in the open, in the cool tropical nights—all this I found back here in Malaya.
>
> In the large Chinese community (40 % of the total population) there was a middle- and upper-middle class, where we found many friends: scholars, painters, calligraphers and musicians. I again set up my Chinese library—minus the large pieces of Chinese furniture like my Mandarin throne seat!—and there I had a constant coming and going of Chinese friends and acquaintances. As a boy I had spoken Malayan fluently, and now the language was quickly coming back. [In the beginning he still worked on it in the evenings in order to perfect his knowledge; Shih-fang also took Malay lessons].

None of these activities stopped Van Gulik from having good contacts with the Dutch people who were working under his aegis. Even though he had obtained his doctorate in Utrecht, he had spent the great part of his student life in Leiden and hence he made sure he celebrated the Relief of Leiden from the Spanish siege in 1573:

> 8-10-1960: Celebrated 3 October in the Huygens' House. I was dressed as a Water Beggar, [one of the guerrilla troops who sailed into the besieged city bringing relief].
>
> My Middle-East and Islamic background-knowledge came in useful with my relations with the Malayan government officials. The relations between the Chinese and Malayan parts of the people being the most important internal problem of the Federation, I could often do useful liaison-work—of course in a quite informal

manner—between those two groups; I was fortunate enough to enjoy the confidence of both sides, and thus could help to smooth out differences. I contributed towards a Chinese chair in the National University of Malaya, pointing out that more Chinese needed to study Malayan culture, and more Malayan[s] Chinese culture. I myself taught there Chinese history, as honorary lecturer, and enjoyed it immensely. As I said earlier, I lack the qualities that make a good teacher, but here I was speaking to a fascinating audience of young Malayan, Chinese and Indians whose views on the past, present and future of Asia interested me profoundly.

Van Gulik certainly did not take any pains to disguise his own vision of the colonial past from these students. Later he was to say to an official who was working on a short history of the Netherlands for foreigners: 'You are unquestionably going about the problem the right way. But one word of advice: make no excuses for our colonial past. When I was posted in Kuala Lumpur, I also spent some time teaching at the university there and I told the youngsters some home truths about our colonial past. You should write your piece about our relationship with Southeast Asia in such a way the students will go to our embassy for a portrait of Jan Pieterszoon Coen to hang above their beds.'

The Van Gulik children have fond memories of their time both in Beirut and in Kuala Lumpur, especially remembering the great freedom they enjoyed. Life was one long party. The offices and schools closed at 1 p.m. and everyone trooped to the club, to swim, sunbathe and play sports. In the evening they would go to the *pasar* (Malay open-air market) and very often they would visit the cinema in Kuala Lumpur, especially to see Chinese films (or ones about Ancient Rome, like *Ben Hur*, which their father so loved).

Van Gulik had very liberal ideas about his children's upbringing. Their parents took them virtually everywhere, including to innumerable informal dinners which could go on until the early hours at the houses of Chinese friends. Now and then Thomas would nod off and then eat some more, just as his fancy took him. This is not to say that their father did take a very great interest in their school-work, which was a crucially important matter. If they had a problem, he would give them all the time in the world and was able to produce a lucid explanation (although he did have rather more difficulty with the exact sciences). At one time, he wrote a number of Latin lessons for Pauline.

Life here, as indeed it was in the Netherlands, was cheerful, easy-going and family-centred, and the Van Guliks were extremely hospitable—living life as it had been in the Indies. In The Hague more often than not when someone paid a visit, for instance a student looking for some information whom Van Gulik had not met earlier, this person was promptly invited to remain for a meal or was taken out to a Chinese restaurant. Although Van Gulik was usually (at least outwardly) imperturbable and never seemed pushed for time, at an early age the children learned that they should not bother him when he was concentrating hard on his calligraphy or some other similar pastime. Were they to do so, he could become very irritable or sometimes even lose his temper.

No matter how easy-going he was, Van Gulik was completely conscious of the dignity of his office and of the responsibility inherent in it. This is reflected in the seriousness of his gaze in official photos and, on one occasion, at a dinner at which he had not been seated at the high table as befitted Her Majesty's ambassador, he lodged a formal complaint. Adroitly, he managed to circumvent a major incident by proposing that the main table be linked to the side tables with ribbons, a solution which a diplomat unfamiliar with Asia might not have thought of so readily.

Although self-confident both as a civil servant and as a private individual, Van Gulik absolutely abhorred pedantry and quashed those who had inflated opinions of themselves and gave themselves airs. On one occasion, when visited by a journalist who was tending to behave rather grandly, Van Gulik stood up suddenly and said: 'What you are asking me about is so complicated I must fetch my secretary.' He disappeared from the room only to re-appear with his gibbon on his shoulder. He addressed the animal earnestly saying: 'What do you think? The gentleman is asking...'

Certainly, Van Gulik's humour could be pretty impish. He made many laugh with his witticisms, often just at the very moment that rather infamous Dutch pomposity happened to been getting the upper hand in a gathering.

He was exceptionally popular among the Malays and, of course, among the Chinese. No sooner had he arrived in Kuala Lumpur than news of his presence was being buzzed around the Chinese community and he began to receive regular visits from Chinese, chief among them people who had known him during his time in China. Here, in Kuala Lumpur, his fame as a performer on the Chinese lute had also preceded him, and on many an occasion the eyes of his staff at the chancellery would be astonished by a most remarkable figure with a lute under his arm, who would then be given a rapturous reception. Frequently, whenever the Van Guliks visited their friend Huang Tu-ch'i and his wife, Robert would play the lute with his mother, the elder Mrs Huang, who always enjoyed this thoroughly. Of course, the Van Guliks also had plenty of contact with Malaysians as well as with foreign (including Dutch) scholars, and there were regular working luncheons with members of the Dutch business community, but above all they chose to spend their time in the Chinese community. Robert opened an exhibition by the painter Miss Lai Foong-mei; at the university he gave a lecture on 'psychoanalysis and *mandalas*' and another on Chinese religions.

His reputation in the Chinese People's Republic was also not inconsiderable; the Chinese ambassador in Kuala Lumpur even offered him a trip to China as guest of the government. However, Dr Van Gulik declined this invitation because he had no wish to revisit China where so many of his best friends had perished.

Had China not become communist, he would have certainly been appointed ambassador there, but at that time the Netherlands had only a chargé d'affaires in Peking and Van Gulik was too high-ranking a diplomat to be considered for the post. Moreover, the fact he was married to a Chinese would have made such an appointment inadvisable at that precise moment in time. By the time there was an exchange of ambassadors between The Hague and Peking he had passed away. This is the reason that, even though he was a Chinese scholar, his diplomatic career leaned more heavily towards Japan than China, and of course Sinology was also a much studied subject in Japan. When it is all said and done, there are many points of contact: unquestionably Japanese is a completely different language to Chinese, but it does use Chinese characters (albeit pronounced differently), supplemented by phonetic syllabaries; it is written with a brush and calligraphy is highly esteemed; furthermore, among the many influences in Japan which originated in China, it is impossible to overlook Buddhism, Confucianism and Taoism.

By this time Van Gulik had so immersed himself in ancient China that he paid only scant attention to the many radical changes happening in the People's Republic. He considered China (including Taiwan) to be one single great cultural area and was not convinced that the division between the Communists and the Nationalists was carved in stone. To a contemporary he remarked: 'Undeniably Communist China and Taiwan are two separate

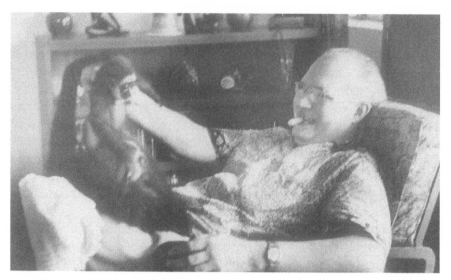

Pl. 25. With the gibbons Piddler and Cheenee, Kuala Lumpur, 1962.

Chinese communities, politically poles apart, but they do have a very good reciprocal relationship. Each knows what the other is thinking and each is aware of exactly what is happening in the other part of China. They can also gauge the weight of each other's threats! As time passes, they will reach an agreement.' And later in an interview with a Dutch newspaper he was to say: 'Chinese culture is in the Chinese blood and will endure for as long as there are Chinese. Whatever they might say about Communism, it is not totally new in China. Earning money for money's sake has always been regarded with the greatest contempt in China. Down the centuries, China has offered everyone equal chances, and the important industries have been state property.'[19]

Kuala Lumpur is the place where Robert's great love of the gibbon (a delicate primate, which he thought more human than ape-like) began and he acquired a number which seem to have become fully fledged members of the family. He was inseparable from the animals, which he regularly brought to the chancellery, and was dreadfully upset if one fell ill or even worse happened. The first time he was given a baby ape (a black gibbon, called Cheenee) by a good friend, the Pakistani ambassador, he was in the habit of bringing the animal to the office with him. The secretary thought him a darling

---

[19]   See *Nieuwsblad van het Noorden*, 27-9-1964.

little animal and she was more than happy to take care of him. The animal had the time of his life, springing from typewriter to telex machine, helping the coffee boy by spilling the beverage and being mothered by the female staff. When he had to settle down to work, the small animal was deposited in a beautiful big box furnished with many air and peep holes in which he would remain sitting as good as gold. However, as soon as visitors arrived he was taken out of the box and was allowed to play with the guests.

> We made many car-trips all over the country, and often stayed on the delightful Island of Penang; so S.F. could point out with satisfaction that her premonition in 1951 [see p. 187] had come true. Penang is indeed a "corner of China"; and S.F. and I are seriously considering making our permanent home there after my retirement—*insha'Allah*—if God wills it!, as the Arabs say. If one builds a house half-way up the mountain, the temperature is neither too cold nor too hot, there are good medical facilities (a point to consider when one is getting older), and it offers an excellent spring-board for visiting Burma, Siam, Indonesia and South China. But these musings belong to the future.

At a later stage Van Gulik once said: 'When I retire, I'm damned if I'm going to have to queue up at the greengrocer's in Holland.'

Whenever he did ponder about where he would retire to in later life, or about the end of his life, he found inspiration in Chinese poetry, for instance, in these two poems by Wang Wei (699-759) which he translated:

THE EVENING OF LIFE

The evening of life brings with it an appreciation of repose
The Ten Thousand Things can no longer disquiet me.
I discover that actually I no longer have any plan,
Other than to return to my old house by the lake.

There the pine-scented wind wafts through my loosened gown
The moon rises over the mountains and sheds its light on my lute.
You ask: 'What is the ultimate meaning of all this?'
Listen, the answer is encapsulated in the song
Of the fishermen, who sail into harbour in the evening mist.

FAREWELL

I mounted my horse and drank a toast to you
Asking you whither your journey would take you?
You said: 'I am tired of life,
I am going to slumber somewhere in the Southern Mountains.
I am going, do not ask how or where,
The White Clouds are everywhere.'[20]

Our favourite holiday-resort was the Rhu Lodge, the government bungalow in Port Dickson. Originally built for the British Naval Commander, after Independence the Malayan government had put it at the disposal of the King, Malayan Ministers of State, and foreign ambassadors. It was a very spacious, comfortable residence, with a magnificent Chinese cook, and a well-trained staff of servants. A bridge connected one end of the enormous garden with a small island in the sea, where stood a tea-pavilion under high cypress trees (the credit for this refinement goes to the Japanese Naval Commander, who used the lodge as resthouse during the Japanese Occupation). Here we spent truly delightful days, swimming and boating every day, and lying on the beautiful beach.

Van Gulik spent the period, from 3 November 1960, to 10 January 1961, in the Netherlands on sick leave and underwent prostate surgery there. While in hospital he kept himself very busy: he corrected the galley proofs of his *Sexual Life in Ancient China* and checked the Latin passages (he had written the more sexually explicit parts in Latin, as these were not intended to be read by all and sundry) with one of his friends who was a classical scholar. He also seized the opportunity to put the final touches to the Dutch version of his novel *The Red Pavilion*. He had a throng of visitors and, the evening before he was discharged from hospital, he invited his friends to dinner at a Chinese restaurant.

Shortly after his return to Kuala Lumpur he was bothered by tachycardia and breathlessness and was given a cardiogram, while an X-ray was made of his thorax. It turned out that there was nothing seriously wrong, but he would have to take things more quietly and,

---

[20] 'White Clouds' are a traditional symbol of a life of retreat. In Hans Bethge's famous edition of *Der Abscheid des Freundes*, this poem is included in Gustav Mahler's large-scale musical composition *Liede van der Erde*. Van Gulik's translation of both these poems is included in *Per Diplomatieke Koerier*, op.cit.

for a short spell, he actually heeded this warning. Nevertheless, he refused to give up chain-smoking.

Later Shih-fang paid a week's visit to Japan, where she visited her '9th sister' and her husband; Robert met her in Port Swettenham (now Port Klang), after which they spent a few days in the refreshing climate of the Cameron Highlands where he played billiards with her. However, it was not very long before his books demanded his attention.

Writing about the Judge Dee books which date from this period, Van Gulik says:

> As regards Judge Dee, Michael Joseph Ltd in London to whom I had sent my "new" novels, *The Haunted Monastery*, *The Red Pavilion* and *The Lacquer Screen*, said that they would publish only one J.D. novel a year and that they thought my three new novels too should make up a volume. I did not like it at all, and decided to publish these books myself. I knew a Mr Ee, an enterprising young Chinese printer in Kuala Lumpur, who specialized in printing cinema-tickets, programs, pamphlets etc. but no books. I persuaded him to enter this field too, beginning with my novel "The Red Pavilion". I spent many most instructive hours in his workshop, selecting the type, the paper, the size of the page etc., and also designing myself the cover. Thus three thousand copies were printed at the—by Western standards—very small cost of 2000 Mal. Dollars, approx. £200.-. I paid Mr Ee 5% for marketing costs. He had no experience for bringing a book onto the market, but his jeeps went every day up and down the country to deliver printed matter, and take new orders. He now gave every driver two dozen copies of my novel, to be sold to everybody who would buy, like one sells apples and eggs! In this most unusual manner the book became widely known, especially among the English-educated Chinese, the Chinese and English newspapers wrote about them and within six months every copy was sold, leaving me a tidy profit! We brought out a second edition and then printed also *The Haunted Monastery* and *The Lacquer Screen*, and Chinese friends began translating these into Chinese. I sent copies also to Hongkong, Bangkok and Japan, and to the U.S.; the favourable reviews convinced me that the "new series" was better than the first, and I wrote a fourth one, *The Emperor's Pearl*; in my last year in Malaya I wrote a fifth, *Murder in Canton*. These I had published in Dutch in Holland. The English editions I would try to place in England, for I had learned that I could not really

manage the marketing of a popular novel, nor could Mr Ee. So I
kept the matter of a re-issue of the three published novels, and the
publishing of the two typescripts pending till my return to Europe.

He also worked on a play, *The Golden Pagoda*, which he discussed
with his friend Professor Alistair Lamb and afterwards sent to
'Gielgud' (almost certainly Sir John Gielgud, the famous English
actor and director), but Gielgud's reaction to it is shrouded mystery.
Be that as it may, later in the Netherlands Van Gulik reworked it into
a puppet play, and it was performed there in this genre.

Van Gulik's report about his life in this period—apparently a very
happy one—gives absolutely nothing away about what he was really
doing in Kuala Lumpur for *Dutch* interests. Relations between the
Netherlands and Indonesia, a neighbour of Malaysia, had now sunk
to their nadir: both countries confronted each other inimically and
even the threat of a war over New Guinea hung in the air. Malaysia
was also dragged into the conflict, and Tunku Abdul Rachman did
his best to act as mediator. Therefore, Ambassador Van Gulik was
certainly not short of work to do. However, as we know from his
closest colleagues, Van Gulik had lost no time in getting it firmly fixed
into his head that the posting to Kuala Lumpur was a piece of cake.
Even if this was not actually the case, it must be acknowledged that
this embassy had to be considered far less an observation post for
Indonesia than it had been represented to Van Gulik in The Hague.
This function had been almost entirely assumed by the consulate-
general in Singapore. The situation is summed up by the fact that
on 17 August, 1960, according to his own notes, Van Gulik had to
be informed by J.G. Kist in a telephone call from Singapore that
Indonesia had broken off diplomatic relations with the Netherlands.

The hours which Robert devoted to the general running of the
embassy were minimal; he prided himself that the embassy in Kuala
Lumpur dispatched fewer telegrams than any other comparable post.
Even though Van Gulik was not entirely convinced of the political
importance of his post, he was always ready to help Dutch people,
not just in business affairs but also in the private sphere. Here, and
in other posts, he invariably showed that he was a caring father-
figure for fellow countrymen who happened to find themselves in
difficulties.

He impressed on his staff that, 'you should never spoil "those
fellows" in The Hague and that should only include half of what
you know in your reports.' This attitude left him all the more time

to spend on matters which captivated his interest far more, like writing the Judge Dee books. Once the spirit had seized him, he was the first to turn up at the chancellery where he let it be known that he did not wish to be disturbed; then the old typewriter on which he worked would rattle away virtually uninterruptedly. Delegation did not bother him one jot and therefore he left much of the work to his closest member of staff, the *chargé d'affaires*, R.H. the Count of Limburg Stirum.

The Count found Van Gulik at his best, completely in his element, when they went away together on an official visit, sometimes in Van Gulik's second-hand limousine, more often on the train. The apogee was a train journey (the road link had been blocked because of the still considerable danger posed by the communist guerrillas in the border area of northern Malaysia and the Isthmus of Kra, southernmost Thailand), of which the final destination was Hat Yai, the provincial capital of Songkhla. In those days, according to Van Gulik, this town was famous for the beauty of the girls who worked there in the various bars and brothels—a place which was roughly the same size as Alkmaar had more than seventy 'houses of pleasure'. He took pleasure in feminine beauty when he was travelling and he impressed on his colleague: what happens at home is sacred; outside, what the eye does not see the heart does not grieve for, was a completely different matter.

He was punctilious in observing official courtesies. On this occasion Van Gulik had got it into his head that, even though Thailand did not fall under his official jurisdiction, he should pay his respects to the provincial governor. He submitted a request and was granted an appointment. With the two of them crammed into a bicycle-rickshaw, the poor driver had to set out on what for him would be a long and arduous journey to the provincial headquarters situated just outside the town. At a certain moment, six motor-cycle police mounted on gigantic Harley Davidsons appeared from the opposite direction to provide them with an escort. The latter cast a suspicious eye over them, rode past, but shortly afterwards turned around and spoke to them.

Van Gulik, who it seems had already managed to master a little of the Thai language, which two days earlier had been a closed book to him, explained who they were, whereupon it turned out that the governor had sent the motor-cycle police to escort the Dutch ambassador to the provincial headquarters. Van Gulik visibly enjoyed the absurdity of the situation and the difficulty the policemen had in trying to keep their motor-cycles balanced as they escorted the exasperatingly slow vehicle.

Although Van Gulik was perfectly well aware that many colleagues did not take him all too seriously as a diplomat, he did become very upset if he was accused of laziness. A Dutch colleague who visited him while passing through Kuala Lumpur was taken to his library where, bursting with pride, Robert showed him his many academic works and his edition of Chinese erotic prints, exclaiming: 'They can say many things about Van Gulik: that he is a bastard, that he is too much of a lady's man and Heaven knows what else, but one thing that can't be said about him is that he is lazy!'

Nor could he be accused of not having enough high-level contacts. He not only got on very well with Prime Minister Tunku Abdul Rachman, his relationship with the King (the reigning Sultan), to whom he always had free access, was precisely the same.

It all began with a conversation about *wayang*. The King remarked that he had heard that Van Gulik was a genuine connoisseur of the Javanese *wayang*. Although the shadow theatre was also part of Malay culture, it was far more widespread in Indonesia where truly large numbers of puppet masters (*dalang*) could be found. Through their choice of their puppets, these *dalang* were sometimes used as political instruments. After all, the stories in this theatre genre teem with both good and bad characters; identifying a particular political leader with one or other hero from the *wayang* repertoire could therefore portray him in a good or bad light.

By this stage the King was beginning to feel rather uneasy about Sukarno's political ambitions, which seemed to envisage Malaysia as an appendage of Indonesia. In his concern, through the intervention of his own puppet-masters, the King wanted to persuade the Indonesian *dalangs* to associate him with a certain character 'X' from the *Ramayāna* epic. Did Van Gulik think that this was a good idea? After pondering the matter a while, delving into his profound knowledge of the Javanese *wayang* theatre, Van Gulik warned that, although he was counted among the heroic characters, X could nevertheless display a few untrustworthy character traits. He went on to explain in some detail why Y or Z might be a better choice for achieving the King's purpose. The King accepted the Dutch ambassador's suggestion.

In 1963-1964 when Barkman was put in charge of the post in Jakarta, he was not aware of any subtle political influence from Malaysia there (and Van Gulik would absolutely not have expected otherwise!); nevertheless, the reverse was true, as the hostile

Indonesian confrontation with that country had just reached its zenith. Be that as it may, the conversation between the King and Van Gulik illustrates the King's admiration for his knowledge, and reflects the atmosphere of trust existing between the two.

On another occasion, an audience with the King was interrupted by a secretary who announced that the representative of Her Majesty's Stationery Office who had handed in a design for a stamp three weeks earlier now had to return to England. He was sitting in the ante-chamber and had sent to enquire if the King had already made a decision. 'Have him wait until I have finished my conversation with Ambassador Van Gulik.' Whereupon the head of state produced the draft stamp: 'I have heard that you also draw. What do you think of the design?' 'Your image is excellent, [Your] Majesty', answered Van Gulik, 'It is a striking likeness. But everything around it, the way in which the denomination and the name Malaya have been reproduced, is less pleasing and in my humble opinion does not come up to standard.' 'Please do explain.' Van Gulik took a piece of paper, sketched a square within which he drew a different garniture to frame the King's portrait. The King's reaction was enthusiastic and a few months later the stamp bearing Van Gulik's design was issued.

These might seem like tall stories, but apparently this is not the case. Nonetheless, this does not rule out that every so often Van Gulik liked to affect playing the fool and dished up what were pure figments of his imagination. For instance, he once had a discussion with a friend about whether it was possible to make an object move simply by staring at it while sunk in deep concentration. People in China had told him that to be able to see this one would have to visit a certain person in Tibet. He had done this and had sat there for five days and five nights, then the lama said: 'Look, it's moving', but this was not so; it did not budge. Interesting... were it not that Van Gulik had never been to Tibet.

On another occasion he told a completely fabricated story about what is supposed to have happened to him in Peking shortly before the Communists arrived there. He could already hear the sound of distant gunfire, and Chiang Kai-shek's troops had withdrawn. That evening, around ten o'clock, the door-bell was rung by a well-dressed Chinese, who said to him: 'You are a well-known, trusted person in this city, which is why I have turned to you. I have here the emperor's pearl [it was the custom for the emperor to wear an enormous pearl on his silk ceremonial cap], you can buy it for [xxx] dollars, because I have to flee.' 'This was something so absolutely incredible,' Van Gulik recounted, 'I was taken completely by surprise because this sort of thing simply could not happen. I said that first of all the pearl would have to be subjected to an examination. But, of course, there was no time for this, the man was in a hurry. To my enormous astonishment, a few years later the pearl turned up in India! After this I began to write my book *The Emperor's Pearl.*'

On 10 October, 1961, the Van Guliks left for the Netherlands again, this time on long furlough. To break their journey, they spent a few days in Bangkok (where he visited an old friend from Peking and Chungking days who had become a Buddhist, the English sinologist and writer John Blofeld) and again in Colombo (from where they visited the Temple of the Tooth and a German monk in a forest hermitage near Kandy). In view of the schooling of the two youngest children (in his diary Pauline and Thomas were still referred to as *kriekjes*—little cherries), it was decided that Shih-fang would remain behind in The Hague, where she purchased a house on the Groot Hertoginnelaan.

Once again this furlough was crammed full of activities, which included plenty of meetings with family and friends, contacts with the ministry, publishers and academic institutions.

In a discussion with Secretary-General Van Tuyll, he happened to mention in passing his contacts with the King of Malaysia. When the former asked him: 'Why don't we get read about such interesting things in your political reports?', Van Gulik answered: 'Well, you know, these are personal matters, more to do with art and with my hobbies; when it's all said and done it is of no interest to the ministry?' Van Tuyll refuted this with the utmost vigour, but once again had to draw the conclusion that Van Gulik was exceptionally reticent about his own personal experiences and private affairs. He consciously made a sharp distinction between his work as a diplomat and his personal life. Not only did Van Gulik not report on such matters, he also made little use of the excellent opportunities he had, something which his closest associates regretted.

On 2 March 1962, Van Gulik flew back to Kuala Lumpur via Tokyo, where Minister Luns had convened a conference of ambassadors in Asia. Barkman, who had been summoned to this conference from Peking, could not remember if Robert took an active part in the discussions, but that he did absorb everything, which was revealed when he, it has to be said in a very friendly tone, ruthlessly dissected the argument of a colleague, leaving not much of it intact. When he did shoot, he invariably hit the bull's-eye.

Back in Kuala Lumpur, he took up his quarters in 'a suite on the eighth floor of the Federal Hotel, an eyrie above both town and countryside', because he was to be transferred in a few months and with this prospect in view he had already packed up his house.

'It's not much fun without family and books, but Calkoen sent me a baby gibbon from Bangkok. An exceptionally loveable animal which I reared with the greatest of care.' This baby gibbon whom he called Mumu, later also called Bubu, was delivered by Thai Airways couched on a bed of orchids on a silver salver!

> 25-4-1962: To chancellery in morning dress, 10-12 to the opening of Parliament. With Mumu to hotel. Installed the little ape in bathroom, lunched alone. Corrected proofs of *The Lacquer Screen* in the afternoon. 4-5 by car to Art Printers and back home, 7-9 reception [given] by the Speaker of Parliament.

When Kist, his colleague from Singapore, and his wife spent a few days in Kuala Lumpur in the same hotel, they had dinner with Van Gulik who, after they had risen from the table, took them to his room for a glass of cognac. 'I have to look after my baby ape,' he said to Noël Kist. 'Would you like to see him?' She accompanied him to the bathroom and saw Mumu sitting in his box in the bath-tub. His tiny nappies were hanging on a washing line to dry. Van Gulik gave the animal his bottle.

He lavished plenty of time on the animal even on the Dutch national day:

> 30-4-1962: Got up late and played with the little ape, 12 o'clock with [the secretary] Mea [Bakker] to the Lake Club, organized flowers etc. for the reception. Swam there alone, afterwards picked up [Chinese] seals, 3-5 rested at home, then to the Lake Club, 6.30-9 National Day celebrations, 9-10 home [=hotel], changed and fed little ape, returned to Lake Club, where ate supper with the Dutch Society [*Nederlandse Vereniging*] until 11.30.

A little while later he wrote to a colleague: 'The writing is going well, the tiny ape, who accompanies me to the chancellery every day composes the political reports, I my tenth detective novel.' The Van Gulik family was reunited for the summer holidays (July-August) and they had a wonderful time together in Malaysia. But then, in Port Dickson where they were holidaying, Bubu died, and Willem recalls that when Bubu passed away it was the first time he ever saw his grief-stricken father cry. In 1964 when Van Gulik wrote the Dutch Book Week free gift, *Vier Vingers*, he dedicated it to 'my loyal friend, the gibbon Bubu'.

Throughout the whole time the Van Guliks spent in Malaysia gibbons played an important role in their lives. Earlier, as a foster family, they had looked after a gibbon which was called Piddler. A game warden had said that it would be good for the animal to live in a group for a while, because he had been left behind alone in the jungle and had developed a mental problem: he clutched at his head whenever he was nervous. Once this had been cured, Piddler was released back into the jungle.

But the end of the holidays came and with it the time for farewell visits:

14-8-1962: with S.F. to palace for farewell visit to the King and Queen.

On 29 August they left Kuala Lumpur for good. At that moment there was no suitable foreign posting available for Van Gulik, and it was also thought that it would be useful for him to work in the Netherlands again to ensure that he did not become estranged from his own country. 'No, I don't yet know,' he wrote to a friend, 'what post will be assigned to me by the alpine ministry. It doesn't really matter, after Kuala Lumpur almost any post will be a promotion. However, first of all I'm going to enjoy my furlough, above all by having myself put in order medically.'

At the ministry in The Hague he was assigned the position of Chief of the Department of Research and Documentation. As this was generally held to a pretty insignificant temporary job until something better came along, the directors of the department were somewhat astonished when he accepted the job immediately, without grumbling. Probably at that moment on account of his many private activities, Robert saw it as a good solution. Moreover, as he said to a colleague: ' It's not the job that makes the man, but the man that makes the job.' Once again he managed to make something of it.

Chapter 15

THIRD PERIOD IN THE NETHERLANDS
1962-1965

It was more than eleven months after his arrival in the Netherlands that Van Gulik would finally make a note on 23 August 1963:

> 9.30 For the first time occupied the chair as Head of Department of Research and Documentation Foreign Affairs.

The head of this department was a function traditionally reserved for a ministerial civil servant and it was unusual for a diplomat to occupy it. Nevertheless, Van Gulik was happy with it; after seven years abroad The Hague made a welcome change, and preferably one which would last three years. His principal motivations in this choice were renewed contact with the Netherlands and the chance for a family reunion.

In the months he had owing him as holidays and paid leave, and indeed thereafter, he plunged into all sorts of activities with his customary energy and enthusiasm and, as usual, he succeeded in using his time profitably. He wasted no time buying a new house and selling the old one so that they could settle in straightaway. Among the rooms in this new home—Ten Hovestraat 88 in the Statenkwatier (one of the best residential parts of The Hague)—one room was set aside as a study housing the accompanying collection of books, Chinese furniture, *objects d'art*, the instruments essential to calligraphy and whatever else should be found in such a room. Throughout the years, his study-cum-library, which oozed character and was invariably given a Chinese name, remained the showpiece of his house and, always differently set up, it invariably made a big impression on every visitor.

Nor were the family pets forgotten. A small, brown capuchin monkey and a small Hussar monkey (*Erythrocebus patas*) were allotted an attic room, because he thought a life without monkeys would be 'sad for the children' (and even more for himself!).

The 19 March, 1964 issue of *Het Vaderland* (an esteemed evening paper printed in The Hague) published an interview with Van Gulik:

'And here I have a hedgehog, eight guinea-pigs and two canaries. A hedgehog is—are you aware?—a mystical animal. Mine (who has just woken up from his hibernation) spends part of the night walking around my apple tree. Every night. And when doing so he describes a perfect circle.' As a matter of fact, referring to this newspaper he once remarked: 'In the morning I read the *Telegraaf* to wake myself up and in the evening *Het Vaderland* to be able to sleep.'

In that period, the ministry was still dispersed over several buildings. His department, where for a very long time there had been complaints about the dreadful lack of space, was situated in the Casuariestraat. Van Gulik lost no time in making some changes: a portion of the books from the library were placed in his room, and the Section Documentation of Newspaper Articles was assigned its own quarters.

From the point of view of his staff, Van Gulik was an exceptionally fine head. He did not have 'to prove himself': they were already aware of how gifted he was. He was 'no pettifogging man who was constantly looking over your shoulder, but a person who assumed that you were competent to do your work.' The memoranda, notes and jottings which the bureaus under his aegis placed before him were dealt with properly and—even more importantly—*quickly*. Any discussion with him about work was invariably brief and was always to the point. Van Gulik behaved 'naturally', he was always himself. His authority was never oppressive but taken as a matter of course. Within the span of a couple of weeks he had had a good talk with every staff member. This gave each and every one the chance to get matters off his chest. After such a talk he knew with whom he was dealing and what sorts of ideas, opinions and feelings were floating around the department. The one gesture above all his staff highly appreciated was that the whole department, over the space of three evenings, were invited to the Van Guliks' house. As his staff pointed out, not unusual for a diplomat but almost unheard of for departmental civil servants. Precisely in this very relaxed atmosphere, the existing hierarchy could be set aside for a few hours. He was happiest when he could surround himself with trust. He arranged that the ex-chancellor from Beirut and the Tibetan scholar M. Ondei, MA, were appointed to his department. Van Gulik's youngest son, Thomas, was set to work there in the holidays, helping to cut out the newspaper articles.

As has already been said, Dr Van Gulik wrote the 1964 Book Week free gift, entitled *Vier Vingers* (later published in English as *Judge Dee at Work*). It tells the story of how for the umpteenth time Judge Dee had managed to solve a number of shady affairs, on this occasion by finding a ring set with a costly emerald, which had been picked up somewhere by a black gibbon and which—as it later turned out—had slipped off one of the four amputated fingers of a murder victim.

His secretary was witness to the way in which this book was written. In between his busy office duties he wrote 'in passing' the text in English using his famous dip pen, first on small filing cards and paper, ornamented with Chinese characters and illustrations he drew himself in the Chinese style. When this had been done, he wrote the text in Dutch. On the cover were two antique puppets from the National Museum of Ethnology in Leiden. This image was photographed in his room during office hours. All this secretive 'fuss' elicited from many of his staff the question: 'What on earth is going on in our head's office?'

Working on a typewriter was not confined to the office. At home Robert was often typing away in his study until deep into the night: this was a familiar sound for eleven-year-old Thomas as he fell asleep in his small bedroom next door. At this time Van Gulik also put the finishing touches to a crime novel which was completely different from his Judge Dee stories: *The Given Day*, illustrated with his own geometrical drawings, into some of which the shape of a woman was occasionally worked. The story takes place in Amsterdam in the 1960s within the space of one day and moments of Zen enlightenment are woven into it.

In the Judge Dee books, the Dutch versions of two novels which had already been published in English were completed: *The Night of the Tiger* and *The Willow Pattern*. In December 1962 Van Gulik spent a morning at Soestdijk Palace, in connection with the translation of *The Chinese Gold Murders* into Spanish by His Royal Highness Prince Bernhard.

Van Gulik thought up yet another form for Judge Dee: he now appeared in a series of comic strips and illustrated stories, which were published both in newspapers and in book form. This possibility had arisen after Van Gulik discovered the expert illustrator Frits Kloezeman.

> 'My eyes were opened up,' said Van Gulik after their first meeting, 'when they came to me with an artist who had studied the illustrations in my novels. I have been fretting myself to death about these drawings, drawn from Ming dynasty examples. I said to him: "Please go ahead and draw a Judge Dee".'

He had finished in five minutes and it seemed very authentic. I was green with envy…, I can sometimes spend hours just on one small hand. I had never looked at comics and I now realized that I had made a mistake. [Comics are] an intermediate form between writing for the stage and writing a script for a film, and it opens up tremendous possibilities for the detective [story].'

He produced the text and gave the artist directions for and examples of Chinese costumes and contemporaneous interiors. The comics were produced so that they were immediately suitable for publication in Japan and China.

'Comics have an enormous advantage,' he concluded, 'in that you can *show* literally everything. We are asking more of the viewer than of the reader of my books. You can bring the character of a person to light visually, and then, on the basis of what we have him see, we leave the combining and deducing to the viewer. [...] With a big blue pencil I cross out everything that is not directly relevant to the story. You reduce a hundred words to twenty and you can still say quite a bit. You are forced to concentrate and to formulate without any distractions. There cannot be one word too much. There is nothing more educational than to have to write within set boundaries. And using a short, to-the-point dialogue, supplemented by plenty of action I am not deviating from the Chinese style.' (*Nieuwsblad van het Noorden*, 28-11-1964)

In 1963-1964, he submitted an article entitled *Monsieur de Wicquefort en zijn Handboek voor Ambassadors* (Mr De Wicquefort and His Manual for Ambassadors) to *Voorpost*, the in-house paper for the *Vereniging voor de Buitenlandse Dienst* (Society for Foreign Affairs), in which he gives a fascinating description of the life and work of this Dutch 'political journalist' (1606-1682). He had written his manual *L'Ambassadeur et ses Fonctions*, to pass the time spent in the Gevangenpoort (the Stadtholder's prison in The Hague), in which he was incarcerated on account of his close ties with Johann de Witt. It is more than likely that Van Gulik saw a kindred spirit in this colourful, talented non-conformist. When De Wicquefort was appointed envoy in The Hague by both the King of Poland and the Duke of Brunswick-Lüneburg-Celle, he occupied, as Van Gulik remarked with scarcely disguised envy, 'the ideal post for a civil servant in foreign affairs, namely that of a Dutch diplomat accredited to his own country'—and thereby free to enjoy all the accompanying facilities and monetary perks.

In the notes of one of De Wicquefort's predecessors, a certain Jean Hotman, Van Gulik came across a passage which revealed that a somewhat thrifty Polish king tried to fob off retiring ambassadors with counterfeit jewels and inferior silverware. However, the Dutch ambassadors were too clever for him; they said they would prefer a promissory note. Van Gulik had this to say about the matter:

> You will agree with me that the Dutch ambassadors of yesteryear were resolute fellows. Picture such an occasion to yourself: with a lump in his throat the foreign head of state has just uttered the hoary words about historical ties, and the *Chef de Protocole* is standing alongside you busy fiddling about with stars and safety-pins, and you say in a matter-of-fact tone: I would have preferred a cheque.

In absolute agreement with the author, Van Gulik abstracted from De Wicquefort's manual that an ambassador should behave with propriety, but this should be a natural dignity, inherent in his personality; not some acquired exhibition of desperately observed formality. In his opinion this would only lead to mistakes being committed.

After having been asked to accept a special teaching commitment in the cultural history of Buddhist countries outside India by the Arts Faculty of the University of Utrecht, he appeared there once a week in his professorial guise. However, the crown on all he had achieved as scholar and writer—the Olympic gold medal for an academic— was his appointment as a member of the Academy of the Arts and Sciences (*Koninklijke Academie van Kunsten en Wetenschappen*). He was installed in the headquarters of the Academy, the Trippenhuis in Amsterdam, on 15 June 1964.

During this Hague time, he played an active part in the local club life. The club *De Witte* became a familiar haunt for meals and intimate games of billiards with friends and family. The *Indische Kulturele Kring* (The Indies Cultural Circle) or *Tong Tong* and the *Haagse Kunstkring* (The Hague Art Circle) brought him into contact with writers, artists and people who knew about the Indies.

In his book *De Koorddansers en Andere Herinneringen* (Tight-Rope Dancers and Other Memories), Rico Bulthuis presents an apt characterization of Van Gulik, whom he had first met at a reception, at which they had had no opportunity to have a conversation.

As I was putting on my coat in the cloakroom, Van Gulik was standing next to me. He handed me his card and asked if I would ring him. He wanted to speak to me [...] A sedate, somewhat nonchalant civil servant from foreign affairs smartly dressed in a dark suit, rather more sturdily built than portly. He wore rimless spectacles. Small lenses with tiny gold hinges in the corners. His almost white moustache was small, and there was an even smaller, virtually unnoticeable tuft underneath his lower lip. The most remarkable feature in that round face was his sharp eyes.

He ushered me in and took me to the first floor, to his study. An orderly junk shop of eastern objects, bronze miniature pagodas, ivory figurines, Chinese porcelain, *kakemono* (scroll paintings) on silk. The many bookcases were crammed full of books, small boxes, specimen drawers and small bronze figurine statuettes. Next to the writing table, against the wall, a Chinese chair made of ebony with a marble seat.

Van Gulik asked me to address him by his first name. Just Robert. He had heard that I was employed by Stols [a well-known publishing house] and wanted to know if it also published detective stories. I denied this and he seemed surprised. Didn't Mr Stols want to make money? He had done well himself, he said, by translating several historical reports of Chinese cases into English, having them printed in Tokyo—at his own expense of course—and selling them [...] at double the rate. Everyone had recouped their costs nicely. And now he was translating the stories into Dutch, as a new publication.

He gave Bulthuis a copy of *Dee Goong An*, inscribed a dedication in it and asked if he knew anything about the animated film industry in the Netherlands. Robert had Walt Disney in mind, Bulthuis noted later, for a film 'about a world trip by Judge Dee on the white screen; copyright Robert van Gulik. He was not without business acumen.'

By this time, he had sought contact with Don Vermeire, a famous Hague puppeteer, in order to have puppets made for a marionette film—Judge Dee as a puppet on the silver screen. 'You [Bulthuis] have written a great deal about puppets and you can advise me.' It seems he was extremely well informed. In the meantime, he was busy smoking a cigar and sprinkling ash over his waistcoat. He struck me as being both on his guard and absent-minded. "I shall fetch some tea. Please do have a look round."

He returned with two cups of tea and a small monkey was perched on his shoulder. I imagined the same thing happening with Bordewijk! The monkey snuggled against Robert's head and made small chirruping sounds. "He wants to make your acquaintance", said Robert.

At the top of his house at the front was a small room which Robert called the monkey cage. He wanted to show it to me, warning me not to hold anything in my hands, because the monkeys would make a grab like greased lightening for it and bite it. In the passageway on the third floor I had no difficulty in guessing where the room was located. Above the door was a square window smeared with faeces, and behind it, it sounded as if everything was being broken apart.

"Please keep behind me," said Robert. He turned the key and set the door ajar so that I could peer inside. Naughty monkeys stared at me, jumped around as quick as lightening and one of them went to swing back and forth on a wash-basin which had been pulled off the wall and hung from a thick lead pipe.

"Dear animals", said Robert. "I'll have the wash basin repaired. It's not doing any harm as the water has been turned off, but the monkeys do like destroying loose objects." He drew a banana out of his coat pocket and threw it inside. He said that the monkeys were not strong. Frequent tuberculosis. They had to be well looked after and a close eye kept on them.

We returned to the study. He showed me books about primates. I still believe that he loved animals and objects more than people. He had written a book about horses. His doctoral thesis.

It [often struck me] that Robert lived in a man's world. If he liked them he called them by their first name. In the company of women, even the wives of his friends, he courteously always addressed them as "madam". Emancipation was a word which he would never say, in whatever language, other than in an ironic tone.'

Van Gulik was a gifted speaker who could fascinate his audience with lectures about his Judge Dee novels and all sorts of other topics.

> 1-2-1964: 10 o'clock to Leiden on the train, 11-12 gave a lecture about the practice of diplomacy for Commemoration Day celebrations.

> 14-2-1964: 7 o'clock to The Hague Art Circle, where gave a lecture about word and image in Chinese painting/calligraphy.

25-3-1964: dinner, afterwards André Peters came. Went together to the Lodge where I gave a talk about Daoism and secret societies.

23-9-1964: 8 o'clock to Pulchri [Pulchri Studios, an important art institution in The Hague], where gave a lecture about the Dutch in Old China for the *Algemeen Nederlands Verbond* [a society which promotes co-operation between the Netherlands and Flanders].

20-10-1964: lunch at home, took train to Arnhem, with military car to the Bilderberg Hotel, where had drinks with [Admirals] Bos, Boon among others. After dinner gave a lecture about Southeast Asia, 11 o'clock brought back to The Hague through the mist in a military car, arrived at 12.30.

Rico Bulthuis (*op cit.*) has provided a lively description of a couple of Van Gulik's lectures.

What Robert really liked was to give talks to small groups. About Japanese calligraphy. He was invited by The Hague Art Circle and brought with him a large number of costly *kakemono* embellished with characters, ink-blocks, brushes and rubbing-stones. On a blackboard he drew Japanese characters with a flat piece of chalk and, to the great astonishment of the audience, praised this extremely complicated, impractical manner of writing as perfect and superior to our phonetic script. He explained that, just as objects, this script clogs our minds and determines our culture. The ideographic script is emotionally laden, abstract and possessed of a rare beauty.

When somebody in the Circle remarked that it was terribly difficult to remember all these small, meaningless signs, Robert was honestly astonished. Not only were these characters pregnant with meaning, it was not at all difficult to remember them. They corresponded to everything in nature and the things which surround us. They were united with these things, said Robert [...].

During drinks that evening he was also asked if he would give a lecture on literature. I waited with bated breath. He could not be such a genius, but during a conversation about narrative prose, just as about painting, it must have been obvious even to a layman that Van Gulik had highly idiosyncratic ideas. Or more aptly, prejudices.

The meeting hall of the Art Circle was packed with interested people when the forum about the thriller was held. Ab Visser had

Bert Japin appointed to be third man behind the table—an amiable, absent-minded man who said no more than ten words the whole evening. Robert had worked out that he was the eldest of us three and *therefore* president of the forum. The first question put by a critical listener was entirely predictable.

"Honoured forum, do you think that the detective novel can be counted as literature?"

Robert wanted to know if this was a serious question. It seemed as if it were going to turn into a fine evening. And indeed it did. I personally think that there are books which are well written and those which are badly written, but that even the best thrillers cannot be classed as literature. Applause from the audience and Robert was beside himself. Did the honoured public think that there was any real literature written in Holland? Could that rubbish produced by that Anna Blaman (Johanna Petronella Vrugt) be considered part of it, with that so-called detective novel which had been inserted into that other unreadable story?

Paul Rodenko [Dutch poet, critic, essayist and translator] was sitting in the audience enjoying himself immensely. Among those present I spotted Gerard B., a civil servant whom I had known slightly a long time ago […]. Gerard sat fuming with annoyance, nudged his neighbour and either shrugged his shoulders whenever anything was said or else tapped his forehead with his index finger. He sprang to his feet […] and walked to the door which he slammed behind him.

Debating with Robert van Gulik when he did not get his own way was a hopeless task. He had craftily said that every writer had to rely on the 'plot' in his novel. Therefore the thriller element could never be denied. "Read Couperus", he said. "*Van oude mensen* (Of Old People). Isn't that a thriller?" "No", said the audience, "it most certainly was not." What was it then? The theme of a thriller was murder. Murder and murder only. A woman writer called out: "I do not read those sorts of books!" And Robert riposted: "Then I advise you to read Dostoyevsky."

At 10 o'clock the discussion was continued merrily in the pub.

On account of his nostalgia for the Indies of yesteryear, he was closely involved in the cultural activities arranged by the *Indische Kulturele Kring* (The Indies Cultural Circle), which had to do with the country of his boyhood. There he was regularly in contact with the great scholar of the Indies, Rob Nieuwenhuis. He also mediated for the

Circle at the embassy of the People's Republic of China, which cleared the path for an exhibition of Chinese paintings. He helped with the selection and hanging of these and personally took responsibility for the Chinese text in the catalogue. The people with whom he mixed in his Hague days formed an interminable procession: both the old friends to whom he remained loyal, among them Theo Rocqué, now in his eighties, and more recent friends, among them the detective writer and journalist Ab Visser and the author Leonhard Huizinga, with whom he developed a close bond.

On account of his diplomatic career and his intensive study of eastern cultures, Van Gulik had been far away from the Netherlands for a very long time. Nevertheless, he felt completely at home. The many changes which had occurred in the Netherlands, many of which he by no means approved, did not upset him; he accepted them philosophically. He lived in another world; domestic politics did not interest him much. In the Netherlands his interest was also completely devoted to cultural matters.

As well as his contacts with family members like his brother Ben and his niece Katy Deys and others, he was in close touch with the Arabic scholars C. Adriaanse and H.H. Dingemans at Foreign Affairs. The historian C. van Wermeskerken often kept him company on strolls along the antique shops in the Denneweg. Despite the fact that there were no diplomatic ties with Taiwan, Van Gulik could not resist a meeting with Dr V.K. Wellington Koo, the famous former Minister of Foreign Affairs and ambassador of the Kuomintang government, and his wife. As far as he was concerned, Koo was not a political but a cultural figure.

> 4-10-1963: With S.F. to Wittebrug [a small area in the dunes between Wassenaar and Scheveningen with a famous hotel and restaurant], where the Wellington Koos were giving a dinner for us and both Schrikkers [a former Dutch diplomat and later promoter of Chinese interests in the Netherlands].

A few days later the Van Guliks gave a return dinner at home with A.D.A de Kat Angelino (a former Indies civil servant who wrote a two-volume work about colonial history). He very rarely relented in the pace of his many social and cultural activities, despite the fact that in this period he was being beset by an increasing number of ailments, above all stomach complaints, and he was demanding too much of himself.

Conscious of the fact of how quickly his children were growing up, just before his arrival in the Netherlands Van Gulik sighed: '*Eheu fugaces labuntur anni!*' (Oh, how quickly the years are flying by!). This was not misplaced as it was now for the last time that the whole family was reunited under one roof. Three still lived at home and the eldest paid regular visits at the weekends and in the holidays. It had been impossible to move Willem to the J.P. Thijsse Lyceum in The Hague so close to his final examinations.

> 22-6-1963: 2 o'clock on the train to Haarlem with S.F.. Willem came to visit the Oolders family [with the good news] of a good result for his Gymnasium A examination.

Pl. 26. Family photo, The Hague, December 1964.

His father was very keen that Willem should do his military service early and the latter was willing. Therefore he began this in August. Willem says that his father thought that the continuity of family traditions was very important and he hoped that his eldest son would become a regular army officer. In December 1962, Pieter was given a place at the Johan de Wit Lyceum in The Hague; Pauline and Thomas were also at school in that city. Van Gulik visited all the schools regularly at set times, spoke with the teachers and helped the children with their homework. The family enjoyed plenty of outings: often eating in restaurants, visits to the zoo and taking family trips. Shih-fang also made a number of trips on her own; after a few short trips within Europe, in the summer of 1964 she also spent three months on family visits in the Far East. This was a twentieth wedding anniversary present.

In a letter to the De Vries family in Tokyo in March 1964, among other things Robert wrote:

> End '64-beginning '65 I hope to go abroad again, because life here is very hard for Frances [=Shih-fang]; generally speaking life is hard enough for the Dutch housewife, but it is naturally worse for Frances, and she misses her social life with Chinese ladies terribly.

And in his pocket diary he noted:

> 26-6-1964: discussions with Van Schelle [Chief DBD = Head of Personnel Services] about Tokyo.

Ten Hovestraat was rented, the monkeys moved to the Wassenaar Zoo, the three sons remained behind, and in a blaze of publicity Ambassador Van Gulik with his wife and daughter left for Tokyo on 22 January 1965. The siren call of Asia proved irresistible.

Chapter 16

THIRD PERIOD IN JAPAN
1965-1967

At every embassy the appointment of a new ambassador is anticipated with trepidation. The situation is something akin to a gamble, at stake is the atmosphere at the post for a number of years. As time goes by, among foreign office staff a general feeling develops about individual heads of post, and those who score less well sometimes have none-too-friendly nicknames bestowed upon them.

Hence it was with a feeling of great relief that the 'second man' in Tokyo, the lawyer W.Ch.E.A. (Wil) de Vries, and his wife were informed, initially by rumour and later officially, that Dr R.H. van Gulik would be the successor to Ambassador N.A.J. de Voogd, who was retiring. The appointment and the request for the *agrément* were made in the middle of 1964.

The Japan which awaited Van Gulik was a very different place to the country which he had left thirteen years earlier. In the 1950s, the Japanese economy had recovered within a very short space of time and, by the beginning of the 1960s, the country was experiencing an astonishingly rapid period of economic growth, one which would make Japan one of the most powerful countries in the world economically in the following decades.

The capital Tokyo had undergone a transformation, of which Van Gulik had gained only a fleeting impression during a three-day visit for an ambassadors' conference in 1962. The impetus behind this transformation was the summer Olympic Games held in Japan in 1964. During the preparations for these Olympic Games, which were opened on 10 October, Japan was caught up in a whirlwind of activities. These were not restricted to the building of the facilities directly related to the games themselves, but extended to the infrastructure in Tokyo, with its 13 million inhabitants. Expressways over large viaducts were constructed right through the city, new stations were built for the underground system, and a railway line was laid down for the spectacular 'bullet train' (the *shinkansen*) between Tokyo and Osaka, which enabled the previously unheard of speed of 250 km per hour to be reached. The hotel accommodation was considerably expanded.

In order to prevent total traffic chaos, most of the work in Tokyo was carried out at night. The detours meant that late in the evening many motorists had difficulty in finding their way home. In fact, beyond the main arteries the jumble of narrow, nameless side-streets had always caused many to head off in the wrong direction and now all this became just that much worse.

It was obvious that Van Gulik seemed to be in no hurry to set off for his new post, for which in fact the *agrément* had already been granted in August, during this hectic period and therefore he did not make any haste. In a letter dated 5 October, he says to his future closest colleague:

> That we shall have Leentje and yourself very close to us makes us less averse to the busy social ado—of which both my wife and I have gradually begun to have more than enough.
>
> From my own person point of view, I had viewed Tokyo more as a *fin de carrière*. The truth is that I feel—don't burst out laughing—still too young for a 'sedentary' post. Therefore I had worked out an alternative, a new ambassadorship for the combination Vietnam-Laos-Cambodia, an area which interests me, buzzing with a cheerful racket wherever one turns and offering possibilities for adventure. In principle S [the Secretary-General] could see something in this, but administrative objections were raised and consequently the minister wanted to keep to Tokyo.
>
> Now, of course Tokyo does offer compensations [...]. Moreover, Korea is a welcome 'addition'; the country and its people have always had a great fascination for me.
>
> We were thinking of flying to Bangkok, either at the end of the year or thereabouts, spending a few days relaxing there and then [continuing on] to Tokyo. Pauline, who is in her first year at secondary school, is the only one of the children who is coming with us; the best place for her in Tokyo will be the Sacred Heart [School]. Willem and Pieter are doing their national service; Thomas would prefer to remain in Holland to finish his primary school.
>
> As you are naturally completely caught up in the Olympic fever, I shall not bother you with practical matters. After all, one should not want to organize too much in advance!

Ambassador De Voogd and his wife left Japan a few days before Christmas, and the arrival of his successor followed hard on his heels. On 5 January 1965, among other matter the latter wrote to De Vries:

> When Doctor Bryan [of the Government Medical Service] checked my wife's health, he thought that she was somewhat run-down and he advised a boat trip to Japan. However, the boats leave either too early or too late. We have now reached a compromise: we shall fly to Karachi with KLM on 22 January, and there we shall embark on the French passenger ship the *Cambodge*, which is due to dock in Kobe on 11 February.
>
> After that we shall have to take up lodgings in the Imperial Hotel [in Tokyo] for a little while, while the residence is spruced up a little.

This was indeed the itinerary which was followed and, on 12 February, the Van Guliks, accompanied by their fourteen-year-old daughter Pauline, finally arrived in Kobe, one of the two most important ports in Japan, delightfully situated between a range of hills and the sea, where a Dutch consulate had traditionally been established.

This institution dated from the first years of the opening up of Japan, after the collapse of the military rule of the Tokugawa *shōguns* and the restoration of the monarchy in 1868. The reign of the Emperor Meiji (1868-1912) marked the beginning of the presence on Japanese soil of European, Americans and Russians on a previously unheard of scale. The strangeness and exotica of Western faces, clothes, way of life, housing, means of transport and all sorts of other curiosities became the favourite subjects for what are known as Meiji prints. In various of these prints of townscapes and scenes in the foreign settlement in Kobe, the Dutch Tricolour, the British Union Jack and the American Stars and Stripes can be seen flying from the mastheads of three oldest consulates there. This former foreign 'concession' still forms the town centre of Kobe. In less than a century, the three cities Kobe, Osaka and the splendid old imperial city of Kyoto, plus the municipalities adjacent to them, have developed into the principal urban conglomeration of western Japan (the *Kansai*), comparable in size to the Tokyo-Yokohama metropolis in the east (the *Kantō*).

The Van Guliks were welcomed and shown around efficiently and in a fitting manner by Nico van Zelm, then acting consul-general. Likewise their arrival in Yokohama, another day's sail, took place as the ambassador had wanted, without the press and without any fuss. Apart from a representative of the protocol, in compliance with the ambassador's wishes only Mr and Mrs De Vries were present to greet them. In the evening over some informal drinks, there was a meeting with the ambassadorial staff in 'House No. 2'.

To those who had known him previously, Van Gulik appeared little changed, perhaps a little greyer and his hair had thinned out. Nevertheless, the same piercing stare behind the rimless glasses, the same sort of moustache and goatee, the inveterate cough, the smoking, a remarkable somewhat muffled voice and an air of authority, similar to that of a teacher who can control the class without raising his voice, had not changed.

From the very beginning of his return to Japan, it was obvious that he felt completely at home, not least because he spoke the language so fluently. Mrs Van Gulik was still a vision of beauty and elegance; but the absence of her former cheerfulness and ready laugh were remarked upon. Daughter Pauline, now grown into a naturally graceful, charming teenager, both friendly and caring, was the apple of her father's eye.

The next morning, Van Gulik inspected the residence and the chancellery, now located in a new wing, which he had not previously known in their present form: 'bathing cabins, not at all in the style of the residence', was his disparaging comment.

Actually the official part began with the ambassador's office in the residence, on one side giving on to the entrance hall to the house, on the other side to the chancellery proper. It was a large, rather gloomy, wood-panelled room, in which all his predecessors had worked. Not Van Gulik! Upon entering, he cast his eye around in silence and then said to his colleague: 'No, old chap, I am not going to sit here, because, if I did, I would always see Pabst's mug in front of me.' He then matched deed to word and unhesitatingly assigned a small salon at the front of his house to be his office. Consequently, the boundary between the chancellery and the residence became even more blurred.

Shih-fang immediately felt less happy there: 'Oh, that residence in Tokyo! Because Robert had set up the small salon as his office and had his study upstairs, both embassy staff and visitors were continually traipsing through the corridors, and you could no longer be sure if you were living in your own home or in an office. What is more, we Chinese are rather superstitious and I thought it was macabre that there was a cemetery located almost right next door to the residence.'

Robert, however, was in his element. A desk for ambassadorial business was placed on one side of the small salon, and on the other side, a second writing-table, on which he wrote his detective stories, was set next to the door into the hall. Thereafter, whenever his closest staff member opened the door, he would look to check where Van Gulik was sitting. If it was on the other side, it was as the ambassador and De Vries went in; if it was to the right of the door, this would be gently closed to await a change of place, because an author must not be disturbed. Once again Van Gulik was living 'three lives', one at each of these desks plus the one in his Chinese study: diplomat-author-scholar.

Opposite the desk at which he dealt with all the embassy business stood one visitor's chair, and at the side of this desk, on his left, was another chair. Usually, when he held discussions with members of his staff (because it was for them that the chairs were intended; guests were usually seated on a small settee), the official concerned was asked to be seated, and in this fashion:

- directly opposite Van Gulik if the person concerned was there to be reprimanded or something else of this nature;
- on the side if it was for a normal or private conversation.

Every month, it was the custom that the ambassador was expected to go through the financial accounts of the post, and endorse and initial all the pages of the cash and bank books. However, Van Gulik did this not by appending his signature or by initialling them, but with his own home-made name stamp in Chinese characters, an innovation for which he had asked and received permission from Foreign Affairs.

Although the study was ready to be used almost immediately, it was almost three weeks before the rest of the house was ready to be moved into, and with the Van Guliks even this did not proceed as it did with most Dutch people:

3-3-1965: Moved from Imperial Hotel to Embassy.

5.30-6.00: Housewarming ceremony [conducted] by Iwagami, Abbott of the Kōmyōgi; followed by the first dinner in our own home.

The appointment with the abbot had been made a few days earlier during a visit to his temple in Kamakura, a coastal town about 50 km from Tokyo, whose most conspicuous attraction is a gigantic, open-air statue of the Buddha. The Kōmyōji—Temple of Light—belonged to the Pure Land sect of Buddhism, with which Van Gulik had been brought into contact before the war through Kachan, his steady girlfriend. The 'pure land' is the paradise which stands in sharp contrast to the little which is pure in our earthly existence. This temple dates from 1243, the heyday of the Kamakura period, when this city was the seat of the government of Japan (1192-1333 CE).

The housewarming ceremony marked the beginning of Van Gulik's life in this residence in Tokyo which was to last slightly over two years. He changed a couple of rooms in the upper storey, which were set aside for a different purpose, beyond recognition. A guided tour of this storey was in fact a stroll along the many and colourful aspects of his activities.

Pride of place was the billiard room, to which he regularly invited three of his staff to play a game; gradually these get-togethers were to turn into hours of cheerful relaxation.

Nevertheless, the most remarkable change was wrought in two adjoining rooms: the innermost windowless, shadowy and stately; the outer a sun-filled veranda offering a view over the garden. Together they formed a 'holy of holies' which he furnished personally and in which he spent a great deal of his spare time. Only specially selected guests were invited to enter these chambers and in them one could imagine oneself in another world. Everything he held dear in the form of Chinese books, paintings, statues, wall hangings, furniture,

Pl. 27. Practising calligraphy in his library in Tokyo.

musical instruments and the accoutrements he needed for his calligraphy had a valued place here and formed an attractive whole.

In the airy outer room, seated on a square ebony stool at a sturdy oblong table, Van Gulik devoted himself to the art of writing with the brush. Chinese calligraphy requires not just hours of practice, it needs a space in which it can be practised, especially if large brushes are used; the characters can be written from top to bottom, or from right to left, and in various writing styles: standard, grass and seal scripts among others. His favourite was the flowing lines of the grass script.

Fig. 12: An example of Van Gulik's calligraphy in 'grass script'.

If he were writing large characters, he usually made two or three copies, of which the best was given way to someone or other and the rest found its way into the wastepaper-basket. Van Gulik was very much aware that the classical Chinese scholar-official, whom he invariably took as his example, should not only write a good style, but should also always be able to express himself in a form which was beautiful.

Of the innumerable fruits of the pens of famous calligraphers that captivated Van Gulik, two deserve a special mention. One exerted such a fascination on Van Gulik that he chose to hang this panel of square characters strategically above his calligraphy table and he often copied the text. It was the work of the Chinese Ch'an (Zen) monk Mu-an— pronounced Moku-an in Japanese—who came to Japan in 1655, eleven years after the collapse of the Ming dynasty in China and became abbot of the Mampukuji, a temple near Kyoto. The four characters mean 'the taste of pure and fragrant tea' (*ch'ing-hsiang ch'a-wei*). It was this temple which introduced the tea ceremony, Ming-style, into Japan where it is still practised today. Mu-an was a colourful figure, under whom the temple—the most Chinese in Japan—reached its heyday. Van Gulik was a great admirer of his personality and his style.

Size-wise, the most dominant piece of calligraphy consisted of two conspicuously large characters (those for good fortune and long life), which actually bore the seal of the famous Manchu emperor Ch'ien-lung (1736-1796). Although Van Gulik, who had a marked predilection for the Ming, was not really very interested in the succeeding Manchu dynasty, perhaps he did feel some affinity with this emperor, who also imitated the classical literati and devoted himself to both poetry and calligraphy.

Fig. 13: The High House of Former Days.

THE HIGH HOUSE OF FORMER DAYS

The high house of former days, the gate to yesteryear:
The shadow of a man returns, [who] recognizes the dusk.
In the inner courtyard, you gave me red love beans as a token of farewell,
I still remember how I would meet you under the blossom of the green peach.
Your delicate eye-brows half creased in a frown, arched like the crescent moon,
Your cicada locks lightly wreathed [your face], as fine as clouds.
Do you still remember how once behind the double curtain and mosquito-net
You burnt the finest quality incense with your own hands?

Chinese poem and calligraphy by Dr Van Gulik

The emperor's two auspicious words hung above a very large Chinese ebony settee, inlaid with mother-of-pearl and into which marble panels were inserted. On it lay a long cushion, clad in dark red brocade, and on one side of it lay a long bolster in the same colour, on which the calligrapher-scholar would sometimes rest his weary head (see back cover illustration).

Heightening the restful atmosphere was a seated Korean Buddha made of gilded wood with downcast eyes, in the pose of contemplation. Van Gulik had placed this in a bay against the background of a red-coloured cloth, and on either hung side scrolls with parallel Zen texts, each bearing seven characters:

> When the clouds disappear from the sky of the mind, shines the moon of the consciousness (= Zen).
> When the spring returns to the earth of the spirit, the flowers of enlightenment spread their perfume.

There is a story attached to the Buddha statue. Van Gulik bought it in the summer of 1950, hence shortly before the outbreak of the Korean War. The price he paid for the beautiful piece of art was incredibly low. He was then overwhelmed by a sense of foreboding that Korea was poised on the brink of a disaster: after all, it is only when threats are of the most serious kind that people are prepared to sell their most precious possessions for next-to-nothing.

On the journey home, as the Buddha statue, all packed up, was ready to be loaded into the aeroplane, a soldier jokingly set his military cap on the swathed head and, as if it were a snowman, stuck a pipe in the place where the mouth would be. Van Gulik was horrified by this and saw this incident as a portent of disaster.

Van Gulik had chosen the upper storey for these studies in the Chinese style so that people would not think, he was wont to say, that they had come to the Chinese embassy.

From time immemorial, the entire terrain of the embassy had belonged to the Temple of the White Snake and, as the oldest inhabitants, under no circumstances would Van Gulik allow the white snakes which still survived to be killed. On one occasion, one of these original inhabitants gave proof of his presence by coiling up on a bench by the swimming pool at the back of the garden.

As 'House number 2', in which the De Vries lived with their three children, was located on the same terrain as the residence, from the very beginning there was fairly intensive intercourse between the

Pl. 28. Niche with Korean Buddha statue, Tokyo, 1967.

two dwellings, not only prompted by embassy matters or official functions, but because both families had known each other for a very long time. Mrs De Vries-Van der Hoeven (Leentje) had first met Van Gulik as a young girl in Harbin in 1935. Later, in the summer of 1942, she and her parents and Van Gulik were all passengers on board the *Tatsuta Maru* as part of the plan for the exchange of Allied and Japanese diplomats.

Van Gulik had also had earlier contact with Leentje's husband, Wil. In 1947 Dr Van Gulik had participated in discussions at the ministry about the training for the foreign service and, in connection with this, he paid a visit to Professor Duyvendak at the Sinological Institute in Leiden. It was already late afternoon and Wil de Vries was just about to leave the reading room of the institute when the librarian advised him to wait a little while before leaving, saying 'Your future is being decided in there.' De Vries did not have the least idea about what his connection was with the man of tall stature, clad in a black coat and hat, who had just walked into Professor Duyvendak's room, where Van Gulik asked if by any chance among the students of Chinese there happened to be two qualified lawyers for the embassy in Nanking. The outcome of this conversation was that De Vries and his fellow student, K.J. Stadtman, were both given posts. Someone who was to arrive there just a bit later—the beginning of 1949—was the future Mrs De Vries, then still Leentje van der Hoeven. She had just done her MA exam in Chinese and had been assistant to Professor Duyvendak before she was dispatched to China as attaché.

Ambassador Van Gulik presented his credentials to the Emperor of Japan on 24 February, 1965. When asked by a representative of the court (the 'Imperial Household') in which language he would address the Emperor on this occasion, without a moment's hesitation Van Gulik had answered: 'In Japanese of course.' And this choice continued in the conversation after the credentials had been handed over. The Emperor was pleasantly surprised that the Dutch ambassador addressed him not in the ordinary, everyday language, but very correctly in formal classical Japanese.

Pl. 29. In the residence after presenting of his credentials to the emperor of Japan; from left to right Jan-Jochem Robertson, Hans Hoog, Mr Naitō of the Imperial Household, Ambassador Van Gulik in diplomatic uniform, Wil de Vries, Wil Pelt, Herman du Marchie Sarvass.

The Dutch ambassador in Tokyo was also accredited to Seoul (Korea), where he also represented the Netherlands in a UN organization, UNCURK (United Nations Commission for the Unification and Rehabilitation of Korea). After the Second World War, as no agreement could be reached with the Soviet Union, which had occupied North Korea, about the formation of a provisional Korean government, UNCURK had been set up with a view to keeping a closer eye on the general elections throughout the whole of Korea. However, as the UN organization was not permitted to enter North Korea, its competence was in fact limited to the South, where the Republic of South Korea was founded after the elections. In June 1951, North Korean troops invaded the South, an action which marked the outbreak of the bloody Korean War. This turned into a test of strength between the United Nations (principally the United States, as well as a number of other countries including the Netherlands) and North Korea, which was supported by the Soviet Union, and above all by the People's Republic of China. In the years 1965-1967, a still-divided Korea was far from being as prosperous as Japan, nevertheless the progress and recovery being made by the country were spectacular.

Van Gulik always journeyed to Korea, where he spent time on no fewer than six occasions in the first year, with visible pleasure. He attended many UNCURK meetings, promoted bilateral affairs (which as a matter of fact were wonderfully taken care of by the local honorary consul, Jan Lenssen) and enjoyed all the culture the land had to offer. His wife accompanied him on the first occasion when he presented his credentials to President Park Chung-hee at the 'Blue House'.

Remarking on the night life, he observed that the traditional institutions of the courtesans survived only in Korea:

> There the young ladies still learn the old dances, like the *Puk-ch'um*: one lady stands between two racks from which are suspended nine different sized drums holding a drumstick in each hand. As she dances she beats the drums—one of the most amazing feats of percussion that I have ever experienced.

He also regretted that in Japan:

> The famous institution of the geishas is in a decline. What attractive young lady will spend five or six years studying Japanese dancing and music if, without any training at all, she will be able to earn 200 to 300 guilders a night as a hostess in a nightclub? All she had to do

is chat and laugh a bit. If she does the horizontal work as well, then she can make as much as 800 guilders!

Not very long after Van Gulik had been posted to Tokyo as ambassador, a large economic mission, led by the Minister of Economic Affairs, J. den Uyl, arrived from the Netherlands on a visit. Among the delegates were the former prime minister Professor De Quay and Sidney van den Bergh, the top man in Unilever. Professor F. Vos accompanied it in his capacity as Japanese expert. The mission also paid a visit to Nagasaki, where there had been a famous Dutch East India Company (VOC) trading-post on the artificial island of Deshima for centuries. During this third posting to Japan, Van Gulik would also often visit the places he knew well, frequently accompanied by the cultural attaché, Charles van der Sloot, who was very familiar with the local situation and was moreover an excellent photographer. Both here and in Tokyo, Van Gulik took every opportunity to stress the inestimable importance of this unique historical fact to bilateral relations. On the occasion of the visit of the trade mission, the ambassador hoped that, as a gesture to promote goodwill, Dutch businesses would make a financial contribution to the Dutch cultural presence in Nagasaki. During a bus tour through the city, Professor Vos and Wil de Vries gave a more detailed explanation of the old historical ties which would form a good basis on which to build in the future. However when the desirability of contributions from the business sector was raised, strikingly their gaze fixed on infinity, they turned their heads and suddenly began to stare out the windows. And to think that, less than a quarter of a century later, millions were spent by the Japanese on 'Holland Village' and the Huis Ten Bosch project—their own celebration of the long historical links between Dutch merchants and Nagasaki!

Where Van Gulik reaped the greatest reward for his work was in his negotiations on behalf of KLM (Royal Dutch Airlines). At that time, the biggest stumbling block was obtaining more aviation rights. If this were to be achieved, it was of the utmost importance to build up a good relationship with JAL (Japan Airlines) but the general management of the Japanese company was not disposed to be particularly forthcoming; in fact it wanted to exclude all competition as far as it possibly could.

Van Gulik hatched a plan. He would invite the whole top echelon of JAL executives *with* their wives (not yet customary in Japan) to the embassy for a meal with the Duijfs, the Tanges, De Quay and Mr and

Mrs De Vries. Duijf was the KLM representative in Japan, Tange the KLM area manager for the Far East. As it was to be such a special occasion, Van Gulik took the utmost care with the details of the preparations for the luncheon. He had the complete background of the JAL directors investigated, including the history of their families and those of their wives. This luncheon, Duijf recounted,

> ...was one of the most exuberantly festive occasions I have ever attended, in spite of the fact the Japanese are said to be so unbending and introverted. This afternoon was subtly dominated by the ambassador. He organized everything and spoke at length with the guests in Japanese. The Japanese sense of humour is different to ours, but this did not trouble Van Gulik one jot. He was especially entertaining, and the Japanese ladies and gentlemen roared with laughter.

This one single luncheon gave rise to a completely different relationship with JAL, which was to prove very valuable to Duijf and Tange in the follow-up. The KLM enjoyed better relations with JAL than any other Western airline company. Later, when former prime minster De Quay and his wife revisited Japan, they and the KLM representative were immediately invited to a dinner at which ladies would be present by the President-Director of JAL. The excellent personal relationships proved to be extremely important to business interests.

On various occasions Van Gulik also did his best for KLM in Korea.

Van Gulik frequently mixed with the Dutch community in Tokyo, was always in high spirits, cracking jokes right and left, and was in fact very unconventional. However, what always impressed everybody the most was his special relationship with the Japanese. Dr Wisse Dekker, the then representative of Philips in Japan, bore witness to this. The first house in which Mr and Mrs Dekker lived was furnished partly in Western and partly in Japanese style, and there they gave dinners for Japanese guests—which could sometimes be rather an uphill battle. The Japanese would stand together talking to each other and when De Voogd, Van Gulik's predecessor, who also spoke Japanese, joined the group, it was immediately obviously that they adopted a different demeanour. When Van Gulik was ambassador, the change was striking. When he approached such a group, all of them just carried on the conversation; it seemed that they had not noticed that a *gaijin* (foreigner) had joined them. Van Gulik was able to chat with them about absolutely everything to do with their daily lives, including which was the best water for making *sake* and so forth.

As the result of a joint venture between Philips and Matsushita, Dr Dekker would sometimes accompany Van Gulik to the *Kansai*, where they would attend the customary geisha dinners. On one such occasion, an older geisha sang a couplet to the accompaniment of her *samisen* (three-stringed guitar) and then wished to withdraw. However Van Gulik said: 'I want to hear the rest.' When it turned out that she did not know this, Van Gulik sang the remaining couplets himself! It was a rousing success!

In answer to a question about Van Gulik's efficacy as a diplomat, Dr Dekker replied as follows:

> His knowledge of Japan was exceptionally wide. He was highly respected by the Japanese and he had very good entrée among them, both naturally very fine and extremely useful to Dutch businesses. Despite this, we did not really find him very beneficial in our business negotiations; at least, we were not always knocking on the door of the embassy. If you did happen to turn up for a visit with a member of the board who was over from the Netherlands, we would leave him shaking our heads. They thought him a bit of a rare bird. The conversation, although entirely pleasant, remained superficial and he would show us his ape and his books. He gave an impression of being more of a scholar than a diplomat. It's my personal belief that he could not see how he could explain Japan—a particularly complex politico-economic subject—to such a visitor in half or three-quarters of an hour, and therefore he did not make any effort to do so. However, if you, as I did, met him on a regular basis, you were able to collect a huge amount of useful knowledge from the conversations you had with him.

In 1970 the great World Exhibition was to be held in Osaka, and in 1966 all the diplomatic representatives in Tokyo were asked to persuade their governments to take part in this Expo '70. In anticipation of the formal agreement of his government, in his own inimitable manner, Van Gulik accepted the invitation immediately. This quick decision proved to have enormous advantages. Of the seventy-six participants which eventually took part, the Netherlands was sixth on the league table. On account of this seniority, the outward and visible signs of which were the hoisting of the flags, the reading out of the participant countries and other such matters of protocol, it was possible to obtain a very suitable location for the Dutch pavilion in a central, well-situated position.

Perhaps a question-mark could be placed about whether Van Gulik's brisk decision to take part actually chimed in with government policy at that time. Certainly the short-lived Cals cabinet had approved the application in principle, but its successor, the interim Zijlstra cabinet, authorized only a trifling sum of 4 million guilders—'and not a cent more'—for the submission; even though 12 million guilders had been set aside for the World Exhibition in Montreal in 1967. The De Jong cabinet, which took office in April 1967, realized that it would be impossible to fund any Dutch contribution with no more than 4 million guilders and decided to withdraw the application for Dutch participation already submitted.

Naturally, under no circumstance would Van Gulik ever have imperilled either his own personal credibility or that of his government: until his departure for the Netherlands in June 1967, he utterly refused to pass on the decision to cancel to the board of the Japanese Expo. Therefore, thanks to the pressure exerted by the business world, a great mistake was prevented: the participation went ahead and was a great success.

Van Gulik's staff were struck that in this and also in the internal relationships within the embassy, the management style pursued could not have been more different to that under his predecessor De Voogd. Whereas the latter always did his best to solve any conflict situations which arose in the embassy by compromise and reconciliation, from the very inception of any such problem Van Gulik made no bones about how the relationships should stand, namely: the way he wanted them to be. His style was authoritarian, but his authority, as was that of Judge Dee in his lifetime, accepted without question. Towards those who were younger and lower in rank, Van Gulik adopted the attitude of the Japanese *sensei*, the teacher, whose proper due was admiration and obedience.

The fact that he could not care less about clothes and often appeared dishevelled did nothing to dispel this. In Tokyo's warm, humid summers, when the air conditioning had broken down for the umpteenth time, he preferred to walk around in white plimsoles, clad in an old pair of trousers and a T-shirt.

Even when he enjoyed a very good relationship with a member of staff, this did not stop him from precisely maintaining values he thought fitting. Godert de Vos (the Third Secretary G. W. Baron van Steenwijk) once returned from an official trip to Korea and was due to meet Van Gulik in Nagasaki, where Godert's wife, Clara, had arrived earlier. However, De Vos was delayed so long that he arrived halfway through a geisha dinner, which made it impossible for him to give a report of his trip. 'Personally, I thought,' said Godert, 'that this could wait until the next morning, but the old gentleman thought otherwise. Clara and I had gone on to a night club with some other guests when he—Heaven knows how—managed to phone me there and ordered me to come to his hotel where I was subjected to a cross-examination. I still respect him for this.'

Van Gulik's conceptions of traditional European and Japanese values applied to all aspects of his conduct. It was up to his subordinates to make sure that a matter was completely, or as completely as possible, in order, remembers Godert de Vos, before the *Taishi* (the ambassador) paid any personal attention to it. Therefore, a given matter could only be broached when some sort of providential act—or something in the Van Gulik tradition which resembled this—seemed to make the occasion appropriate. Should the matter need to be investigated, the conditions required for a mutual agreement had to be sounded out and the Japanese partners or opponents thoroughly prepared. Van Gulik reserved the dotting of the i's for himself, to be done in the manner he thought best. One must never venture beyond the pale with him, because such behaviour could land one in serious trouble, and Van Gulik made this patently clear. And, if one could believe his own comments, the consequences would endure until the end of the Earth and, if possible, even beyond.

'For as far as I was able to observe,' writes Godert de Vos, 'he was without fear. He must have been a difficult man to live with and he did nothing to make things any easier for himself. I imagine he lived a very independent life. It is a pity that this sort of giant among men appears to belong to a dying breed.'

Van Gulik was not on first-name terms with any of his staff and he addressed them by their surnames; he would only call the ladies by their first names if he had known them as children. He was certainly not always an easy man, and he dominated his surroundings in no uncertain terms, to which Pauline, who loved her father dearly, bears witness. She was also frequently struck by the fact that his personality was so completely different to the average 'phlegmatic Dutchman'.

No matter how informal he could often be, Pauline was given evidence of this side of his character on a number of occasions. Once a person from Hong Kong who was visiting Tokyo was to dine with Van Gulik; the appointment had been made long in advance. However, when Pauline came downstairs at dinnertime, she saw that places had been laid only for her father and herself. When she asked where Mr X was, Father answered abruptly: 'He has left. He arrived unannounced with a lady friend, whom I had not invited.'

He was a man of strong likes and dislikes. In the latter event, he could be thought to have been rather mild if he restricted himself to expressing this with a streak of malicious form of humour. The unfortunate foreign visitor who sat next to him at a Japanese dinner with cramps in his legs and who had consumed what to his taste were ghastly items of food could be told by Van Gulik, in a serious, admonitory tone: 'People will think it very unmannerly if you do not eat up that small twig of cherry blossom [which was lying on the table as decoration].'

When asked if he was a Christian or a Buddhist, Pauline said:

> I think a little bit of everything. It did not matter to him if the higher power, God, was worshipped via Christianity, Islam or Buddhism. Occasionally he would burn some incense in front of our statue of the Buddha, but I think he only did this as a gesture of respect, nothing more than that. He taught us children that before God all people, of whatever race, creed, rank or standing, were equal. For instance, he thought it not right that St Paul had condemned homosexuality.

After Chungking, Robert and Shih-fang were perhaps happiest in Lebanon and Malaysia, especially in the latter country. The atmosphere there was carefree and, as described earlier, there was a large Chinese community in Malaysia, where Shih-fang felt she did not have to hide her Chinese-ness; she could even wear a Chinese dress, the *cheong-sam*. In contrast, in Japan she was not able to be herself and felt chronically unsettled. Rightly or wrongly, she often had the impression that, because of her origins, many Japanese did not take her seriously as the wife of the Dutch ambassador. 'At that time I was plagued with headaches, and the medicine prescribed by the physician made me completely dull-witted.'

From his conversations with her and with others, Barkman drew the conclusion that it was difficult for Mrs Van Gulik to adapt herself to a foreign country, but elsewhere this had never been such a great problem because her husband was so very 'Chinese' and everywhere they went, the Van Guliks gathered many Chinese friends and acquaintances around them. Unfortunately matters turned out differently for her in Japan, where Robert also lived his 'Japanese life' with the people of that country. And there, according to daughter Pauline, she also suffered 'under the strain of his Japanese past.'

As a matter of fact, at all the posts in foreign countries to which she followed her husband, Shih-fang did her utmost to help him, not only by easing his innumerable activities but also in fulfilling the by-no-means easy task of being a diplomatic wife. Quite apart from this, to bring four children into the world and raise them as well as possible under the circumstances was an exceptional achievement. Everywhere she happened to go, she was undeniably a 'lady', with an air of distinction, but keeping herself modestly in the background.

Years later, in 1989, when she and her son Willem were interviewed by the editor of a Taiwanese magazine, *Kuang Hua* (*Sinorama*), the editor commenced the interview by saying:

> Westerners say that genius is a 'gift of God'; in the eyes of the Chinese people a genius is an 'exiled Immortal'. However, in both East and West the word 'lonely' is invariably associated with 'genius'. What was it like to be the wife of a genius—the partner of an 'exiled Immortal'?

Mrs Van Gulik had been the wife of a diplomat long enough to be able to skirt around that question deftly, with a subtle smile.

A very special fellow inmate of the embassy in Tokyo made the whole of life there very different during Van Gulik's time there. She had been personally met in Yokohama by Robert. The little lady who at that time became part of the daily life at the embassy was Ginger, alias Jinja, a young blond gibbon with a dark face and dark hands and feet. From the very first day Mrs De Vries' daughter, Michèle, always crazy about animals, was inseparable from the ape, until the moment she was bitten on the cheek, something which was never repeated. Although Ginger never harmed anybody, Van Gulik warned his staff that they must not laugh and show their teeth in her presence, because if they did Ginger would think that they were angry and could become angry herself.

Robert idolized the animal (see front cover illustration) and, one fine day, when in his presence at the office Jinja came and sat on De

Vries' lap and gave him a hug, the latter carefully loosened her hold with the admonitory words: 'Go away Ginger, your master is green with envy, and that is bad for my career.'

Godert de Vos made a similar remark:

> Honestly, I think that Van Gulik was rather jealous by nature [...] and not just of his prerogatives and protégés, but also of his personal relationships. What was his, was his. Furthermore, the gibbon Jinja could do no wrong in Van Gulik's eyes. Everybody knew that, including the Japanese police, who formulated the complaints of the people living in the neighbourhood with the greatest care, it was said.

After a dinner for gentlemen, whenever the ambassador thought that the moment had come for the guests to wend their way home, he fetched his gibbon from upstairs. She descended the wide monumental staircase hand in hand with her master and shook the hand of each guest as a sign that the end of the evening had arrived. In the time which still remained, with a long elegant black finger Ginger spooned the remaining sugar out of the porcelain government coffee cups on the table. During this delicate exercise not one coffee cup was ever broken.

In the summer months, when Ginger was put in an aviary in the garden during the day, on a few occasions she escaped either on the way there or the way back. When she did so, she swung most elegantly along the overhead power cables, sometimes to the Japanese cemetery (if there was food to be found on the graves), sometimes to neighbouring houses in which bits of this and that were also grabbed and devoured. She was as light as a feather and it was astonishing how incredibly little gibbon there was under such a luxuriant coat. On one such escapade, the ambassador sat a very long time in a cane chair on the lawn in his garden with a banana held high in his hand, waiting patiently until Ginger, driven by the pangs of hunger, allowed herself to be caught.

It was in this third Tokyo period that Van Gulik worked on his last scientific publication, *The Gibbon in China*, which he completed there but did not live to see in its printed form. In his Foreword he explains what inspired him to write this book. Since time immemorial, a mysterious link had been considered to have existed between man and nature; throughout the centuries the gibbon has been constantly immortalized in Chinese literature and painting. The gibbon occupies a special place in the culture of the Far East, and Van Gulik found inspiration in investigating the traces of this animal in the various art forms of China, Korea and Japan.

Alongside this romantically inspired academic work, in Tokyo he also continued writing detective stories. Here he finished *The Phantom of the Temple*, which he had begun earlier. According to his own account, he devoted more attention to Judge Dee's three wives at the request of his reading public. What is remarkable is that, in the daily lives of these three, hardly ever was a false note struck; the situation remained ideal, free of quarrels or backbiting, a real marital utopia.

He also bundled together eight short stories including one new one ('He Came with the Rain') to make one book, *Judge Dee at Work*. To this he added a chronological table of Judge Dee's activities throughout the years, as Van Gulik had invented and described these in fifteen novels and eight short stories. This was to signal that this book was the end of the whole series. However his English publisher asked for more, and therefore he wrote two more novels: *Necklace and Calabash* and *Poets and Murder*.

A younger colleague and poet, Maarten Mourik, took the trouble to gather together a number of contributions by diplomat authors into an anthology, *Per Diplomatieke Koerier* (By Diplomatic Courier; *op. cit.*), among them a few poems translated by Van Gulik from Chinese and Japanese, including his well-known *By the Hot Springs at Odawara*. On 20 October 1965, Van Gulik wrote to him that he very well understood how much time and trouble this had cost him,

> All the more so because, in this instance your collaborators have been diplomats—an underdeveloped group in the population who it is true do give themselves airs, but lack the capacity for teamwork which all the other primates have. I myself, after I have undertaken collaborative academic work, have repeatedly sworn a solemn oath that I would never do it again; but, nonetheless, I have revoked this every time, because despite all the headaches it is such pleasant work. [...] Now I'm gradually beginning to get settled here, I hope I'll be able to commence writing again. As you know, writing is like smoking opium; difficult to begin, but even more difficult to kick the habit!'

In view of his wide interest in oriental studies and Asian art, it was no wonder that he spent a great deal of time with people who shared this passion. He was one of an extended circle of friends and acquaintances composed of Japanese and foreign scholars; he also made essential contacts in Korea. He showed a warm interest in the activities of such societies as the Asiatic Society of Japan, the *Oastasiastische Gesellschaft* and those groups which were involved in *Rangaku* (Dutch Studies), among them Professors Seiichi Iwao and Ogata Tomio, as well as Dr Shoichi Nagashima in Nagasaki. He became president of the Asiatic Society and also gave lectures there; on one occasion, giving a talk about the gibbon.

Among his best friends was Nick Carter and his wife (he was American, a self-made man, and an authority in the field of Asian art), with whom he often dined out and visited antique shops. Among his colleagues were also many orientalists such as the famous scholar of Japanese, Professor Edwin O. Reischauer, United States ambassador, and his Japanese wife; and the Chinese ambassador (Taiwan) Chen Chih-mai, Chinese scholar and calligrapher, an old friend from Chungking days, and his wife.

Of course there were the men and women who were passing through, visiting Tokyo temporarily. The visit of Prince Aschwin, the brother of Prince Bernhard, the husband of Queen Juliana, and his wife Princess Simone, deserves a special mention. Pauline van Gulik recalls that her father preferred not to lodge with colleagues or friends; nor did he like to have them stay. He wanted to be free and consequently always preferred a hotel. One exception to the rule was Dr Boon and his wife, with whom he gladly stayed in Rome; they also lodged with him in Tokyo. When Prince Aschwin and his wife came, Van Gulik reserved a hotel for them. However, it turned out that they could not go there on the first day of their visit, and therefore they spent a night in the residence. This visit was such a success they remained and the hotel was cancelled. Actually, they had known each other for awhile and shared many interests. Prince Aschwin was a sinologist and an art connoisseur, especially of Chinese paintings; he was Assistant Curator of the Asian Department of the Metropolitan Museum in New York.

Leonhard Huizinga and Jan Lenssen were another two who were welcome to stay with Van Gulik. The journalist and writer Huizinga was an exceptionally witty man, with whom Van Gulik could get along very well. With his brownish complexion, small moustache and impeccable four button bespoke suits he appeared rather eastern, consequently Japanese often addressed him in Japanese. Van Gulik allowed him to read his 'autobiographical notes', and toyed with the idea that Leonhard Huizinga might write his biography.

Pl. 30.With Leonhard Huizinga and son Willem on the Chinese settee, Tokyo 1965.

The businessman Jan Lenssen, honorary consul in Seoul, felt very much at home in Asia. He had a tremendous sense of humour, was a good conversationalist and *bon vivant*. Importantly he knew how to behave with Koreans. Whenever Van Gulik went to Korea, Lenssen organized everything for him and they did a great deal together; it was probably because of this good relationship that Robert visited Korea so often and with such great pleasure.

Whenever international billiards tournaments were held in Tokyo, as a great fan of the game Van Gulik naturally attended the contests (as a matter of fact the only ambassador to do so). Belgium was represented by Ceulemans, whom he promptly invited to dine at home and with whom he played a few frames. The Dutch judo champion Anton Geesink, who visited Japan on a number of occasions, was also a very welcome guest of the Van Guliks'.

Ever since 1949 Robert had enjoyed a special bond with his literary friend Etsuko Teruyama, who had translated his *Chinese Gold*

Murders and *Chinese Bell Murders* into Japanese and she deserves a special mention as an important personality in Van Gulik's life. On both her father's and mother's side she had descended from samurai families, in which a strict upbringing, acquiring good manners and observation of all the rules of etiquette formed important parts. Although it was still the custom that girls married young, she was one of the first female students to attend Waseda University. She chose to study Chinese history, concentrating on the Tang dynasty. She later married a fellow student, Ikeda, who died young. Before the war she had worked for the British Council, whose head was then the famous student of Japanese, Frank Hawley, and it was there that she developed a deep interest in English language and literature. When Hawley returned to Tokyo after the war as the *Times* correspondent, she went to work for him again. Soon she was also working for Van Gulik, every Wednesday morning; they used to discuss such matters as Japanese texts, illustrations and use of language.

She was an attractive woman, not perhaps what one would immediately call a beauty, but extremely feminine, refined and well dressed. She was a person who loved company and merriment, who would do anything for her friends, and always remained modestly in the background. Even though she had been strictly brought up in the conduct befitting her time and social class, because of her interest in Chinese culture, English language and literature, her association with foreigners and later her Roman Catholic faith, she was also something of an outsider and a pioneer.

In Van Gulik's third period in Tokyo, Etsuko helped him in innumerable ways and a deep affection developed between them. Her greatest assistance to him was with his book about the gibbon. When Robert was afflicted with eye problems and unable to read, she read everything to him; without her help this work would probably never have been finished. They used to enjoy practising calligraphy together. On one occasion when something had gone wrong, he said to her: 'Your characters look like the footsteps of spiders which have trodden in the ink pot.' She also used to visit Robert and Shih Fang for lunch and afternoon tea, or she went to the cinema with them and their children Pieter and Pauline.

Van Gulik continued to be an inveterate film-goer. On one occasion he took his staff with him to see a Japanese film during office hours: 'If you want to learn about Japan, you really must see this.' This is why he saw *Irezumi* (Tattooing) twice. It was a story about a woman who had been sold into prostitution and had a tattoo of a spider which covered the whole of her back. The film showed how, under the influence of this evil spider, she took the most appalling vengeance on those who had plunged her into her misery.

Once again in this Japanese period, just as in the old days, this non-conformist ambassador did not deny himself the pleasure of wandering through parts of Tokyo in which 'the ordinary man' sought his pleasure. Cautiously the police informed the embassy that it was responsible for his safety and it would be better were the ambassador not to visit dangerous areas of a questionable character, but Van Gulik shrugged it all off. There he would meet all sorts of interesting people and made friendships which perhaps meant more to him than those on a higher level. Once in a *sushi* bar, he happened to make a critical remark to the *sushi* boss about the glass *sake* bottles—surely traditionally they should have been porcelain. A Japanese regular—a simple trader or labourer—who overheard this was so impressed by it that, when he heard who Van Gulik was, he had a portion of expensive *matsutake* mushrooms delivered to his home. That Japanese became a regular guest at the embassy.

With the exception of official and unofficial visits to Nagasaki and the *Kansai*, Van Gulik made a regular habit of fleeing Tokyo around Christmas. Among these excursions, he and his wife, Pieter and Pauline visited Cambodia, where they spent five days viewing the splendid temple complex of Angkor Wat, from where they returned to Japan after a short stop-over in Hong Kong. Occasionally they would spend a weekend at the mountain resort of Nikko, and in 1966 Shih-fang and the children made very good use of a small summer cottage at Hayama on the coast. Willem spent only the summer holiday of 1965 in Tokyo, but Thomas was present during both summers. Willem wrote:

> I completed the period of my military service after a twenty-four-month training in the Cavalry, followed by being a platoon commandant of troops in the 43rd Tank Battalion on 't Harde (Sytzama's Hussar Regiment). My parents left for Japan half a year before my discharge. Afterwards, as a reward for my national service, I was allowed to spend a couple of months in Japan, but on one condition: I had to study. Therefore, in the summer of 1965 my father enrolled me at Sophia University in Tokyo for seminars on the history of East Asia and the religious history of Japan.
>
> Father was kept extremely busy with all his social obligations, but nevertheless on various occasions there was still time to "go

out on the town" with him in Tokyo and explore the nightclubs.

In the Japanese part of the residency garden was an *azumaya*, a small Japanese tea pavilion with a thatched roof; there we had many conversations, and there for the first time I noticed that we could talk about the culture of East Asia. My return to Japan as an adult, after having lived there so many years ago as a child, was like the closing of a circle. Father wanted me to study law in Leiden, but everything changed a year later. I chose to study Japanese and Chinese. And then, just at the moment that our fields of interest coincided, my father's early death prevented me from being able to profit from his enormous knowledge in this field of study.

For Pauline the regular times for meeting her father were straight after school, in the office (that is to say in the residence!) for afternoon tea. Pauline was worried about his eating habits, and often checked the drawers of his desk to see that no sweets or nuts were hidden there. Afternoon tea was always a merry mixture of chatter and gossip. Every so often they would also go out:

10-3-1966: Holiday for the wedding of Princess Beatrix, 6-7.30 reception for all Dutch people, 8 o'clock to Holland Ball with Pauline in her first long frock, home 11.30.

There were other receptions to which Pieter and Pauline or one or the other accompanied their father. He also made sure that they made enjoyable trips in both Japan and in Korea.

Just as of old, Robert remained a great lover of bookshops and antiquarian booksellers. The place he loved best of all was Yushima Seidō. This 'Hall of the Saint' in Yushima was founded in 1690 as a centre for the veneration of Confucius and as an academy at whose centre was the study of neo-Confucianism. Services were held to venerate Confucius. In another space, separate from the temple and set up in a very businesslike way, there is still a Chinese antique shop-cum-restaurant, and lessons in Chinese cooking are still given there. Van Gulik said in jest that Yushima Seidō had been founded by the Tokugawa to prove that the Earth was square. The Chinese had once had such a conception of the Earth, as they did of a rounded vault of Heaven.

He spent many a Sunday there and was especially interested in scroll paintings. One whole wall was divided up into pigeon holes and in each of these was a painting, which one could pull out oneself and look at. He did this systematically and also bought this and that. This cultural activity could be combined with delicious dining—which was handy on a Sunday, on which the household staff had their day off.

He did not allow physical problems, however unpleasant they must have been, to interfere with the activities closest to his heart. Certainly he went out less and retired to bed earlier, and he also occasionally delegated more to his staff. He had regular consultations with his general practitioner and was examined by specialists in all sorts of fields. His allergy, bronchial complaints, his stomach, his back and above all his eyes caused a great deal of trouble.

Despite all this he remained optimistic and, on 14th May, wrote to his cousin Katy Deys that he was planning to fly to the Netherlands with Pieter and Pauline on 15 June, while Shih-fang would travel by boat; they were hoping to fly back to Tokyo at the end of July, and to take Thomas with them for his month-long holiday. Six weeks was long enough for them to do everything they needed to do back in the home country. The last few days before their departure were pretty full of social engagements, including the lunch Van Gulik gave for the Dutch Chamber of Commerce and the opening of the office of the agricultural attaché, at which he gave a speech and attended a reception.

15-6-1967: 2 o'clock the printer Saito comes to fetch the Ms [manuscript] of the ape book [*The Gibbon in China*], afterwards packed, 9 o'clock to Haneda [Airport] with Pieter and Pauline, coffee with the staff of the embassy, 10.30 left for the Netherlands.

Leaving the airport somebody remarked: 'The ambassador has gone into orbit', and everyone returned home absolutely convinced that he would return very shortly.

Chapter 17

ILLNESS AND DEATH

When I shall die
Who will mourn me?
Only the black crows from the mountains
Will come to grieve over me.
But the mountain crows
Will also not lament me:
They will bewail the inaccessibility of the offering cakes
On my death altar.

Translated from the Japanese by R.H. van Gulik[21]

Robert van Gulik had a talent for putting matters, including the sadness of loss, into perspective and he had a strong personal awareness of the transience of all worldly things.

As said, on 15 June 1967 he flew from Japan to the Netherlands where he lost no time in ringing up his friend Dr Waalkens, the otolaryngology specialist at the Red Cross Hospital in The Hague:

'Jan, can I come to see you as early as this afternoon?'
'Why, what's the matter?'
'I think I have lung cancer; in Japan they say it is tuberculosis and are treating me with INH [Isoniazid, an anti-tuberculosis drug], but I'm not happy about it. They are skilled doctors, but their cancer statistics do not give a true picture of the reality. If you have lung cancer, they say that it is tuberculosis and if it hopeless, they send you to a priest, thereby ensuring their cancer statistics are kept low.'

Waalkens immediately rang the lung specialist Van der Drift, and X-rays were taken the very next day. These did indeed confirm that it was lung cancer, and that it was located in the right *pars intermedia*. A bronchoscopy was performed. This revealed that the disease had spread, among other sites to the liver and the bones. It would seem that the tumour was very long established.

---

[21] From *Per Diplomateke Koerier*, Amsterdam 1965, p. 130

Van Gulik wanted to be precisely informed and it turned out that he had a state-of-the-art knowledge of all manner of medical details. For years he had suffered from chronic respiratory symptoms and was especially allergic to dust; Waalkens had washed out his maxillary sinuses on various occasions.

> 8-7-1967: Feel ill, to Red Cross Hospital where [I had] an X-ray and was admitted, 4 p.m. the children come bringing clothes etc.

In hospital he received a constant stream of visits from family and friends, all of whom he kept in complete ignorance about the true nature of his illness.

> 21-7-1967: At 9 o'clock the [lung specialist] Dr Van der Drift and [the physician] Dr Cost come to give me a report. First 2 Endoxan [drug used for the treatment of some cancers] injections.

'When he heard the truth of the matter,' Doctor Waalkens recounted, 'he asked the lung specialist and me: "How long do I have to live?" We said: "No longer an half a year at the most, at the very most." (In fact it was just two months). To which he reacted by saying: "Then I'll have to work damned hard. Do you have a room for me in the hospital? If so, I want to have a desk there, and I shall be under your care every day and I can finish my work." Whereupon he was assigned a two-bed room in the Red Cross Hospital; instead of a second bed he had a desk and a couple of armchairs and it was here he took up residence. He was administered an intensive course of Endoxan.

Waalkens had very close contact with Van Gulik: 'I dropped in on him every day, after consultations, and we would sit and chat for half an hour about the most diverse topics. It was only then I realized what a remarkable person he was. He was literally well informed about everything. He was then working on the book about apes [*The Gibbon in China*]. It was here he put the finishing touches to it and it was published on the day he died. In the hospital he not only wrote his last Judge Dee novel, but also his Judge Dee comic strips for *De Telegraaf* [with the drawings by Frits Kloezeman], and sometimes he would ask me—as he had previously done—whether some fact or other was medically correct. Everything had to be perfect, everything had to tie in perfectly.

'We had the craziest conversations. And—he returned to this very often—he believed in the occult. He could also talk endlessly about telepathy. As a down-to-earth person who hails from Groningen, I did not believe in it; I had seen all sorts of tricks which were used in it, and this sent him into gales of laughter.

'Talking of telepathy, one of the very best stories is the following. After he had already been with us a while he had his sister-in-law to visit. One afternoon he said triumphantly: "Jan, now I've wrong-footed you. Telepathy does exist. I can prove it to you. Nobody in the family knows what I have, and I have told *nobody*. When my sister-in-law asked: 'Robert what do you have?' I replied, 'A form of tuberculosis.'"

"But it's been dragging on for so long now, you should have been cured quite a while ago," she said. "We know a man in Zeist, a clairvoyant who also heals people, and he says that all he needs is something which you have about your body on a daily basis."

"So I gave her my spectacles case. And, lo and behold, this afternoon my sister-in-law came back and said that I have lung cancer and that it is in the right lung. Don't you think that's amazing?"

'This really irritated me and I decided to investigate. Then one day a government medical officer happened to ring up to ask for information about a patient. This should never be passed on by telephone, unless you are very well acquainted with the doctor and know that it is alright to do so. Nevertheless, it gave me an idea. I went to the Radiology Department and asked if anyone had made enquiries about Van Gulik. And, yes indeed this had happened, a week earlier a 'medical officer' had rung up and asked for information about Van Gulik "on behalf of Foreign Affairs". He had asked that the X-ray report be read out to him, and they had done this!

'I told Robert all about it, and we had a good laugh together. Robert said: "That's what makes you so interesting, you really investigate something and then it turns out that not everything is what it appears to be. You unravel the puzzle completely; it's just like a detective story!"

'He sometimes did a little calligraphy, but not really very much. Nor did he have very many books; indeed there was not much room. Nevertheless, he was constantly occupied with writing; he worked tremendously hard those final months, and in the last weeks he was overtaken by an enormous sense of urgency and worked as a man possessed; he toiled the livelong day.

'Speaking about his marriage he once said: "I married Shih-fang not only because I was in love with her and loved her deeply, but also because I thought: were you to mix the wisdom and erudition of the East with our Western civilization, surely something very special must emerge from it." Of course at that time the children were much too young to know "what would emerge", but he was extremely curious about it. I asked: "You're not looking at this from a scientific point of view, a sort of breeding programme?" "No certainly not, absolutely not," he said, "but I thought that these were the two most exquisite things that you could combine." Actually I often thought of him as a Chinese, he was sometimes more Chinese than European.

'I admired him tremendously. Just imagine that you are suffering lung cancer and that you don't have much longer to live, and that you shut yourself up and work full tilt, without a murmur of complaint. This had to be finished; that had to be rounded off. Conversations with him, even at this time, were never boring, they were invariably inspiring, and you could have a good laugh with him; he had an enormous sense of humour. Everything he said was well considered, he never spouted nonsense. He was a man whom I often think about.'

In this period Van Gulik also seized the chance to spend plenty of time with his family and friends. During the first month in hospital—apparently he was allowed to move about freely—he would very frequently go out to lunch with his wife and children or take afternoon tea with them or they would all eat Chinese food in the evenings, either at home or in a restaurant, sometimes taking friends with them.

> 4-8-1967: Second Endoxan tablet after breakfast. Injection for neuralgia. 12.30 with Dr Waalkens to pick up his wife, then S.F. and Pauline, all lunched together in the *Witte Paviljoen* [summer quarters of the club *De Witte* in Scheveningen]. Afterwards home worked on Chinese typewriter. Willem came. Early dinner at home and Willem took me back to hospital.

For a long time he had toyed with the idea of spending his retirement in Penang. Later his thoughts turned more towards Japan, but now he realized that all these plans would come to naught. On 8 August he wrote to Wil de Vries in Tokyo that, upon all the medical advice, he had 'definitively decided to relinquish my original idea of remaining in Japan for very many years yet to come, indeed even retiring there.' And in a letter of the 22nd he continued: 'I have now had to relinquish my ideal of ending my days in the East, because I shall have to remain under the best, prolonged medical care. If I had no wife and children, I would retire somewhere to a mountain in Japan, but under the present circumstances this is naturally impossible; as the father of a family one does have certain responsibilities! I have resigned myself to this, and here in The Hague I shall also not expire of boredom.'

From 15 August he was back at home, even though he often still had to go to the hospital for check-ups and treatments. He played billiards with his three sons. 'From time immemorial', wrote Willem, 'billiards was a great pastime of father's. The reason I became a special member of the New or Literary Club (*Nieuwe of Literaire Sociëteit*) *De Witte* during my national service (1963-1965) was so that I could play there with my father at the weekends. In my secondary-school time I had already played my fair share of billiards, but it was in *De Witte* my father taught me all the finer points, including all the appropriate exclamations which are part of the game. Double shots of Dutch gin were the usual accompaniment.'

Van Gulik attended a conference at the Ministry about the forthcoming visit to Japan by an Amsterdam delegation. He also bought a new car and fixed up the insurance.

> 15-8-1967: 10 o'clock maxillary sinus washed out, 12 o'clock Willem came, home together where lunched together, rested in the afternoon, with Willem and Pauline into town in the rain, bought a Taunus car at Auto Service, evening dinner at home and watched TV.

There were a hundred and one things which needed to be done and everything should carry on as usually as possible. Nobody was allowed to notice what was the matter with him. He wanted to spare his family all worries. Later his wife said: 'I feel very upset that I did not know then what the matter was.' When Barkman answered: 'He did not want to saddle you with this burden, and you could not have done anything about it', she said, 'That's true, but during that final period I would have treated him differently.'

> 20-8-1967: Slept in, 11-12 with Thomas in the new car to Lingeman [the teacher's family with whom Thomas boarded and where he had continued to live during this furlough], rested afternoon, 7 o'clock with S.F., Pieter and Thomas to the *Witte Paviljoen*, where had dinner, 8.30 home.

> 25-8-1967: 12 o'clock with S.F., Pieter and Pauline to Wassenaar Zoo in our own car, where we lunched, 3 o'clock home.

26-8-1967: 11.30 Leonhard Huizinga and wife came to visit, 4 o'clock Thomas home, all dined together at home with Willem and [Willem's wife] Yvonne.

On 29 August, he wrote to his American friend, the art collector Nick Carter:

'[…] It has been detected here that for over a year I have been suffering from a treacherous disease which is incurable and this will limit the length of one's life. Here [in the Netherlands] I was immediately admitted to one of our best hospitals and have undergone six weeks' intensive treatment. I have now been discharged and am going out everywhere just as before, only twelve kilos lighter! Luckily it seems that my illness is susceptible to the new, very powerful drugs, and hence the process has been stabilized. However, nobody knows for how long; according to the statistics for no longer than a few years.

'Personally this news has not upset me greatly; I have had a rich and happy life and have no cause for complaint. Nevertheless, I have been forced to make some necessary changes to all my plans, first and foremost to ensure that the interests of my wife and children are secure. I have relinquished all my treasured plans to spend the rest of my life in the East; we have once again installed ourselves in our own house in The Hague, and Pauline and Pieter will continue their studies here in the Netherlands. The Ministry of Foreign Affairs has given me three months' sick leave, until 1st November. If my condition continues to be as satisfactory as it is now, the Ministry wants me to return to Tokyo for two to three weeks to wind up my mission and to make my farewells officially. Later—once again as long as my health remains good—I shall be appointed a councillor at the Ministry, a high position which is not bound to strict office hours and [does not involve] exhausting activities. In the meantime, I have assembled all my capital in the Netherlands so that, should anything befall me, my wife and children will have no difficulty in settling the estate. The only problem is my art collection.'

After a short discursion about his plans for this art collection and an offer to Carter, giving him first choice to take over a number of *objets d'art*, Van Gulik goes on:

'The strange thing about my illness is that it causes me no pain or distressing side-effects; it is the powerful medicine (Endoxan) which does occasion some pain and unpleasant side-effects. Nevertheless, I drive round in the small car which I have bought, play billiards and attend conferences at the Ministry. It is a strange life! My wife and children know that I am seriously ill, but naturally I have not told them the whole truth. As a matter of fact, this would be irresponsible, because sometimes (in 20 per cent of the cases) the disease can be kept at bay for several years. However, this is the exception, and we should reckon on the normal rule which varies between six months and a year. Please do not say anything to your wife or anybody else about the real situation, of which only my Minister of Foreign Affairs has been informed. [...] My book, *The Gibbon in China*, is being printed in Tokyo at the moment. I am very happy that I have been able to complete this labour of love.'

At the beginning of September Van Gulik was once again admitted to hospital, where he continued to work for ten days; afterwards he returned home for a short while, but as early as the 22nd—much sooner than either he or his doctors had expected—his condition became critical and he was taken to hospital by ambulance, where he died two days later.

Only when a condolence register was opened in the embassy in Tokyo did it truly emerge with just how many diverse people from different circles and strata of society he had been in contact; people the majority of whom knew absolutely nothing about each other and of their relationship with Van Gulik, as if they were placed in separate, non-communicating compartments. Not only did Japanese ministers, civil servants and diplomatic colleagues come to sign the register, but from Tokyo and other places farther afield came artists, art connoisseurs, antiquarian booksellers, taking their place alongside publicans and other denizens of the pleasure quarters.

His son Pieter later (1-10-1967) wrote:

'Now that we were all reunited, these last few months my father wanted to live with us normally. Because nothing more could be done for him, he came home. I am dreadfully sorry that I did not know this [what a short time he had to live], because I could have profited so much more from these last months with him. But, this was exactly what he did not want; he bore the heavy burden alone. Now I also understand why it was so difficult for him to blow out the fifty-seven candles on his birthday, less than two months ago.

'One consolation is that he did not suffer greatly. This was because, at his own request, he was administered morphine for the pain, to allow him to get on with his work. He wanted to round off everything: his financial affairs, his books, his art collection and

Foreign Affairs. I know that the end also caught him unawares. At the end of this month he had very much hoped to be able to go to Japan and settle his affairs there. Even despite his illness, he had asked the doctors to give him their consent for his departure, so that he could round off all his outstanding work.

'One consolation at least in this time of affliction is that my father passed away as he had always hoped to do. He died in harness. The evening on which his condition became critical, he put the finishing touches to his last Judge Dee story, which has since appeared posthumously [*Poets and Murder*].

'On Friday morning 22 September my father again felt poorly and was suffering from an awful headache and drowsiness. After that the end came quickly. Father lapsed into a coma and was suffering from a lack of oxygen. Fortunately I had already warned the hospital and he could be taken there in good time. Later the doctors told me that the cancer had spread to the brain and this is what had now caused a crisis. Only my father's iron determination prevented him dying that same day. He fought so terribly hard, on Saturday morning he regained consciousness. Despite some light paralysis, he could still speak, see and hear. He told his doctor and friend, who had been a pillar of strength to him, that he realized the end was very near. Nevertheless, he was reconciled to this, because he would once again meet his old Chinese and Japanese friends, and he had attained all he had wished to achieve. His only worry was about us, the children, who would now all be left on their own.

'All of us visited him and we talked to him and said our goodbyes. Although his spirit was somewhat dimmed, he recognized us and bade us take heart. On Sunday his condition deteriorated again; he hardly spoke, but his expression and smile showed that he recognized us. We could see quite clearly that his body was exhausted. During the afternoon he once again slipped into a coma and he passed away completely at peace at 20 past 8 in the evening of 24 September 1967. His face had become so much younger and was so tranquil I am happy to be able to carry this image in my memory.'

Years earlier Van Gulik once said to Iwan Verkade that he had plans to write the exact opposite of his *Sexual Life in Ancient China*; this would be a book about death. He was already collecting data for it: Chinese poems and stories from all periods whose theme was death. He had said to Verkade: 'Some poems are so beautiful they send shivers down your spine.' When the latter visited him at home

in 1967 and asked him—unaware of how ill he was—whether he
was planning to finish that book, the answer was, 'No, old chap, it
is beyond me. It is too close to me.'

'…I am tired of life,
I am now going to slumber, somewhere in the Southern Mountains,
I am going, ask not how or whither,
The white clouds are everywhere and eternal.'

BIBLIOGRAPHY[22]

1. Books in the field of science; translated works.

Uhlenbeck, C.C. and R.H. van Gulik; *An English Blackfoot Vocabulary based on material from the Southern Peigans*, Amsterdam: Verhandelingen de Kon. Akademie van Wetenschappen te Amsterdam, New Series, Vol. XXIX, No. 4, 1930.

Uhlenbeck, C.C. and R.H. van Gulik; *A Blackfoot-English Vocabulary based on material from the Southern Peigans*, Amsterdam: Verhandelingen de Kon. Akademie van Wetenschappen te Amsterdam, New Series, Volume XXXIII, No. 2, 1934.

Van Gulik, R.H.; *Urvaçī, an ancient Indian play by Kālidāsa, translated from the original Sanskrit text, and provided with an introduction*, The Hague: Adī Poestāka, 1932 (in Dutch).

——; *Hayagrīva, the Mantrayanic aspect of horse-cult in China and Japan, with an introduction on horse-cult in India and Tibet*, Leiden: Brill, 1935 [reprinted under the title *Hayagrīva, Horse-Cult in Asia*, Bangkok: Orchid Press, 2005].

——; *Mi Fu on Inkstones, a translation of the Yen-Shih, with an introduction and notes*, Peking: Henri Vetch, 1938 [reprinted Bangkok: Orchid Press, 2006].

——; *The Lore of the Chinese Lute; an essay in ch'in ideology*, Monumenta Nipponica Monographs, vol. 3, Tokyo: Sophia University, 1941. [reprinted Bangkok: Orchid Press, 2011].

——; *Hsi K'ang and his Poetical Essay on the Lute*. Monumenta Nipponica Monographs, vol. 4, Tokyo: Sophia University, 1941.

——; *Ming-mo i-seng Tung-Kao-ch'an-shih chi-k'an: Collected works of the Ch'an master Tung-Kao, a loyal monk of the end of the Ming period*. Chunking: Commercial Press, 1944.

---

[22] This abbreviated biography lists primarily those publications referred to in the present work. For a complete bibliography of all of Dr van Gulik's publications, books, essays, reviews, etc. one should refer to the work of A. M. Evers, listed herein.

——; *Dee Coong An, three murder cases solved by Judge Dee. An old Chinese detective novel translated from the original Chinese with an introduction and notes*. Printed for the author, Tokyo: Toppan Printing Co., 1949.

——; *Ch'un-meng So-yen, Trifling Tale of a Spring Dream. A Ming erotic story, published on the basis of a manuscript preserved in Japan*, Lit. D., Tokyo: privately printed in 200 copies, 1950.

——; *Pi-hsi t'u k'ao, Erotic Color Prints of the Ming Period, with an essay on Chinese sex life from the Han to the Ch'ing dynasty, BC 206 – AD 1644*, (privately published in 50 copies: Tokyo, 1951), in 3 volumes: part I: English text, xvi + 242 pages; Part II: Chinese text, 210 pages; part III: Hua-ying-chin-chen, reprint of a Ming erotic album, 24 prints with 24 accompanying Chinese texts.

——; *De Boek Illustratie in het Ming Tijdperk* [Book Illustration in the Ming Period], The Hague: Nederlandse Vereniging voor druk- en boekkunst, 1955 (in Dutch).

——; *Siddham; an essay on the history of Sanskrit studies in China and Japan*, Sarasvati-Vihara Series, Vol. 36, Nagpur: International Academy of Indian Culture, 1956.

——; *T'ang-yin pi-shih, 'Parallel cases from under the pear-tree', a 13th century manual of jurisprudence and detection*, Sinica Leidensia, Vol. X, Leiden: Brill; 1956 [reprinted under the title *Crime and Punishment in Ancient China*, Bangkok: Orchid Press, 2007].

——; *Chinese Pictorial Art as Viewed by the Connoisseur. Notes on the means and methods of traditional Chinese connoisseurship or pictorial art, based upon a study of the art of mounting scrolls in China and Japan*, Serie Orientale Roma XIX, Roma: Istituto Italiano per il Medio ed Estremo Oriente, 1958.

——; *Scrapbook for Chinese Collectors. A Chinese treatise on scrolls and forgers - Shu-hua-shuo-ling - Translated with an introduction and notes*, Beirut: Imprimerie Catholique, 1958 [reprinted Bangkok: Orchid Press, 2006].

——; *Sexual Love in Ancient China. A preliminary survey of Chinese sex and society from ca. 1500 BC till 1644 AD*, Leiden: Brill, 1961.

——; *The Gibbon in China. An essay in Chinese animal lore*, Leiden: Brill, 1967.

2. Detective novels, fiction

——; *The Chinese Bell Murders*, written in English between 1948 and 1951 (London: Michael Joseph, 1958); first appeared in Japanese in the magazine Tantei kurabu (= detective club) under the titles *Hangetsukai no satsujin, Soin no himitsu* and *Tsurigane no himitsu* (translated by Ms Etsuko Ikeda), Tokyo: Kyoeisha, 1955; Dutch edition, The Hague: Van Hoeve, 1958.

——; *The Chinese Maze Murders*, written in English in 1950 and published in Japanese in the same year under the title *Meiro no satsujin* (translated by Prof. Yoshio Ogaeri), Tokyo: Kodansha, 1950; subsequently translated into Chinese by the writer himself and published under the title *Ti Jen-chieh ch'i-an*, Singapore: Nanyang yin-shua-she, 1953; Dutch edition, The Hague: Van Hoeve, 1956.

——; *The Chinese Lake Murders*, written in English between 1952 and 1957; London: Michael Joseph, 1960; Dutch edition, The Hague: Van Hoeve, 1959.

——; *The Chinese Gold Murders*, written in English in 1956, London: Michael Joseph, 1959; Dutch edition, The Hague: Van Hoeve, 1958; Japanese edition, titled *Ogon no satsujin* (translated by Mrs Etsuko Numano), Tokyo: Kodansha, 1965; Spanish version (translated by HRH Prince Bernhard), Madrid: Aguilar, 1965.

——; *The Chinese Nail Murders*, written in English in 1958, London: Michael Joseph, 1961; Dutch edition, The Hague: Van Hoeve, 1960.

——; *The Lacquer Screen*, written in English in 1958, Kuala Lumpur: Art Printing Works, 1962; Dutch edition, The Hague: Van Hoeve, 1962.

——; *New Years' Eve in Lan-Fang*, a collection of Judge Dee short stories, privately printed by the author, 200 copies, Beirut: 1958; Dutch edition The Hague: Van Houvre, 1958.

——; *The Haunted Monastery*, written in English between 1958 and 1959, Kuala Lumpur: Art Printing Works, 1961, Dutch edition, The Hague: Van Hoeve, 1962.

——; *The Red Pavilion*, written in English in 1959, Kuala Lumpur: Art Printing Works, 1961; Dutch edition, The Hague: Van Hoeve, 1961.

——; *The Emperor's Pearl*, written in English in 1960, London: William Heinemann, 1963; Dutch edition, The Hague: Van Hoeve, 1963.

——; *The Monkey and the Tiger*, Judge Dee short stories written in English in 1963, William Heinemann: London, 1965.

——; *Murder in Canton*, written in English between 1961 and 1962, London: William Heinemann, 1966; Dutch edition, The Hague: Van Hoeve, 1964.

——; *The Willow Pattern*, written in English in 1963, London: William Heinemann, 1965; Dutch version first as a series in De Telegraaf, Amsterdam: 1964, later by Van Hoeve: The Hague, in book form.

——; *The Phantom of the Temple*, written in English in 1965, developed into a novel based on previously written comic strips for Swan Features, Amsterdam, London: William Heinemann, 1966; Dutch edition, The Hague: Van Hoeve.

——; *Judge Dee at Work*, a collection of Judge Dee short stories written in English between 1958 and 1961, London: William Heinemann, 1967.

——; *Necklace and Calabash*, written in English in 1966, London: William Heinemann, 1967; Dutch edition, The Hague: Van Hoeve, 1967.

——; *Poets and Murder*, written in English in 1967; published posthumously, London: William Heinemann, 1968.

3. On the life and works of R.H. van Gulik

Evers, A. M. (comp.); *A Bibliography of Dr. R.H. van Gulik*, Boston: The Department of Special Collections, Boston Universities Libraries, 1969 [reprint 1983].

Van de Wetering, Janwillem; *Robert Van Gulik, His Life, His Work*, limited edition, 350 copies, Miami Beach: Dennis McMillan, 1987.

various contributors; *Orientations Magazine – The Robert Hans van Gulik Issue*; Vol. 12, No. 11, Hong Kong: November 1981.

INDEX

Lightning Source UK Ltd.
Milton Keynes UK
UKHW011941030222
398153UK00003B/810